Discover Washington
and Seattle with Kids

DISCOVER WASHINGTON
& Seattle
with KIDS

Rosanne Cohn &
Suzanne Monson

JOHNSTON
ASSOCIATES
INTERNATIONAL

P.O. BOX 313
MEDINA, WASHINGTON 98039
(206) 454-3490

Discover Washington and Seattle with Kids
First Edition
© 1995 by Rosanne Cohn and Suzanne Monson

ISBN 1-881409-07-4

Cover art and book design by Mike Jaynes
Production and typesetting by Kate Rose
Researcher/Editor: Shelly Arenas
Maps by Marge Mueller

JASI
Post Office Box 313
Medina, Washingon 98039
(206) 454-3490 FAX: (206) 462-1335

Printed in the United States of America

Library of Congress Cataloging-in-Publication Data

Cohn, Rosanne.
    Discover Washington and Seattle with Kids / Rosanne Cohn and
Suzanne Monson. -- 1st ed.
        p.   cm.
    Includes index.
    ISBN 1-881409-07-4
    1. Washington (State) -- Guidebooks.   2. Family recreation -
-Washington (State) -- Guidebooks.   3. Seattle (Wash.) -- Guidebooks.
4. Seattle Region (Wash.) -- Guidebooks.   5. Family recreation -
-Washington (State) -- Seattle -- Guidebooks.   6. Family recreation-
-Washington (State) -- Seattle Region -- Guidebooks.   I. Monson,
Suzanne, 1961-   . II. Title.
F899.3.C58   1995
917.9704'43--dc20   95-24327
                                                        CIP

To Larry with thanks and love.

— Rosanne Cohn

To my parents, who introduced me to Washington's wonders when I was a child; and to my husband, who is helping me to introduce our children to the same joys now that we are parents.

— Susanne Monson

Acknowledgements

The authors would like to give special thanks to the following people who assisted In researching and writing this guide:

Shelly Arenas; Beth Hapala; Rex Hapala; Marlene and Hap Hapala; Karla Lapinksi; Seattle Times travel editor John Macdonald; Michelle Mackey; Dori, Kelsey, Haley and Keegan Monson; Patty Ray; Patti Seebeck; Mike Seigel; Jane Shannon; Tony and Mika Ventrella; and the Washington State Division of Tourism.

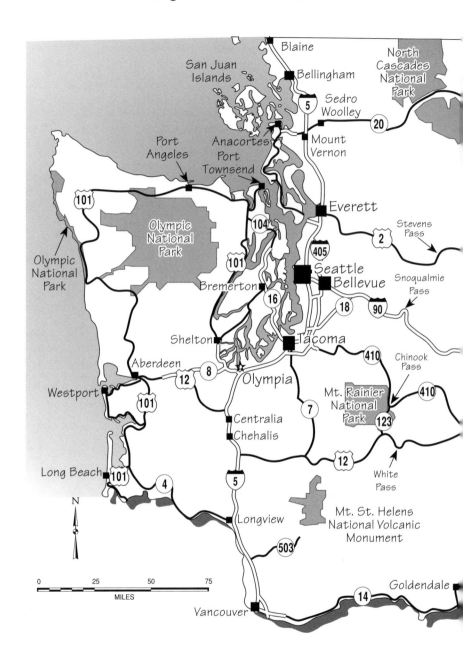

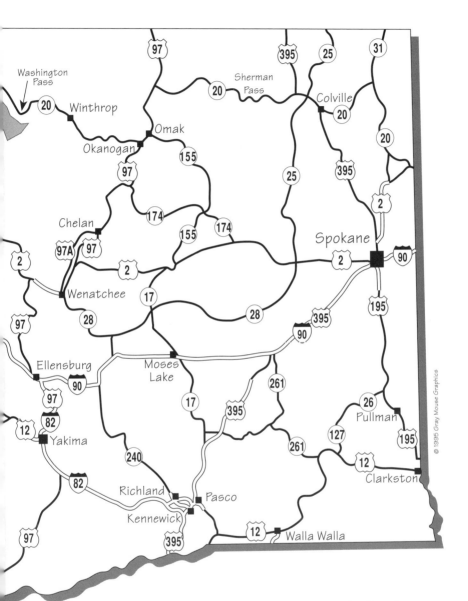

Washington
Pass

20 Winthrop

Omak

Okanogan

97

Sherman
Pass

20

395   25   31

Colville
20

20

155

Chelan

97A 97

2

174

155 174

25

395

Spokane

2

90

2

Wenatchee 17

28

28

90

395

195

Ellensburg

90

97

97 82

12 Yakima

Moses
Lake

17

395

261

26

Pullman

127

261

195

12

Clarkston

240

82

Richland Pasco

Kennewick

97   395

12   Walla Walla

© 1995 Gray Mouse Graphics

WASHINGTON

Table of Contents

Foreword

We are about to launch another first....*Discover Washington and Seattle with Kids!*

With the tremendous success that *Discover Seattle with Kids* — the first family guide in the state — has enjoyed through six editions over the past 18 years, it was only natural that our horizons would expand to include the entire state of Washington. Suzanne Monson brings a new, refreshing and thoroughly professional expertise to this new, seventh edition.

Seattle and the Puget Sound area have grown over the years to become a giant playground for families. *Discover Washington and Seattle with Kids* has reflected those changes and, having been showcased on the *Seattle Times'* best seller list every year for the past ten, has reflected the changing needs and interests of the families in our communities.

We have offered a wide variety of selections, as well as creative and diverse opportunities for families to enjoy, and have always kept in mind that we must meet the needs of many types of families. Over the years, we have grown from being a "kids" book to an "everyone's" book, and have found that young adults and seniors also love to explore and discover the wonderful world of Washington.

We hope that you enjoy our new adventure.

Rosanne Cohn

Introduction

I t becomes clear after spending time with kids that they are natural explorers. What most children need, however, is a skilled navigator. That's where you — the parents and grandparents — can step in. In fact, adults who discover new destinations, events, and activities with children may be surprised at their own renewed sense of curiosity. Exploring places with a child sheds a new light on the familiar.

As your child's chief navigator, you know that traveling with kids takes some planning. That's where this guide comes in. Here you'll find hundreds of activities, destinations, and events across Washington state — aimed primarily at kids aged 3 to 13 years, but including listings for younger children as well.

In this guide, original author Rosanne Cohn has updated many of her favorite destinations and attractions within King County, including extensive details about Seattle. I've added hundreds of features from the state's surrounding four corners and numerous stops in between. While researching this book, we attemped to find places that illustrate the state's geographic and ethnic diversity. We have also highlighted programs and facilities for the physically challenged.

After being invited to help write *Discover Washington and Seattle with Kids*, childhood memories of summer vacations traveling throughout the Evergreen State with my own parents were especially vivid. It has been a thrill to relive these memories, exploring new places with my husband and daughters, and knowing that other families will have the pleasure of discovering Washington's greatest treasures as well.

The more our family explores small towns across the country and new cities across Washington state, the more I discover about our own children. Discovering Washington state has become a gift we continue to give to each other.

Happy traveling!

Suzanne Hapala Monson

Tips for Traveling with Kids

Before leaving home on your adventure, remember that part of the excitement of discovering new places is the anticipation, so involve the whole family — including the kids — from the onset. Here are a few tips:

- Mark the dates for the trip on the calendar so that your child can have fun watching the approaching vacation.

- Many children by the age of 8 have acquired the proper telephone manners to call tourist or visitor agencies to request information and maps. Before making the call, have them practice what they'll say. Make sure they know their address and the days or month you will be traveling. Encourage them to tell tourist officials that they're looking for things kids their age can enjoy. Often, the agent will take a little extra time to recall things their own children or their neighbor's children like to do.

- Refer to the resources listed in the appendix at the back of this guide. If your child requests the travel information, materials will be addressed to them when they arrive in the mail. Make a point of opening the package together and spending time reading or looking at the pictures.

- Encourage your child to ask for an extra map when calling any of the listings or resources in the appendix. The first map is for the driver; the other is for the kids. This way, children can chart their own course with a highlighter pen or tape a piece of wax paper over the top and trace the route with an ink pen. As kids follow road markers on their map, they're less likely to pester the driver about how much farther it is to the final destination.

- Have the kids start a scrapbook before you leave. Reserve pages for photographs, ticket stubs, the child's drawings of things she's seen, and other special memorabilia. A shoebox decorated by your child before the trip will serve for larger collectibles. It's compact, and fits easily into a suitcase, backpack, or vehicle trunk.

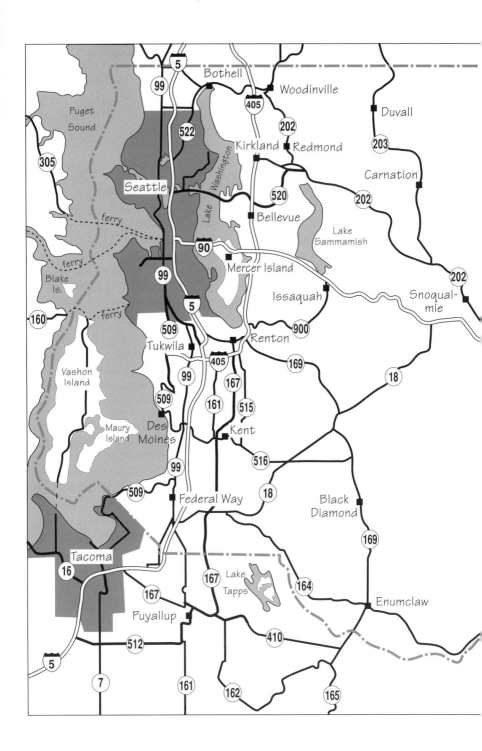

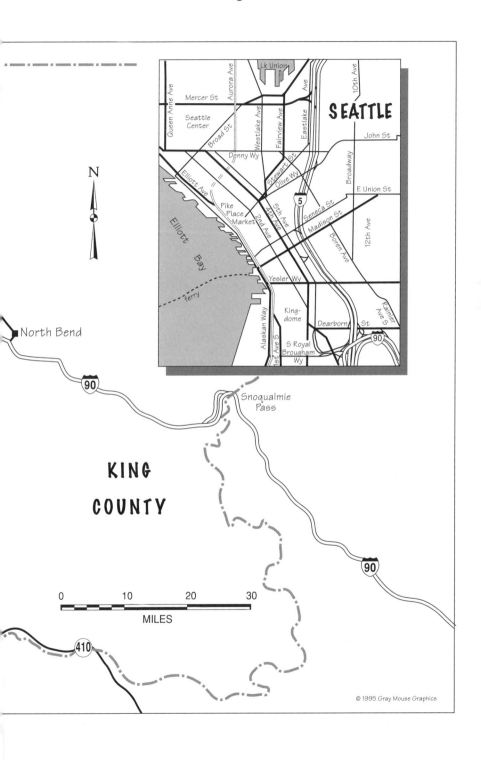

© 1995 Gray Mouse Graphics

Families love to explore the spirit of old Seattle during Bill Speidel's Underground Tour at Pioneer Square.

Downtown Seattle

From the International District and Pioneer Square to the retail shopping corridor and Seattle Center, downtown Seattle is like a patchwork quilt. Each section has its own look and texture, but is connected by smooth seams to complement its neighboring parts.

Though downtown communities can be diverse, as a whole they offer wonderful parks, great shopping, fun restaurants, and rich urban cultural centers. In this chapter, listings are categorized in these geographic areas: Pioneer Square, the International District, Pike Place Market, downtown's retail core, and the Seattle Center area. Attractions in the city's outlying residential neighborhoods appear in Chapter 2.

Pioneer Square

Pioneer Square and its turn-of-the-century buildings are especially interesting to out-of-town visiting families, but there's always some new shop, restaurant, gallery, or event to attract locals as well.

The triangular park at First Avenue and Yesler Way marks Seattle's first settlement. Yesler Way was originally called "Skid Road" because logs were dragged down its steep slope to a steam-powered lumber mill (where Magic Mouse Toys now stands).

Great Destinations

Bill Speidel's Underground Tour

Location: *610 First Ave., Doc Maynard's Public House*
Phone: *206-682-4646*
Days/Hours: Daily year-round but schedule changes seasonally.
Wheelchair/Stroller Access: *Yes, for the lecture; not on the tour*

Beneath the hustle and bustle of Pioneer Square streets there lies a ghost town — but it's not the kind haunted by spooks and goblins. This is more a tour of the spirit of old Seattle, rebuilt after the fire of 1889. You'll start at Doc Maynard's Public House with a 20-minute seated introduction before leaving on a 90-minute walking tour along underground sidewalks built in the 1890s. Some of Seattle's most interesting history is buried here, and the guides lace these legends with rib-tickling stories. Teens and pre-teens get a kick out of hosting their birthday parties here. Reservations are recommended, especially in the summer. Arrive with a flashlight and wear comfortable shoes. The only restroom stop along this tour is at Doc Maynard's. Light lunches are available before and after the stroll. There are five blocks of rough ground and a few steep flights of stairs. Toddlers and pre-schoolers may not find this tour interesting, and maneuvering young walkers could prove to be a challenge. Admission is $5.95 for adults, $4.87 for seniors, $4.33 for students 13 to 17, $2.51 for students 6 to 12, and free for kids 5 or younger.

Klondike Gold Rush National Historical Park

Location: *117 S. Main*
Phone: *206-553-7220*
Days/Hours: *9 a.m. to 5 p.m., daily; closed Thanksgiving, Christmas and New Year's Day.*
Wheelchair/Stroller Access: *Yes*

This storefront museum is the smallest National Park west of the Mississippi. Visitors see how bells jingled on Seattle tills and coffers filled as nearly 100,000 miners shopped here on their way to the 1897-98 Alaska Gold Rush. Films presented in the auditorium include Charlie Chaplin's "The Gold Rush" (3 p.m. each first Sunday of the month). Park rangers guide free one-hour walking tours of the Pioneer Square Historic District at 1:30 p.m. on Saturdays, from Memorial Day to Labor Day. Children younger than 12 must be accompanied by an adult. Appointments are required for large groups.

Seattle Kingdome

Location: *201 S. King*
Phone: *206-296-3128*
Days/Hours: *11 a.m., 1 p.m., and 3 p.m., Monday through Saturday, mid-April through mid-September. (Group tours of 25 people or more are available during the rest of the year with appointments made at least two weeks in advance.)*
Wheelchair/Stroller Access: *Yes*

Home of the Seahawks and the Mariners, the 60,000-seat Kingdome is a behemoth covered stadium hosting dozens of other events as well. It attracts thousands of visitors each year for the Home Show, the Boat Show, sell-out concerts, and noisy monster-truck rallies. Have a look at what's behind the scenes of this arena during one-hour tours. Guides escort visitors to a sports locker room, the press boxes, the arena floor, and the sports museum. The museum displays collectibles from one of the game's all-time great wide receivers — retired Seahawk Steve Largent —and memorabilia from the former Rainiers and Pilots baseball teams. Wear comfortable shoes because you'll be covering a lot of ground. Admission is $4 for 12 years or older, and $2 for those younger than 12.

Seattle Mariners

Location: *Home games in the Kingdome; administrative offices at 83 S. King St., Suite 300*
Phone: *Call Ticketmaster for tickets at 206-622-HITS; administrative offices at 206-628-3555*
Days/Hours: *Game times vary during April through September season; offices open 8:30 a.m. to 5:30 p.m., Monday through Friday.*
Wheelchair/Stroller Access: *Yes*

There's more than just baseball happening during a Mariner game in the Kingdome. Fans can watch the antics of the Mariner Moose mascot, play along as guessing games and colored hydroplane boats appear on the larger-than-life computerized DiamondVision screen, and munch on concessions, ranging from popcorn to pizza. Behind right field, near Aisle 11, you'll find a kids' arcade with video games and baseball card booths. Watch for free promotion giveaways, including a jersey, ball or bat. When ordering tickets, ask about childrens general admission seating on Level 300, and two-for-one family nights — which are on selected Mondays during the season. For $5, fans 14 or younger can join the Mariners' Club. They'll get posters, club newsletters and more. Gates open two hours before the first pitch. Batting practice and infield activities are fun for kids to watch.

Seattle Seahawks

Location: *Home games in the Kingdome; administrative offices at 11220 N.E. 53rd St., Kirkland*
Phone: *Call Ticketmaster for tickets at 206-628-0888; administrative offices at 206-827-9777*
Days/Hours: *Game times vary on Sundays, mid-August through late December, with post-season playoffs possible in early January.*
Wheelchair/Stroller Access: *Yes*

Bone-crunching action kicks off in the Kingdome when the Seattle Seahawks take on other National Football League competitors. (The team's training camp is in Kirkland, but practices are closed to the public.) There are no discount admission prices for children, so expect to pay from $20-$35 each for tickets.

Smith Tower

Location: *506 Second Ave.*
Phone: *206-682-9393*
Days/Hours: *10 a.m. to 10 p.m. daily, elevator to the Chinese Room when no meeting is in progress.*
Wheelchair/Stroller Access: *Yes*

From the time it was built in 1914 until the early 1960s, the 42-story Smith Tower was the tallest building west of the Mississippi River. Unlike today's high-rises, the Smith Tower still operates manual elevators. After soaring to the 35th story, an observatory offers a 360-degree view of the city, Elliott Bay, and Puget Sound. Visits are self-guided and cost $2 for adults and children 12 years and older, and $1 for seniors and kids younger than 12 years.

Amtrak's Mount Baker International

Location: *King Street Station, one block northeast of the Kingdome*
Phone: *800-872-7245*
Days/Hours: *Leaves once daily in the morning and returns in the evening; departures may vary.*
Wheelchair/Stroller Access: *Yes*

Zoom between Seattle and Vancouver, B.C. in high-speed style aboard the first international rail link along this route in many years. A state-of-the-art train uses a glide system to run faster than most trains with an even smoother ride. Capable of traveling 140 mph, the train goes about half this speed to meet U.S. regulations. Aisles are wide enough for strollers and some seats swivel toward tables so families can face each other and play cards or board games. There's a dining car on board and restrooms are equipped with diaper changing facilities. Most of the scenic route is along the Puget Sound.

Look for brief stops in Edmonds, Everett, Mount Vernon and Bellingham. Roundtrip fares are $42 for adults and $26 for children. Departure times may change, but the 4 1/2-hour ride leaves Seattle around 7 a.m. each morning and departs Vancouver at about 6 p.m. daily. Call for reservations.

Places to Eat

Cow Chip Cookies

Location: *102 First Ave. S.*
Phone: *206-292-9808*
Days/Hours: *9 a.m. to 6 p.m., Monday through Saturday; noon to 5 p.m., Sunday.*
Wheelchair/Stroller Access: *Yes*

If you're looking for a snack while you stroll, these really big, really crunchy cookies should please you and the kids. Take some home after a busy day touring the Pioneer Square area.

Grand Central Baking Co.

Location: *214 First Ave. S. in the Grand Central Arcade*
Phone: *206-622-3644*
Days/Hours: *7 a.m. to 6 p.m., Monday through Friday, and 9 a.m. to 5 p.m., Saturday and Sunday, in the deli; 11 a.m. to 3 p.m., Monday through Saturday, in the restaurant.*
Wheelchair/Stroller Access: Yes

Yummy cinnamon rolls, great desserts, hearty homemade soup, whole and half sandwiches (including peanut butter and jelly) and a rustic European Italian-style bread have created a devoted clientele at Grand Central Baking Co.

Places to Shop

Champion Party and Costume

Location: *124 Denny Way*
Phone: *206-284-1980*
Days/Hours: *9 a.m. to 7 p.m., Monday through Friday; 9 a.m. to 6 p.m., Saturday; 11 a.m. to 5 p.m. Sunday.*
Wheelchair/Stroller Access: *No*

For Halloween, birthdays, and costume parties, this place has it all. Buy or rent a wacky costume, then select the other party goods needed to host a big shebang! There's also colorful crepe paper, a wide selection of piñatas, stickers for all occasions, balloons, party favors, and much more.

Elliott Bay Book Company

Location: *First Avenue South at South Main Street*
Phone: *206-624-6600*
Days/Hours: *10 a.m. to 11 p.m., Monday through Saturday;*
noon to 6 p.m., Sunday and holidays.
Wheelchair/Stroller Access: *First floor only (the bookstore)*
Children's readings and special programs for kids are commonplace on Saturday mornings at this venerable old bookstore. Parents love this place for the bargain loft and well-stocked shelves for themselves, and kids adore the wooden playhouse. The downstairs cafe is cozy and quiet, and patrons often have their noses in books or magazines while eating. Even though there's no children's menu, soups and half-sandwiches are well-suited to younger tastes. The fare is served cafeteria style, which minimizes the wait for your food.

Glass House Art Glass

Location: *311 Occidental Ave. S.*
Phone: *206-682-9939*
Days/Hours: *10 a.m. to 5 p.m., daily.*
Wheelchair/Stroller Access: *Yes*
Visitors often break into a sweat just thinking about the hot work performed here. Watch the glassblower work from 10 a.m. to 3 p.m. (with an 11:30 a.m. to 12:30 p.m. break for lunch) in front of a gas furnace heated to 2,000 degrees. Blowers follow the same procedure artisans have used for nearly 3,000 years. Using little more than melted sand, designers create ingenious glass objects. There are glass forms of all sizes here, from small perfume bottles to large sculptures. Tours are casual and available to groups of 20 or fewer.

Great Winds Kite Shop

Location: *402 Occidental Ave. S.*
Phone: *206-624-6886*
Days/Hours: *10 a.m. to 5:30 p.m., Monday through Saturday;*
noon to 5:30 p.m., Sunday.
Wheelchair/Stroller Access: *Yes*
With more than 400 kites to tempt you, this shop specializes in matching people to just the right kite for them. Located three blocks west of Pioneer Square's underground bus terminal, it's a popular place for both serious and amateur kite fliers. The shop staff is happy to answer questions about flying or kite-building. Kite history, construction, and flying classes are available by appointment.

Magic Mouse Toys

Location: *603 First Ave.*
Phone: *206-682-8097*
Days/Hours: *9 a.m. to 9 p.m., Monday through Saturday; 10 a.m. to 6 p.m., Sunday.*
Wheelchair/Stroller Access: *First floor only*
   Magic Mouse Toys is a superb collection of international games, puzzles and playthings. Most visitors can't leave without hugging at least one of the big furry stuffed animals. This is more than just a run-of-the-mill toy store limited to goodies for kids — games for serious competitors attract adults as well.

Wood Shop Toys

Location: *320 First Ave. S.*
Phone: *206-624-1763*
Days/Hours: *9:30 a.m. to 5:30 p.m., Monday through Saturday; some extended hours in November and December.*
Wheelchair/Stroller Access: *First floor only*
   This family-owned shop offers an eclectic collection of toys found in few other places. Jack the Woodsman greets visitors at the door. Inside the shop, marionettes and colorful nutcrackers imported from Germany line the shelves. In addition to the popular wooden and Russian toys, you and the children will be delighted with the "furry folk" collection of nearly 35 animal puppets. A pair of bears known as Fred and Zeke are favorites here. Staff members will bring things down to you if your stroller can't manage the stairs.

Places to Play

Waterfall Park

Location: *Main Street at Second Avenue South.*
Wheelchair/Stroller Access: *Partially*
   This vest-pocket park is an oasis on a summer day. Water cascading over massive rocks drowns out all street noises, and tables and chairs under a glass-covered shelter offer a serene place for a picnic. Privately built and maintained by the Annie E. Casey Foundation, the park commemorates the original offices of the United Parcel Service.

The International District

Asian restaurants of all sizes and types, shops filled with exotic merchandise, and tiny grocery stores packed with familiar and unusual items are but a few of the wonders that beguile visitors in this compact, historic neighborhood. Once called Chinatown, it's now home for families of a wide range of Asian descent. The arrival of new cultures has broadened the array of shopping and eating adventures in what is now called the International District.

During Seafair in early August, join hundreds of Japanese Americans celebrating Bon Odori. For more than 90 years, spectators have gathered to tour the Buddhist Temple at South Main Street between 14th and 16th avenues south. Nearby, families will find Japanese foods and traditional dancing and drumming.

Great Destinations

Chinatown Discovery Tour

Location: *Write to P.O. Box 3406, Seattle, WA 98114*
Phone: *206-236-0657*
Days/Hours: *Flexible.*
Wheelchair/Stroller Access: *No*

Hidden treasures of Seattle's International District are revealed during a three-hour guided walking tour led by Seattle native Vi Mar. This charming lady tailors each tour to what the group wants. Trip departures often hinge on the weather, but lunch is always included. At least 10 adults are required for each tour, but special arrangements can be made for smaller families. The tour is best for children 5 years or older. Reservations are required. Call for prices and a schedule.

Wing Luke Asian Museum

Location: *407 Seventh Ave. S.*
Phone: *206-623-5124*
Days/Hours: *11 a.m. to 4:30 p.m., Tuesday through Friday; noon to 4 p.m., Saturday and Sunday.*
Wheelchair/Stroller Access: *Yes*

Seattle's Asian community dates back to 1860. Tours of this unique, ethnic history museum may be self-guided or with a docent, by appointment. Guided tours are loaded with information interesting to kids. Exhibits, which change every two months, feature Asian folk art and crafts. Guides will describe how these items reflect

Asian culture. Special hands-on activities for children relate to the visiting exhibits. Admission is $2.50 for adults, $1.50 for seniors and students 12 or older, 75 cents for children 6 to 11, and free to kids 5 or younger.

Places to Eat

King Cafe

Location: *723 S. King*
Phone: *206-622-6373*
Days/Hours: *11 a.m. to 5 p.m. daily, closed Wednesday.*
Wheelchair/Stroller Access: *No*
Dim Sum, something of a Chinese smorgasbord, is served hot and fresh in the upstairs dining area of King Cafe. Kids will be entertained by the fact that dishes come up on a dumbwaiter and are quickly distributed throughout the room. You can select what you want from the offerings as they appear. Seating is limited, but worth a weekend family outing.

House of Hong

Location: *409 Eighth Ave. S.*
Phone: *206-622-7997*
Days/Hours: *11 a.m. to 3 p.m., Monday through Friday; 10:30 a.m to 3 p.m., Saturday and Sunday.*
Wheelchair/Stroller Access: *Yes*
A generous restaurant with slightly formal decor, House of Hong offers 70 types of dishes and Dim Sum. Lined with comfortable booths, this restaurant specializes in family gatherings.

Ocean City

Location: *609 S. Weller*
Phone: *206-623-2333*
Days/Hours: *Dim Sum served from 9 a.m. to 3 p.m., daily.*
Wheelchair/Stroller Access: *Yes*
Ocean City offers over 30 dishes and provides highchairs and booster seats for the little ones. The restaurant's outside decor is colorful with striking carvings. The great advantage of Dim Sum is that children can look first, then choose what appeals to them, instead of selecting from a menu. You'll watch the wait staff pushing carts filled with small dishes of fried, steamed or baked beef, pork, fish and vegetables. First-timers may want to try fried Fun Gow, a crescent-shaped type of egg roll (also available steamed); Gin Dau, a

sweetish, sesame-covered dough filled with red-bean paste; and steamed Hum Bow, a white baked dough usually filled with a tangy barbecue sauce. Most dishes contain two to four portions, easily divided among a family. This way kids get to take a bit of everything and parents can avoid the "clean your plate" routine.

Places to Shop

Uwajimaya

Location: *Sixth Avenue South at South King Street*
Phone: *206-624-6248*
Days/Hours: *9 a.m. to 9 p.m., Monday through Saturday, and 9 a.m. to 8 p.m., Sunday, June through Labor Day; 9 a.m. to 8 p.m., daily, the rest of the year.*
Wheelchair/Stroller Access: *First floor only*

You'll feel like you've flown to the Pacific Rim when you venture through the doors of Uwajimaya. This Asian department store is a colorful expanse filled with foods, gifts, art and clothing. Cooking connoisseurs — and those who would like to be — come here for regularly-scheduled classes in the secrets of Far East cuisine. Kids are fascinated by the exotic fish and foods. Be sure to visit the bakery for freshly-made cream cakes and other tasty treats. There's also a deli with take-out food available, including Hum Bow, sushi, egg rolls, and hot entrees. Uwajimaya also has a smaller outlet in Bellevue, at 15555 N.E. 24th.

Places to Play

International Children's Park

Location: *Seventh Avenue South at South Lane Street*
Wheelchair/Stroller Access: *Yes*

This little playground is among the most charming in the city. A slide spirals down a mound of rocks into a huge bed of sand while a delightful dragon stands guard.

The Waterfront/Alaskan Way

Sights, sounds and smells blend together, beckoning visitors to Seattle's waterfront. Ferries sail across Elliott Bay, spraying a fine saltwater mist behind them. Brightly colored flags flap on ships of international origin docked here. Seafood restaurants cook up Seattle's specialties for hungry diners.

Much has changed since 1897, when the waterfront was the city's primary working harbor. Most industry has moved south to Harbor Island now, but Alaskan Way piers have been refurbished for varied uses, such as the Aquarium at Pier 59. From Pier 69, the high-speed catamaran Victoria Clipper sails between Seattle and the picturesque provincial seat of British Columbia. Harbor excursion boats depart from Pier 55. Seattle's fireboats dock at Pier 53. And Pier 52 at Colman dock is the point of departure for Washington State Ferries to Bremerton and Bainbridge Island.

Waterfront piers 49 to 70 are numbered from south to north. It's fun to take the Waterfront Streetcar from the International District (Fifth Avenue at Jackson Street) or Pioneer Square (Main at Occidental) all the way to the north end of the waterfront for an overview of the offerings, and then stroll back along the bay. Call 206-553-3000 (select Customer Service) for trolley details.

Great Destinations

Coast Guard Museum

Location: *1519 Alaskan Way S.*
Phone: *206-217-6993*
Days/Hours: *9 a.m. to 3 p.m., Monday, Wednesday and Friday; 1 p.m. to 5 p.m., Saturday and Sunday.*
Wheelchair/Stroller Access: *Yes*

You and the children can learn about the work and history of the U.S. Coast Guard at this interesting museum. Navigational aids, including a magnetic compass, ship models, Arctic ivory and a four-foot-high Fresnel lens made in France for a Puget Sound lighthouse are all on display here.

Coast Guard Vessel Traffic Center

Location: *Pier 36*
Phone: *206-217-6050*
Days/Hours: *8 a.m. to 4 p.m., daily. Tour hours flexible; call for information.*
Wheelchair/Stroller Access: *Yes*
    The center's important mission is to prevent collisions, groundings, and other marine mishaps in Puget Sound. The Coast Guard monitors the waters from Cape Flattery (on the Pacific Ocean) to Olympia (at the south end of Puget Sound) round-the-clock by radio. Drop in anytime between 8 a.m. and 4 p.m. and watch personnel at work through a viewing window. The tour includes a guide and a 20-minute film; call in advance for times.

Argosy Cruises
(formerly known as Seattle Harbor Tours)

Location: *Pier 55*
Phone: *206-623-1445*
Days/Hours: *Schedules vary; call ahead.*
Wheelchair/Stroller Access: *Yes*
    See the water from the water! Here's a unique and educational way to explore Seattle's waterways and learn more about its maritime industries. A one-hour narrated harbor tour cruises through Elliott Bay and the Duwamish waterway, offering an up-close view of the shipyards, cargo docks, freighters, tugboats, anglers, and more. Tours are $13.75 for adults, $6.50 for those 5 to 12 years, and free for those younger than 5 years. A longer 2 1/2 hour "Cruise the Locks" tour travels through the Hiram M. Chittenden Locks, Shilshole Bay, Lake Union, West Point and Elliott Bay. This tour costs $21.50 for adults, $11.50 for those 5 to 12 years, and is free for those younger than 5 years. Argosy also offers 90-minute Lake Washington cruises, departing from the Kirkland Marina on the Lake's east side. Fares are $16.75 for adults and $6.50 for children.

Tillicum Village on Blake Island

Location: *Sail from Pier 56*
Phone: *206-443-1244*
Days/Hours: *Call ahead; schedules vary.*
Wheelchair/Stroller Access: *Yes*
    Sample Native American hospitality at Tillicum Village on Blake Island after cruising across the inner sound from Pier 56. Out-of-town visitors and locals alike find this an entertaining and

educational four hours. After the cruise across Elliott Bay, guests are treated to an Indian-style salmon dinner, tribal dancing, and 45 minutes of free time to explore the pristine island's totem poles, masks and carvings. If you're lucky, a tribal artist will be designing a new piece while you visit; most take time to tell you about their work. It's possible to spend the better part of the day exploring this quintessential Puget Sound island, ending up with dinner and an evening cruise back to Seattle. Ask for details when you call for reservations. Tillicum Village is also accessible through Kitsap Harbor Tours from Bremerton. Reservations are recommended. Admission is $45 for adults, $29 for teenagers, $18 for students 6 to 12, $9 for kids 4 and 5, and free to those 3 or younger.

Seattle Aquarium

Location: *Pier 59*
Phone: *206-386-4320 and 206-386-4300*
Days/Hours: *10 a.m. to 7 p.m., daily, Memorial Day through Labor Day; 10 a.m. to 5 p.m., daily, Labor Day to Memorial Day.*
Wheelchair/Stroller Access: *Yes*

Peer into the habitats of Pacific Northwest sealife at the Seattle Aquarium. Tanks of fish and mollusks make a great family escape on a rainy afternoon, and the outdoor exhibits are especially popular in the summer. The life cycle of the Northwest's vital salmon is told at the "Journey of the Salmon to the Sea" exhibit. Look under the microscope at the tiniest creatures which start the food chain, or plunge little (and big) hands into the "touch tank" to stroke the starfish and sea urchins.

The "Sea Birds" display mimics an authentic habitat. Nearby, the sea lions and seals always seem to be putting on a show for their audience, much to the delight of the kids. Rest your feet in the domed aquarium room, where you are surrounded on all sides and overhead by tanks filled with an array of sea creatures.

Self-guided tours take anywhere from an hour to several hours. Admission is $6.75 for those 19 or older, $5.25 for seniors, $4.25 for students 6 to 18, $1.75 for children 3 to 5, and free to those 2 or younger. A $40 annual family pass may be the most affordable option for your family. Ask about a combination Woodland Park Zoo/Seattle Aquarium pass if you visit frequently. Discounts are also available for King County residents and groups of 10 or more.

Omnidome

Location: *Pier 59*
Phone: *206-622-1868 and 206-622-1869*
Days/Hours: *Shows air between 9:30 a.m. and 9:55 p.m., daily.*
Wheelchair/Stroller Access: *Yes*

Realistic sights and sounds flood your senses in the curved mega-screen IMAX theater in the Omnidome. Screenings of movies with nature themes are shown here, but they change frequently so call ahead to see what's playing. Admission is $6 for adults, $5 for seniors and youths 13 to 18, $4 for kids 3 to 12, and free to those 2 or younger. Ask about combination tickets for the Omnidome and Aquarium. You must arrive 10 minutes before show time to be seated.

Spirit of Puget Sound

Location: *Leaves from Pier 70*
Phone: *206-443-1442*
Days/Hours: *Lunch cruises between noon and 2 p.m., and dinner cruises between 7 p.m. and 10 p.m., Monday through Saturday; and 6 p.m. to 9 p.m. on Sunday, during the summer months; schedule shortened during cooler months; call ahead for required reservations.*
Wheelchair/Stroller Access: *Yes; alert the staff when you make your reservation*

Especially popular with out-of-town visitors, this narrated cruise tours Magnolia Bluff, Todd's Shipyards, Alki Point, Blake and Bainbridge islands, and includes a buffet lunch or dinner. The lunch cruise includes cultural and historical happenings in and around Elliott Bay and the Puget Sound area. Dancing and entertainment are provided on some cruises. Kids will love whooping it up in the Congo line! Admission ranges from $23.95 to $45.25 for adults, with a 10 percent discount for seniors. Children 3 to 12 pay half-price; those 2 or younger sail for free.

Victoria Clipper

Location: *Pier 60*
Phone: *206-448-5000*
Days/Hours: *Schedules vary; call ahead.*
Wheelchair/Stroller Access: *Yes*

This high-speed, passenger-only catamaran travels to Victoria, B.C. in less than three hours. With several daily departures between Seattle and Victoria, it's possible to make this a day trip. There's plenty to see and do within walking distance of the Canadian harbor. Don't miss the Royal British Columbia Museum located half a block away from the tenninal. A full-scale model of a Victorian-era town, a rain forest display, and an outstanding collection of native Canadian art and history are just some of the museum's many features. Nearby, you can sip high tea at the Empress Hotel, visit the lovely Crystal Gardens atrium, ride a double-decker bus, or tour the fragrant Butchart Gardens. Round trip fares on the Clipper range from $73 to $89 for adults; children's fares are half price.

Washington State Ferries

Location: *Pier 52*
Phone: *206-464-6400 or 800-84-FERRY*
Days/Hours: *Schedules vary; call ahead.*
Wheelchair/Stroller Access: *Yes*

Downtown Seattle's Washington State Marine Highway System ferry terminal is the departure point for three of the ferry system's routes. Catch a vehicle ferry to Bremerton or Bainbridge Island, or a passenger-only ferry to Vashon Island. The one-hour ride to Bremerton offers time to explore the ferry, view Seattle's skyline or enjoy a picnic onboard. Vehicles aren't necessary on the other side because there's walking access to Bremerton (or to Winslow on Bainbridge Island). For a special treat, return on an evening ferry and see the city lights against the night sky. Fares vary according to the season; summer rares are higher, but are still a bargain, especially the passenger-only rate which starts at $3.50 for adults and $1.75 for kids 5 to 12 years. Those 5 years or younger ride free. Walk-ons and car passengers pay only on the Seattle side; rates for vehicles with drivers, which start at $7.10, are charged on both sides.

Places to Eat

Ivar's Acres of Clams

Location: *At Pier 54*
Phone: *206-624-6852*
Days/Hours: *11 a.m. to 11 p.m., daily, Memorial Day through Labor Day; 11 a.m. to 10 p.m., Sunday through Thursday, and 11 a.m. to 11 p.m., Friday and Saturday, the rest of the year.*
Wheelchair/Stroller Access: *Yes*

A statue of the late Ivar Haglund, one of Seattle's most colorful characters and successful restaurateurs, stands outside this waterfront eatery. Ivar's is famous for clam nectar, fish and chips, and other seafood favorites, plus warm cups of red or white clam chowder on brisk Seattle days. There are two dining options. Inside, the restaurant offers views of the waterfront activity. Outside, the bar offers quick service and a chance to feed leftovers to the sea gulls. The waterfront trolley stop across the street is named "Clam Central Station."

The Frankfurter

Location: *Pier 55*
Phone: *206-622-1748*
Days/Hours: *9 a.m. to 9 p.m., daily, Memorial Day through Labor Day; 9 a.m. to 5 p.m., daily, the rest of the year.*
Wheelchair/Stroller Access: *Yes*
Wieners, franks, hot dogs or foot-longs — no matter what you call them, this place has them! Eat them plump and juicy just the way they are, or slap on an assortment of condiments. There are nearly a dozen *Frankfurter* stands throughout the city and in East King County. The ones near Green Lake and the University District are especially popular.

The Salmon Cooker/The Crab Pot

Location: *Bay Pavilion at Pier 57*
Phone: *206-624-1890*
Days/Hours: *11 a.m. to 10 p.m., Sunday through Thursday, and 11 a.m. to 11 p.m., Friday and Saturday, Memorial Day through Labor Day; 11 a.m. to 9 p.m., Sunday through Thursday, and 11 a.m. to 10 p.m., Friday and Saturday, the rest of the year.*
Wheelchair/Stroller Access: *Yes*
The Salmon Cooker is the street-side eatery and the Crab Pot offers full-service dining inside. You'll have a wide choice of top-quality Pacific Northwest seafood. After dining, browse the Bay Pavilion's shops. Your children will love taking a ride on the vintage carousel found here.

Steamers

Location: *Pier 59*
Phone: *206-624-0312*
Days/Hours: *10 a.m. to 10 p.m., Sunday through Thursday, and 10 a.m. to 11 p.m., Friday and Saturday, Memorial Day to Labor Day; extended hours 10 a.m. to midnight during Pier 62 summer concerts; 10 a.m. to 6 p.m., Sunday through Thursday; 10 a.m. to 8 p.m., Friday and Saturday.*
Wheelchair/Stroller Access: *Yes*
While *Steamers* caters mostly to the hamburger and fish and chip trade, they have added salads, charbroiled chicken, fish, and

cioppino-style soup. Eat inside or take your food to the nearby Waterfront Park.

The Old Spaghetti Factory

Location: *2801 Elliott at Broad; across from Pier 70*
Phone: *206-441-7724*
Days/Hours: *Lunch served 11:30 a.m. to 2 p.m., Monday through Friday; open 5 p.m. to 10 p.m., Monday through Thursday; 5 p.m. to 11 p.m., Friday; noon to 11 p.m., Saturday; noon to 10 p.m. Sunday.*
Wheelchair/Stroller Access: *Yes, except restrooms*
Children feel like they have hit the jackpot when they're seated in the 1917 Birney Car at The Old Spaghetti Factory. This inexpensive pasta place is frequently crowded on weekends. Diners savor the spaghetti and a variety of sauces while relaxing on velvet-covered sofas under red Tiffany lamps. Crayons and placemats intended for coloring decorate each table. Bring your own cake if you're celebrating a birthday and the wait staff will sing "Happy Birthday." Spumoni ice cream is served with all orders. Reservations are not accepted.

Places to Shop

Ye Olde Curiosity Shop

Location: *Pier 54*
Phone: *206-682-5844*
Days/Hours: *9 a.m. to 9:30 p.m., May through mid-October; 9:30 a.m. to 6 p.m., Monday through Thursday, 9 a.m. to 9 p.m., Friday and Saturday, and 9 a.m. to 8 p.m., Sunday, the rest of the year.*
Wheelchair/Stroller Access: *Yes*
The hosts and chief residents of this honest-to-goodness curiosity shop are Sylvester and Sylvia, a pair of six-foot-tall mummies. Part museum, part curio shop, part Ripley's Believe-It-or-Not and part tourist gift shop, this establishment has been in the hands of the Standley family since 1899. Four generations later, the family still scours the earth for the strange and unusual. Even those with the best vision will probably need a magnifying glass to read one of the finest exhibits here: the Lord's Prayer carved on a grain of rice! This shop been a perennial kid (and adult) favorite since its earliest days.

Waterfront Landmark

Location: *Pier 55*
Phone: *206-622-3939*
Days/Hours: *9 a.m. to 6 p.m., Labor Day to Memorial Day;
9 a.m. to 9:30 p.m., Memorial Day to Labor Day.*
Wheelchair/Stroller Access: *Yes*
    Admittedly commercial, Waterfront Landmark is a store stocked with wonderful things to see and buy. You and the young ones can run your fingers through thousands of colored, tumbler-polished stones in an open display case or talk to the very big stuffed bears huddled in the corner. Look for the authentic Indian headdress on the wall. You can also munch on 13 varieties of fudge made on the premises or admire a display of totems by Northwest carvers.

Bay Pavilion

Location: *Pier 57*
Phone: *206-623-8600*
Days/Hours: *10 a.m. to 9 p.m., daily.*
Wheelchair/Stroller Access: *Yes*
    Visit Seattle's only indoor carousel, sample delicious fudge at Seattle Fudge, shop for souvenirs, and enjoy some Seattle sourdough bread — and that's just what's on the first floor! On the second floor you'll find a food court with varied ethnic eating options. The Pavilion is an all-season kind of place — in the wet, wintery months you can come in out of the rain and warm up while having fun; and on summer weekend afternoons you'll find free live music featured on a large deck area outside.

Sandpiper Gift Shop

Location: *Pier 59 next to the Aquarium*
Phone: *206-624-2835*
Days/Hours: *10 a.m. to 8 p.m., daily, Labor Day to Memorial Day;
10 a.m. to 6 p.m., daily, Memorial Day to Labor Day.*
Wheelchair/Stroller Access: *Yes*
    Being the official aquarium gift store, you can expect to find lots of items relating to sea life here, including stuffed animals, toys, and books. You'll also find plenty of northwest specialties, such as items made from Moun St. Helen's ash. Looking for a T-shirt to commemorate your visit to the aquarium and/or Seattle? There's a great selection of colorful shirts, sweatshirts, and baby rompers here.

Pier 70

At the waterfront's north end, Pier 70 is a cavernous building. Built in 1901 by Elton Ainsworth and Arthur Dunn, the pier was a full-fledged ocean terminal for steamship lines until 1910. The Coast Guard leased it until 1954. Since then, it has attracted visitors to its interesting shops and places to eat. Shops here reflect Pacific Northwest and Pacific Rim flavor and feel. Don't miss the main level restrooms with their wonderfully nostalgic flush chains — a good place to stop with kids for a bathroom break.

Places to Play

Waterfront Park

Location: *Between Pier 57 (Bay Pavilion) and Pier 59 (Seattle Aquarium)*
Wheelchair/Stroller Access: *Yes*

This park doesn't have any grass to roll around on, but kids will enjoy the water fountain near the aquarium and parents will be happy to have a place to sit and rest. There are also walkways and stairs that lead to observation decks, offering great views of the water and the Olympic Mountains. (Be sure to bring your camera.)

Myrtle Edwards Park

Location: *Alaskan Way, just north of Pier 70*
Wheelchair/Stroller Access: *Yes*

Walk north from the parking lot that's adjacent to the Pier 70 complex, and you'll find this delightful grassy waterfront park. There are two paved paths here, one for biking and one for walking. The trails continue 1.25 miles to Elliott Bay Park. Along the way you'll pass a fishing pier (Pier 86), a grain terminal, and a giant rock sculpture that children can't resist climbing.

Pike Place Market

The oldest continuously operating farmers' market in the country, Pike Place Market is in the heart of the seven-acre Market Historical District. This dearly-loved part of the city functions as a shopping destination for Puget Sounders from all walks of life. Its main entrance at First Avenue and Pike Street is the gateway to stands run by dozens of local crop growers, more than 250 shops and restaurants, and nearly 200 artisans displaying their fine handicrafts. You and the kids will be thoroughly entertained listening to street musicians and watching the eclectic mix of loyal market-goers. Third-generation seafood vendors toss fish across their stall and over patrons' heads to the counter where it's wrapped. These stalls are especially fascinating to youngsters who have only seen the cut and wrapped variety of fish.

The Pike Place Market is open year-round, 9 a.m. to 6 p.m., Monday through Saturday, and 11 a.m. to 5 p.m., Sunday. You can reserve space on a guided tour or browse at your own pace. The Market office can give you a map. Family walking tours of the market are scheduled for the last Saturday of each month; reservations are required. Call 206-682-7453 for details. These tours vary from 30 minutes to an hour, depending on the ages of the children.

Nearby Market Park at Virginia Street and Western Avenue is not recommended after dark. However, during the day it offers a waterfront view, spanning from Pier 59 to Pier 64.

Places to Eat

Deluxe BBQ

Location: *Main Arcade; opposite De Laurenti's*
Phone: *206-624-2511*
Days/Hours: *9 a.m. to 6 p.m., daily.*
Wheelchair/Stroller Access: *Yes*
Stop here if your palate craves barbecued ribs, chicken or pork. Teriyaki chicken is served here as well. It's tasty and messy, just the way kids like it!

Chocolate and Ice Cream Delight

Location: *Soames Dunn Building*
Phone: *206-441-8877.*
Wheelchair/Stroller Access: *Yes*
Just the place on a warm summer day! You can enjoy delicious ice cream treats by the cone or by the dish, plus wonderful sodas, sundaes and floats.

Cucina Fresca

Location: *1904 Pike Place*
Phone: *206-448-4758*
Days/Hours: *9:30 a.m. to 6 p.m., Monday through Saturday; 9:30 a.m. to 5 p.m., Sunday.*
Wheelchair/Stroller Access: *From arcade side*
 Pasta, antipasto and regional entrees are made fresh daily. Everything is take-out, and all but the bread is sold by the pound. Children love the "Space Needle Noodles."

El Puerco Lloron

Location: *On the Hillclimb*
Phone: *206-624-0541*
Days/Hours: *11:30 a.m. to 8 p.m., Monday through Thursday; 11:30 a.m. to 9 p.m., Friday and Saturday; noon to 6:30 p.m., Sunday.*
Wheelchair/Stroller Access: *Take the elevator from Western Avenue*
 Inexpensive and authentic Mexican food is what you'll find here. Tasty food is served cafeteria-style, making this "fast food," but this is not a chain restaurant.

Procopio's

Location: *On the Hillclimb*
Phone: *206-622-4280*
Days/Hours: *9 a.m. to 11 p.m., Sunday through Thursday; 9 a.m. to midnight, Friday and Saturday.*
Wheelchair/Stroller Access: *Take the elevator from Western Avenue*
 Delicious gelato, Italian panini sandwiches, salads, luscious desserts, and a full line of espresso drinks promise something to satisfy the taste buds of every member of your family. The extensive gelato flavors are somewhat exotic, including loganberry, clove, watermelon, and ginger. But not to worry — there's usually good old chocolate available, too!

The Shy Giant

Location: *Corner Market Building*
Phone: *206-622-1988*
Days/Hours: *10 a.m. to 5:30 p.m., Monday through Saturday; 11 a.m. to 5 p.m., Sunday.*
Wheelchair/Stroller Access: *Yes*
The Shy Giant is a long-time market favorite for yogurt, waffle cones and ice cream. If you're trying to watch your fat intake, try the non-fat yogurt. Kids love the fresh fruit and natural puréed fruit yogurt, made on the premises.

Three Girls Sandwich Shop & Bakery

Location: *Sanitary Market*
Phone: *206-622-1045*
Days/Hours: *7 a.m. to 5:30 p.m., daily.*
Wheelchair/Stroller Access: *Yes*
Casual, but delicious, Three Girls is a lunch stop and bakery. Perch on a stool if you want to eat in, or carry your meal out. Choose from dozens of homemade breads and bagels. Children like both the sandwiches and the yummy sweets served here.

Places to Shop

City Kites/City Toys

Location: *On the Hillclimb*
Phone: *206-622-5349*
Days/Hours: *11 a.m. to 5 p.m., Sunday through Friday; 10 a.m. to 6 p.m., Saturday.*
Wheelchair/Stroller Access: *Take the elevator from Western Ave.*
Even if you've never flown a kite in your life, you have to appreciate the variety and names of kites available: whooses and rippers, bow biters and puddlejumpers, zube tubes, loony tunes, and more. There doesn't seem to be a color in the spectrum missing among the 75 kites and 20 air toys displayed here. Along with the kites, there are shelves full of playthings for kids of all ages.

Cost Plus Imports

Location: *2103 Western Ave.*
Phone: *443-1055*
Days/Hours: *9 a.m. to 9 p.m., daily.*
Wheelchair/Stroller Access: *Yes*
Here's a good alternative if the hustle and bustle of the market becomes just too much. This big, bright store is just a couple blocks

from the main market and has a huge selection of imported furniture, housewares, baskets, and home decor, as well as some toys, clothes, and assorted knick-knacks. They offer their own line of coffee beans and teas, and there's always a fresh pot featuring one of the many varieties for you to sample. Perhaps best of all, Cost Plus has an extensive selection of reasonably-priced packaged foods imported from all over the world.

Craft Emporium

Location: *Minus 1 Level*
Phone: *206-622-2219*
Days/Hours: *10 a.m. to 6:30 p.m., Monday through Saturday; 10 a.m. to 6 p.m., Sunday.*
Wheelchair/Stroller Access: *Yes*
Here you'll find thousands of colored stones in countless shapes, colored and metallic pipe cleaners, miniature collectibles, craft ribbon, and unusual supplies for the craft-minded or creative party giver.

Emerald Earth Toys

Location: *Post Alley Market*
Phone: *206-447-9566.*
Wheelchair/Stroller Access: *Yes*
While small in floor space, this shop is chock-full of interesting toys, with a heavy emphasis on educational and scientific toys and games.

Golden Age Collectables

Location: *Minus 1 Level*
Phone: *206-622-9799*
Days/Hours: *10 a.m. to 6 p.m., Monday through Saturday; 11 a.m. to 5 p.m., Sunday.*
Wheelchair/Stroller Access: *Take the elevator from Western Avenue*
If comic books, posters or baseball cards are a passion for someone in your group, this is the place to come to add to a collection. The shop has recently added a myriad of games to its shelves.

The Great Wind-Up

Location: *Economy Market*
Phone: *206-621-9370*
Days/Hours: *10 a.m. to 5 p.m., Monday through Saturday; noon to 4 p.m., Sunday.*
Wheelchair/Stroller Access: *Yes*
You don't have to be a kid to play with the wind-up, blow-up, stuffed and movable toys that fill this little shop!

Market Magic Shop

Location: *Minus 1 Level*
Phone: *206-624-4271*
Days/Hours: *9 a.m. to 6 p.m., Monday through Saturday; 10 a.m. to 5:30 p.m., Sunday.*
Wheelchair/Stroller Access: *Yes*
Before you can say "abracadabra," you'll be drawn into this magical world of prestidigitation. This store caters to the magician in all of us, and it's especially fascinating to youngsters eager to learn a few tricks.

Central Business Corridor/Retail Core

With the arrival of new shops, parks and other features, the face of downtown Seattle is rapidly changing. December's holiday shopping season is especially exciting in the retail core when store windows and street trees are decorated for the season. In Westlake Park, a 19th-century carousel of painted horses awaits with free rides for all ages. Rides on horse-drawn carriages provide an up-close view of downtown's festive decorations. A number of stores feature musicians playing Christmas carols to put shoppers in the holiday spirit. Summers bring a multitude of international travelers and colorful street vendors and musicians. Local businesses and the Downtown Seattle Association sponsor free lunch-hour "Out to Lunch" concerts from June through Labor Day.

Metro's tunnel station at Westlake Center provides an underground link between Seattle's leading department stores and beyond. The overground Monorail connects downtown with the Seattle Center.

Take a short stroll south to the new Harbor Steps. Several flights of stairs, separated by fun fountains to splash in, descend from the foot of University Street at First to Western Avenue. You can't miss the Seattle Art Museum's "Hammering Man" statue pounding away near the top.

Great Destinations

Frye Art Museum

Location: *704 Terry*
Phone: *206-622-9250*
Days/Hours: *10 a.m. to 5 p.m., Monday through Saturday; noon to 5 p.m., Sunday and holidays; closed Thanksgiving and Christmas.*
Wheelchair/Stroller Access: *Yes*

The Frye Art Museum, located a few blocks north of the retail core, features seven small galleries. (Closed for remodeling, this musuem will re-open in October 1996.) The first three house Charles and Emma Frye's original collection of 19th- and 20th-century paintings. The others are devoted to contemporary art and traveling exhibits, which are replaced monthly. Admission is free, as is parking at 705 and 707 Terry Street. The museum is set up for self-guided tours with a printed gallery guide. Groups may arrange docent tours by appointment.

Seattle Art Museum

Location: *100 University St., between First and Second avenues*
Phone: *206-654-3100 (recorded information); 206-654-3137 (TDD); and 206-625-8900*
Days/Hours: *10 a.m. to 5 p.m., Tuesday, Wednesday, and Friday through Sunday; 10 a.m. to 9 p.m., Thursday; closed most Mondays except Fourth of July, Presidents Day, Memorial Day and Martin Luther King Jr. holidays; closed Thanksgiving, Christmas and New Year's Day.*
Wheelchair/Stroller Access: *Yes, from First Avenue store entrance; not from museum entrance*

The four floors of the Seattle Art Museum (known locally as SAM) represent an international mix of masterpieces. The museum's retail store is located on the first floor. The second floor is dedicated to special exhibits; the third floor to art from Asia, the Near East, Africa, Oceania and the Americas; and the fourth floor exhibits European and North American art. Locals and visitors alike rave about the fine collection of Northwest Coast Native American pieces on the third floor.

Kids 6 to 10 years gain a deeper appreciation for many of these pieces with the help of the Family Guide Book. This guide suggests museum routes, and features photographs of displays children should see in each area. Other pages recommend activities the child can undertake to help understand particular works.

The Museum also offers Second Saturday for Families, which occurs — you guessed it — on the second Saturday of each month. Special hands-on workshops from 11 a.m. to 1 p.m. are featured on these days.

Guided tours are at 2 p.m., Tuesday through Saturday; 2:30 p.m., Sunday; and 7 p.m. Thursday. The sign language program is offered on the first Sunday of each month. Sign language interpreters are available for other programs with two weeks' notice. Admission to SAM is $6 for those 12 or older; $4 for seniors, and free to children younger than 12 when accompanied by an adult. Your admission also entitles you to a free visit (within two days) to the Seattle Asian Art Museum at Volunteer Park. Admission is free the first Tuesday of each month and free to members. Call the office for membership details.

Seattle Public Library

Location: *1000 Fourth Ave.*
Phone: *206-386-4636 (information) or 206-386-4190*
Days/Hours: *9 a.m. to 9 p.m., Monday through Thursday and 9 a.m. to 6 p.m., Friday and Saturday year-round; 1 p.m. to 5 p.m., Sunday, September through May.*
Wheelchair/Stroller Access: *Yes*

Tour the city's main library branch at noon, Wednesday, and 2 p.m., Saturday. Seattleites check out nearly 6 million books, audio selections and other materials from the library's 1.9-million-volume collection each year. The Children's Department alone circulates about 2,500 videos a month. Look for the new computerized systems which can perform vast amounts of research in just minutes, or jump on the "information super-highway" aboard Internet. Can't figure it out? Your kids can show you how!

Places to Eat or Stay

Four Seasons Olympic

Location: *411 University St.*
Phone: *206-621-1700.*
Wheelchair/Stroller Access: *Yes*

Whether for a stroll or for a stay, families will enjoy the grand elegance of the Four Seasons Olympic Hotel. Overnight guests will find everything from Nintendo games to infant bathtubs. Cribs arrive with teddy bears ready for hugging during your stay. Guests may ask for special hotel tours for children, including a peek inside the pastry kitchen.

The Children's Tea, offered daily in the Garden Court restaurant, is a favorite of guests. It features a selection of petit fours, fruit breads, and scones served with Devonshire cream and strawberry preserves, and a steaming pot of tea, all for $8.25. A Winnie-the-Pooh brunch is featured every Sunday morning from 10 a.m. to 1:30 p.m. VCR showings of Winnie-the-Pooh films entertain the kids while they dine from child-sized plates, using silver and glassware made for small fingers.

During the Christmas holidays, the lobby is filled with festive Yuletide trees, each adorned with decorations marking the names of patients at Children's Hospital and Medical Center. Also in December is the Teddy Bear Suite, featuring a room decorated with bears, bear and more bears. Visit the suite during the day to see the bear ornaments, the tea table, and other delightful decor. Ask for directions at the front desk.

Westin Hotel Market Cafe/Westin Hotel

Location: *1900 Fifth Ave.*
Phone: *206-728-1000*
Days/Hours: *6 a.m. to 10 p.m., daily (Market Cafe).*
Wheelchair/Stroller Access: *Yes*

The posh Westin Hotel is a great place to bring kids. Its Market Cafe offers a delightful children's menu on a 16-page coloring book plus three crayons. For kids 12 or younger, there are four special breakfast selections and a dozen lunch or dinner entrees. Service can be leisurely here, so allow plenty of time. They have highchairs and boosters.

For guests staying in the hotel, the Westin Kids Club offers special gifts to children of all ages. Rooms are child safety-proofed, and guests are provided with a complementary copy of KidStar magazine. Turn to Seattle's kids' radio at 1250 AM to hear local entertainment and information geared to families.

Places to Shop

Westlake Center

Location: *1601 Fifth Ave.*
Phone: *206-467-1600*
Days/Hours: *9:30 a.m. to 9 p.m., Monday through Friday; 9:30 a.m. to 7 p.m., Saturday; 11 a.m. to 6 p.m., Sunday.*
Wheelchair/Stroller Access: *Yes*

Though certainly not the only place to shop in Seattle's expanding downtown retail core, Westlake Center is definitely a must-see. Three floors of shops offer an array of choices: upscale boutiques, housewares, lingerie, gifts, jewelry, clothing, and much more. Family favorites include the Disney Store, 'Lil People, Natural Wonders, and The Sweet Factory. When you're ready for a snack or meal, take the open escalator up to the third floor "Pacific Picnic" food court area. Here you can choose from more than a dozen food vendors, featuring international cuisine (Chinese, Japanese, Middle Eastern, and Italian, to name a few) as well as American (burgers, sandwiches, hot dogs, soups, and more).

Places to Play

Freeway Park

Location: *Seneca at Sixth Avenue, next to the Convention Center.*
Wheelchair/Stroller Access: *Yes*

Billed as Seattle's hanging gardens and designed to restore pedestrian access between First Hill and the downtown area, Freeway Park provides a peaceful greenbelt in the heart of the city. (It's beautiful during the day, but not a safe place in the early morning or after dark.) Twenty seven thousand gallons of recycled water rush over the fountains each minute. It's hard to believe that the freeway is just below. Freedom Plaza at the park's east end is an open grassy area designed for children. Naramore Fountain, south of Seneca, was designed by Seattle sculptor George Tsutakawa and donated by the late Floyd Naramore, a Seattle architect concerned about freeway noise effects on the city. During the summer, weekly brown-bag concerts are held at noon. For a schedule of events, call the Downtown Seattle Association, 206-623-0340.

Westlake Park

Location: *Fourth Avenue at Pine Street.*
Wheelchair/Stroller Access: *Yes*
This red-brick park is in the heart of the retail shopping core. During the warmer months, visitors relish the mist from the fountain walls. In December, a vintage carousel is erected for shoppers to enjoy. A narrow bridge through the center of these fountains is a favorite for kids who can't resist getting wet.

The Seattle Center

When John F. Kennedy was president and most TVs were black-and-white, Seattle hosted the 1962 World's Fair at the newly created Seattle Center. Now several decades old, this 74-acre site is still a center for arts, science, and entertainment for the region.

Once a Northwest Indian tribal gathering spot for ceremonial feasts, the center is now a gathering spot for a broader range of cultural and community festivals. The mid-summer *Bite of Seattle* is a weekend music and food fest. Labor Day weekend's *Bumbershoot* music festival attracts thousands of music fans. December's *Winterfest* features ice skating and other holiday entertainment.

Seattle Center is also home to other cultural offerings. The new Charlotte Martin Seattle Children's Theater is an architectural masterpiece at the west corner of the grounds. Look for Pacific Northwest Ballet and Seattle Symphony performances here. Outstanding productions can also be found at the Bagley Wright Theatre, Opera House, and Intiman Playhouse. As you stroll the grounds, be sure to set aside some time for the International Fountain, a lighted, musically-synchronized waterworks extravaganza. Kids can play and splash in designated areas at its base.

Seattle Center is open year-round, but some exhibits and areas operate seasonally. See specific listings below or call the events line at 206-684-8582.

Ethnic and Cultural Festivals

Location: *Seattle Center House, Flag Pavilion, Center grounds*
Phone: *206-684-7200, general information*
Days/Hours: *Varies.*
Wheelchair/Stroller Access: *Yes*

After hosting 10 million visitors and more than a dozen nations at the 1962 World's Fair, the Seattle Center continues to serve as a regional center for ethnic and cultural celebrations. Some of the most popular annual events are listed below. Except as noted, festival activities are free.

Festival Sundiata (February). At the Center House and Flag Pavilion, this three-day weekend celebration focuses on African and African-American cultures, with art, music, readings, and special activities for kids.

Irish Festival (March). For this weekend event, the Center House comes alive with entertainment, workshops, Irish music, traditional dancing, and contests for kids.

Cherry Blossom & Japanese Cultural Festival (April). Tea ceremonies, flower arranging, origami, calligraphy, martial arts, doll exhibit, games, music, Awa Odori folk dancers, and food are featured at this weekend festival, held at the Center House and Flag Pavilion.

Seattle International Children's Festival (May). A week-long event, this childrents celebration features some of the world's finest performing companies from Taiwan, Australia, Germany, Brazil, Japan, Russia, Bolivia, Uganda, Canada, Sweden, the U.S., and other nations. Performances are held throughout the Seattle Center campus. Admission fees are charged for performances, but there are also free Activity Centers provided by corporate sponsors. Tickets range from $5 to $13, depending on the performance. Weekday events are often sold-out to school groups so a special family day is held on the last day (Saturday) of the festival. Call 684- 7346 for info.

Philippine Festival (June). The three-day weekend festival with Filipino arts, crafts, food, and entertainment, is held at the Center House.

Fiestas Patrias (September). This weekend event celebrates Mexican and Latin American independence with dance, music, ethnic foods and exhibits. Activities are held at the Center House and Flag Pavilion.

Festa Italiana (October). This weekend Italian festival features exhibits, demonstrations, entertainment, bocci ball and grape stomp competitions. It's held at the Center House and Flag Pavilion.

Great Destinations

Boeing Spacearium

Location: *Pacific Science Center*
Phone: *206-443-2850*
Hours/Days: *Varies; call ahead.*
Wheelchair/Stroller Access: *Yes*

The most popular seats in this theater on the floor. That's because most viewers prefer to recline on the carpet while they enjoy laser light show displays set to music on 4,500 watts of compact disk-quality sound. These shows are typically best suited to teens and adults because regularly scheduled music is heavy metal and grunge. Call the hotline periodically to hear about occasional classical music shows, too. Tickets run $3 to $8, depending on the show's time and day. Discounts are available for groups of 15 or more.

Fun Forest

Phone: *206-728-1585*
Days/Hours: *Noon to midnight, daily, Memorial Day through Labor Day; weekends only, spring and fall; closed November through January.*
Wheelchair/Stroller Access: *Yes*

The head-spinning, stomach-turning, let-me-try-it-again Jet Spin ride is the newest addition to this amusement park for all ages. There's a section of rides for tiny tots, and a popular mini-golf course. An arcade of carnival games offers players a chance to win stuffed animals. Popcorn and cotton candy stands offer between-rides snacks. Admission is free, but tickets for rides cost 85 cents. Rides vary in the number of tickets required.

IMAX

Location: *Pacific Science Center*
Phone: *206-443-IMAX*
Days/Hours: *Daily from 11 a.m., plus evening shows on weekends.*
Wheelchair/Stroller Access: *Yes*

On a screen three and a half stories high and 60 feet wide, viewers are nearly engulfed in the action of films projected here. Nature and science are the general themes. Shows change periodically, so call for a current schedule. Most shows are an hour long. Matinee admission is $5.50 for those 14 or older, $4.50 for seniors and students 6 to 13, $3.50 for children 2 to 5, and free to kids younger than 2.

Monorail

Location: *Terminals at Fifth Avenue and Pine Street at the third floor of Westlake Center and at the Seattle Center near the Space Needle*
Days/Hours: *9 a.m. to midnight (summer), 9 a.m. to 9 p.m., Sunday through Thursday, and 9 a.m. to midnight, Friday and Saturday, the rest of the year.*
Wheelchair/Stroller Access: *Yes*

It's just a two-minute ride between the Seattle Center and Westlake Center in downtown's retail shopping area on this attraction that's very popular with the younger set. The glass cars ride on tracks elevated by concrete pillars, offering a bird s eye view of downtown.

Pacific Science Center

Phone: *206-443-2001 (exhibit, IMAX and Laser Show updates)*
Days/Hours: *10 a.m. to 6 p.m., daily, mid-June to Labor Day; 10 a.m. to 5 p.m., Monday through Friday, and 10 a.m to 6 p.m., Saturday and Sunday the rest of the year.*
Wheelchair/Stroller Access: *Yes*

Eye-catching arches identify the Pacific Science Center, a cluster of five buildings that surround reflecting pools. The complex is an arena for exceptionally well-designed scientific displays and demonstrations for visitors of all ages.

The new permanent Tech Zone offers virtual reality games, robotics, and computers that become games for visitors. There are dozens of permanent hands-on exhibits, as well as several rotating exhibits. Favorites include the August Bubble Festival, the

Photo by Carol Harrold

Tech Zone, a permanent exhibit at Pacific Science Center, shows children how to become computer artists.

Halloween weekend haunted science center, and — most popular of all — Thanksgiving weekend's Model Railroad show. Admission prices include the science center, the Planetarium and IMAX or laser show. Those 14 and older pay $8, seniors and students 6 to 13 years pay $7, children 2 to 5 years pay $5.50, and disabled visitors or those 2 years or younger are admitted free.

Seattle Children's Museum

Location: *Lower level of Seattle Center House*
Phone: *206-298-2521 (recorded info.) or 206-441-1768 (reservations)*
Days/Hours: *10 a.m. to 5 p.m., daily, Memorial Day through Labor Day; 10 a.m. to 5 p.m., Tuesday through Sunday, the rest of the year.*
Wheelchair/Stroller Access: *Yes, on the first level from the east and west sides*

The largest children's museum in the state just tripled in size! Designed as a hands-on, participatory learning and play place for kids, the $4.15 million expansion is chock full of fun. Everything is made to be smelled, touched, picked up, and examined.

Permanent displays include a child-sized neighborhood with a fire truck, grocery store, restaurant and more. Adults are encouraged to play along with kids here. Be sure to visit the Imagination Station, a drop-in art studio where museum visitors meet professional artists and try their hands at an art medium. Infants and toddlers will enjoy Little Lagoon, a padded toy area for climbing and romping.

The mechanical world in the new addition will delight everyone. You ll see construction blocks, pipes, balls, conveyor belts and pulleys. Another new section includes a wilderness area, international village, a historical time zone station, a contemporary culture zone, an improved storytelling area, a discovery bay for toddlers, and a resource area for teachers.

Admission is $3.50 for those 1 year or older, and free to those younger than 1 year. Call ahead about group or birthday party rates for groups of 10 to 15 kids.

Seattle Children's Theatre

Location: *Charlotte Martin Theatre*
Phone: *206-441-3322 (tickets)*
Days/Hours: *Call ahead for performance schedules.*
Wheelchair/Stroller Access: *Yes*

Since 1976, the Seattle Children's Theatre has been presenting lively performances, including favorite old classics and fascinating contemporary productions, and has produced more than 50 original works for young audiences. Hearing-impaired director Howie Seago and his acting brother Billy also present special productions for deaf audiences. Classes in mask-making, comedy, movement, and dance for children 4 1/2 to 19 years are available each quarter.

Seattle Sonics

Location: *190 Queen Anne Avenue N.*
Phone: *206-281-5800 (administrative office); tickets also available through Ticketmaster at 206-283-DUNK*
Days/Hours: *Pre-season games begin in October; regular season starts in November and runs through mid-May. Game times vary.*
Wheelchair/Stroller Access: *Yes*

The Sonics' National Basketball Association home games will be held at the Tacoma Dome during a coliseum facelift (and roof- and wall-lift, for that matter). They'll return to their remodeled Key Arena home court in 1996. Kids of all ages love the slam-dunking action. Half-time entertainment can be nearly as fun, when fans whose names are drawn may compete in hoop shoot contests to win prizes. Admission prices range from $7 to $60, and are always subject to change. Call the ticket office for current information.

Seattle Thunderbirds

Location: *2505 Third Ave.*
Phone: *206-448-PUCK(7825) for tickets*
Days/Hours: *Office open 9 a.m. to 5 p.m., Monday through Friday, September through March.*
Wheelchair/Stroller Access: *Yes*

For a team that plays on the ice, this semi-pro hockey team can get really hot! Fans like sitting right behind the players' box to hear the coach bark directions. The season runs from October through March. Watch for cross-state rivalries in Spokane and Tri-Cities.

Space Needle

Phone: *206-443-2100*
Days/Hours: *7 a.m. to midnight, Monday through Saturday; 8 a.m. to midnight, Sunday.*
Wheelchair/Stroller Access: *Yes*

Glass elevators whisk you up 520 feet to the Observation deck, or 500 feet to the revolving restaurant in mere seconds. Enjoy the 360-degree view of the city, sound, mountains, and outlying islands (if it isn't raining!). The Needle is a magnet for both visitors and natives. Four gift shops at street level sell local and regional souvenirs. Admission is $6.50 for adults, $5.75 for seniors, $4 for students 5 to 12, and free to those 4 or younger. See the Space Needle Restaurant listing for dining information.

Places to Eat

Seattle Center House

Days/Hours: *11 a.m. to 6 p.m., daily, Labor Day through Memorial Day; 11 a.m. to 8 p.m., Sunday through Thursday, and 11 a.m. to 9 p.m., Friday and Saturday, the rest of the year.*
Wheelchair/Stroller Access: *Yes*
This is a popular place with families, rain or shine. More than 50 shops offer gifts and an international scope of specialty foods. Watch a fudge maker at work, drink anything apple flavored, and sample Asian, Middle Eastern or plain old American food. Eateries are on the main floor's perimeter and upper balcony. Shops carry both traditional and funky souvenirs.

Entertainment — available almost daily — often includes excellent local bands, energetic dance groups, and classic films. You can watch (for free) a variety of activities in the performing arts area on the main level. On the lowest level you'll find the Seattle Children's Museum.

Space Needle Restaurant

Phone: *206-443-2100*
Days/Hours: *11 a.m. to 11 p.m., daily.*
Wheelchair/Stroller Access: *Yes, except restrooms. There's a restroom for the disabled on the 100-foot-deck; take elevator*
Your eyes aren't playing tricks on you. The restaurant on top of the 605-foot-tall Space Needle is continually revolving, providing a 360-degree view while you remain seated. Prices are somewhat upscale, but locals and out-of-town visitors make it a special-occasion-visit with children. A kids' menu features chicken, spaghetti or fish. Save room for the Lunar Orbiter dessert. For a souvenir, order the Space Needle punch. It's served in a plastic Space Needle cup that the kids can take home.

Helpful Phone Numbers:

Seattle/King County Convention and Visitors Bureau, 206-461-5840

Seattle Parks and Recreation Department information and recreation scheduling, 206-684-4075

Seattle Parks and Recreation Department Youth Sports Information, 206-684-7091

Washington State Ferry System, 206-464-6400

RIMENTAL

Children of all ages enjoy "flying" the real aircraft of the Hangar exhibit in the Museum of Flight.

Greater Seattle Neighborhoods

Surrounding the downtown core, Seattle's residential communities also offer destinations the entire family is sure to enjoy. These neighborhoods originated in the 1880s, when trolleys made suburban life more accessible. City planners jumped on the bandwagon and developed amusement parks, picnic grounds, dance pavilions, sports fields, zoos and groomed beaches. To this day, appealing parks are some of the best features in Seattle's well-established neighborhoods.

North of downtown, you'll find Magnolia and Queen Anne. Magnolia's name is something of a misnomer. It was named by early settlers who mistook the madrona trees in the area for magnolias. Neighboring Queen Anne was named after the architectural style favored by its early residents.

Beyond Magnolia — north of Lake Union and the ship canal — are Ballard, Wallingford, Fremont, Green Lake, Greenwood and several other neighborhoods northwest of Seattle. Interstate 5 separates these communities from dozens of enclaves to the northeast, including the University District, Sand Point, and Lake City.

East of the city center are Madison Park and Capitol Hill. Farther south, Mount Baker, Seward Park, Beacon Hill, and Rainier Valley are a melting pot of the city's diverse ethnic mix.

West of the downtown core is West Seattle, where the city's love affair with water is evident in its parks, beaches, and ferry terminals. Fauntleroy and other neighborhoods spread out from West Seattle.

Magnolia and Queen Anne

Great Destinations

Discovery Park

Location: *In Magnolia at 36th Avenue West and West Government Way*
Phone: *206-386-4236*
Days/Hours: *Dawn to dusk, daily; visitors center open 8:30 a.m. to 5 p.m.; closed major holidays.*
Wheelchair/Stroller Access: *Yes*

When the army abandoned most of Fort Lawton in 1973, the city developed this premier piece of real estate into a 500-acre park that is actually four parks in one: cliff, beach, meadowland and forest. A good first visit with the kids is the Wolf Tree Nature Trail, a self-guided educational walk. Look for a brochure at the Visitors Center near the park's entrance. Park naturalists lead nature walks at 2 p.m. on Saturdays. While it's wise to call ahead and confirm, reservations are not needed.

Discovery Park has many nesting birds — some quite rare — as well as other small wildlife. Educational programs include "Bird Observation Tours" and "Meet the Ranger." Call for a schedule of modestly-priced group programs about polliwogs, spiders, and snakes planned for pre-schoolers and children in kindergarten through eighth grade.

Daybreak Star Art Center/United Indians

Location: *North side of Discovery Park*
Phone: *206-285-4425*
Days/Hours: *10 a.m. to 5 p.m., Wednesday through Saturday.*
Wheelchair/Stroller Access: *Yes*

The upper level of this Native American center houses a collection of artwork from Northwest Indians as well as other North American tribes. Look for beadwork, baskets and Kachina cornhusks, and Seminole and Miccosukee dolls. There's also a major collection of contemporary works by Indian artists, featuring large murals and sculpted pieces. October through April, the second Saturday of the month, organizers host an Indian Art Mart between 10 a.m. and 4 p.m. Crafts created by Native Americans are sold here. For tours, group rates for children are available. Parties of more than four need reservations.

Pea Patch Program

Location: *425 Elliott Ave. W.*

Phone: *206-684-0264*

The Pea Patch Program, administered by the Department of Human Resources, is a back-to-nature program; a modern version of the Victory Garden. Families work together to plan, plant, and work their garden plots. New gardeners can get help from the Master Gardeners available at patch sites. Pea Patches are scattered in 17 locations within city limits and leased on an annual basis. Call for information on plot sizes and prices. The Gardenship Fund sponsors plots for those in need. Don't miss the granddaddy of potlucks, the Harvest Banquet, held in September by city Pea Patchers celebrating their harvest.

Seattle Funplex

Location: *Near Magnolia at 1535 15th Ave W., just west of the Magnolia Bridge*

Phone: *206-285-7842*

Days/Hours: *Daily; hours change seasonally.*

Wheelchair/Stroller Access: *Yes*

Designed for families of all ages, Seattle Funplex offers indoor mini-golf, video games, batting cages, go-carts and laser tag for older children and adults. Toddlers will love the play area and "jungle bouncer," an inflatable arena of soft plastic floors and mesh walls designed for jumping and tumbling. There's also a full service concession. Special group rates and birthday party packages are available. There is a $2 cover charge after 9 p.m., Friday and Saturday. There is no entrance fee the rest of the time; however, each game is individually priced.

Places to Play

Bhy Kracke

Location: *On Queen Anne at Bigelow Avenue North and Comstock Place*

Neighborhood children love the playground at this little park (pronounced "by cracky"). Parents will enjoy the lattice-laced arbor as they sit and watch the kids at play. During spring, the steep, ivy-covered hill abounds in azaleas and rhododendrons, and it offers a splendid view of the city all year long.

Places to Eat

Chinook's at Salmon Bay

Location: *At Fisherman's Terminal, just south of the Ballard Bridge*
Phone: *206-283-HOOK(4665)*
Days/Hours: *7:30 a.m. to 10 p.m., Sunday; 11 a.m. to 10 p.m., Monday through Thursday; 11 a.m. to 11 p.m., Friday.*
Wheelchair/Stroller Access: *Yes*
 With a great view of the Seattle Fishing Terminal as the drawing card, Chinook's is a popular seafood stop. Little Chinooks get a placemat menu with crayons and their choice of fish 'n chips, prawns, burgers, or a grilled cheese sandwich. Scones are a favorite here, too.

Northwest Neighborhoods

 Public art is one of the distinctive features of Northwest Seattle. Kids love the great Viking statue on Ballard's Shilshole Avenue. The sculpture of patient bus riders in Fremont, "Waiting for the Interurban" — is regularly decorated by locals, and one of the most photographed sites in the city. The Troll that likes to eat cars (but doesn't scare kids) emerges from under the north end of the Aurora Bridge between Wallingford and Fremont. These landmarks — and so much more — are what give this region a special personality.

Great Destinations

The Bathhouse Theater

Location: *7312 W. Greenlake Dr. N.*
Phone: *206-524-9108 and 206-524-9109 (recorded information)*
Days/Hours: *Noon to 7 p.m., Tuesday through Sunday at box office.*
Wheelchair/Stroller Access: *Four steps at entry; staff will assist*
 This popular theater group produces at least two productions a year suitable for children, including a musical in the summer. Admission prices vary — call for information. No babies, please.

Bergen Place

Location: *In Ballard at 22nd Avenue Northwest and Northwest Market Street.*
Wheelchair/Stroller Access: *Yes*
Named after Seattle's sister city in Norway, this Ballard community gathering place was dedicated by King Olav V during his 1975 visit. The plaza is cobbled in brick and has a pavilion used for outdoor concerts and community festivals.

Gas Works Park

Location: *Near Wallingford at Northlake Way and Meridian. From Aurora Avenue, take Northlake Way east and follow Lake Union's north shore.*
Wheelchair/Stroller Access: *Yes*
What was once an old gas works plant is now a park of rolling hills featuring the machinery used years ago — only today it's sandblasted and attractively painted. Kids can climb all over the wheels and gears of this unique playground. Before you leave, climb to the top of the highest hill to look at the sundial and catch a spectacular view of downtown Seattle. On the Fourth of July, Gas Works Park is one of the best sites in the city to watch fireworks displays. There's plenty of parking here for picnickers, kite-fliers and those who use the park as a launching point for the paved Burke-Gilman Trail (popular with bicyclists, pedestrians and in-line skaters).

Green Lake

Location: *East Green Lake Drive North at West Green Lake Drive*
Days/Hours: *Dawn until dusk.*
Wheelchair/Stroller Access: *Yes*
This tree-lined, lakefront park is a major draw for active recreationalists as well as casual strollers and park-goers. The lake is wrapped by a meandering 2.8-mile asphalt path. Half is dedicated to pedestrians, the other half to bicyclists and skaters. At the park's north end, the trail weaves near a wading pool which is filled with laughing children in the summer.

Green Lake's northeast side is home to tennis courts, playfields, an indoor swimming pool, gymnasium, canoe and paddleboat rentals, a sandy beach with a lifeguard (summers only) and a community center. Classes for swimming and other recreation and leisure activities are taught by city park personnel. Behind the community center there's a playground with a dozen swings and other equipment.

The northwest side of the park offers fishing piers where anglers try to reel in some of the trout stocked annually. The Bathhouse Theater and an island game preserve are also on this side of the lake. Picnic tables, lawn bowling, horseshoes and a pitch-and-putt course make up the park's south side.

Lake Washington Ship Canal and Hiram Chittenden Locks

Location: *In Ballard at 3015 N.W. 54th St. From Elliott Avenue, cross the Ballard Bridge to 15th Avenue Northwest. Turn west on Market Street and drive about 15 blocks*
Phone: *206-783-7001 and 206-783-7059 (tours)*
Days/Hours: *10 a.m. to 7 p.m., daily, June through September; Visitors Center open 11 a.m. to 5 p.m., Thursday through Monday, October through May; tours at 1 p.m. and 3 p.m. daily.*
Wheelchair/Stroller Access: *Yes*

Visitors often catch the boating bug after a stop at the Government Locks on the Lake Washington Ship Canal. The Visitors Center is one of the city's most popular tourist attractions. It offers five different slide programs and a working model of the Locks. Thousands of boats pass between Lake Washington and Puget Sound via these locks each week. Since weekend boating began in 1916, traffic has exceeded expectations.

Tours begin in the Visitors Center with the history of the locks, then take you to the immaculately landscaped gardens before winding up at the locks. The tour includes viewing the fish ladder where visitors learn about the life cycle of salmon. Children will be fascinated by the underwater view of the fish ladder, where they can watch salmon return to their spawning grounds.

Commodore Park, adjacent to the locks on the south side, is completely fenced and a delightful park setting. The park and grounds at the north side of the locks close at 9 p.m. daily. Ramps to the fish ladder aid physically challenged visitors. Adjacent grounds are well-lit, with convenient restrooms and bike racks.

Appointments are required for group tours, which usually last about an hour. Tours are available for anyone 5 years or older and include a fair amount of walking, so wear comfortable shoes and warm outer clothing in cool weather.

Nordic Heritage Museum

Location: *In Ballard at 3014 N.W. 67th*
Phone: *206-789-5707*
Days/Hours: *10 a.m. to 4 p.m., Tuesday through Saturday;
noon to 4 p.m., Sunday.*
Wheelchair/Stroller Access: *Yes*

Scandinavian Americans take great pride in the immigration story told on the self-guided tour through this museum. Using vivid displays, the tour retraces Swedish, Danish, Norwegian, Finnish and Icelandic treks across the Atlantic to Ellis Island. From there, many immigrants stopped in the Midwest before finally reaching the West Coast. Displays highlight how the immigrants fished, farmed and logged when they arrived in the Northwest. Each country is represented by its own display room on the second floor.

Curators here are dedicated to teaching history to children and often use weekend theatrical performances, art and music demonstrations to pique kids' interests. Call ahead to find out what's happening. Admission is $3 for adults, $2 for seniors and college students, $1 for students 6 to 16, and free to kids 5 or younger. Admission is free the first Tuesday of the month.

Woodland Park Zoo

Location: *Between Green Lake and Ballard on Phinney Ridge at Fremont Avenue North*
Phone: *206-684-4800 for recorded general information*
Days/Hours: *9:30 a.m. to 6 p.m., daily, April through September;
9:30 a.m. to 5 p.m., weekdays, October and March; 9:30 a.m. to
4 p.m., weekdays, November through February; zoo opens at 8:30
a.m. on weekends and holidays.*
Wheelchair/Stroller Access: *Yes; rental equipment is also available*

Ranked one of the top 10 zoos in the country, the Woodland Park Zoo is a stop guaranteed to please young and old alike. From carefully replicated natural habitats to flower gardens, there's something here for everyone. Kids of all ages take delight in the Family Farm, where they pet some of their favorite animals. Watch out for the friendly goats — they'll pick your pocket, eating whatever they find in there!

A specially designed and nationally acclaimed Asian tropical forest is home to the Great Elephants. Kids love exploring the dark, warm Nocturnal House, where bats, unusual snakes, spiders and

Photo by Karen Anderson
Everyone enjoys petting the animals in the
Family Farm Contact Yard in Woodland Park Zoo.

other creatures of the night live. Giraffes and zebras roam in the Africa-like savanna. Everybody will enjoy watching the Great Apes frolic together. The newest area is the six-acre *Northern Trail of Alaska* exhibit featuring river otters, brown bears, wolves, elk, mountain goats, bald eagles and snowy owls.

Woodland Park Zoo also creates temporary homes for traveling exhibits, which are featured for two to six months. Visiting animals as part of this program have included golden monkeys, koalas and pandas. Spring is especially popular here because of the influx of baby animals, as well as the Rose Garden next door being in full bloom.

There are two important rules at this zoo: no pets except Seeing Eye Dogs are allowed; and don't feed the animals, because their diets are strictly controlled. If you get hungry, however, there are concession stands selling hot dogs, popcorn and soft drinks. Or you can visit the new Food Court, which features such vendors as Burger King and Cinnabon.

Admission is $7 for adults, $5.25 for seniors and college students, $4.50 for the disabled of any age and students 6 to 17, $2.25 for kids 3 to 5, and free to those 2 or younger. Ask about a small discount for King County residents and an annual pass. A $3 ($1.50 during winter months) parking fee is charged in zoo lots.

Places to Play

Carkeek Park

Location: *North of Greenwood at Northwest Carkeek Park Road and Ninth Avenue Northwest, near Northwest 110th Street*

Carkeek is a wilderness park of 180 forested acres resting on a hill above a beach overlooking the Puget Sound. European-style playground equipment attracts young children, and riding high on the swing set near the picnic shelter offers incredible views for all ages. A hiking trail with a view of the Olympic Mountains runs to the hill's edge. Just inside the main gate is an archery range for those with their own bows and arrows. Model airplanes are welcome on the grassy area — check with the parks department for competitions in the spring and summer. Permanent fire pits are available on the beach. Dangerous railroad tracks running through this park have been fenced off. A pedestrian bridge links the beach and park.

Licton Springs Park

Location: *North 97th Street at Ashworth Avenue North*

This site, just a few blocks west of North Seattle Community College, was once an historical Indian health spa with a natural mineral spring. Look for the tree house, play area, wetlands trails, wooded walking paths and restrooms in this peaceful park.

Woodland Park

Location: *North 50th at Green Lake Way North*

This greenbelt is adjacent to the zoo and just as large. Three pedestrian bridges connect the park's upper and lower sections. Wooded trails and pleasant picnic areas with grassy hills overlooking Green Lake are accessible from parking lots off Aurora Avenue and from North 50th Street. Lower Woodland Park is devoted to tennis courts, soccer and softball fields, and the Seattle Parks and Recreation office.

Places to Eat

Bruegger's Fresh Bagel Bakery

Location: *7200 E. Green Lake Dr. N.*
Phone: *206-522-0902*
Days/Hours: *6:30 a.m. to 7 p.m., Monday through Friday; 7 a.m. to 8 p.m., Saturday and Sunday.*
Wheelchair/Stroller Access: *Yes*
    Tasty bagels and an indoor play area for younger children await families at this bakery across the street from Green Lake. Try a sandwich and soup combo or slather one of Bruegger's tasty spreads on your bagel for a fun meal. There are three other Bruegger's: 7695 S.E. 27th St. in Tabit Square on Mercer Island, 4517 University Way N.E. in the University District and 1301 Madison on First Hill.

Dick's

Location: *In Wallingford at 111 N.E. 45th St.*
Phone: *206-632-5125*
Days/Hours: *10:30 a.m. to 2 a.m., daily.*
Wheelchair/Stroller Access: *Yes*
    A Seattle fast-food restaurant for 50 years, Dick's is a city landmark when it comes to burgers, fries and milkshakes. Root beer floats and nearly a dozen toppings for ice cream sundaes attract sweet lovers. Families find Dick's to be a great place for a quick, tasty meal. This is a popular place for pre-teens as well as those teens who can drive. Dick's also has restaurants on Capitol Hill, Queen Anne, Lake City and north of Ballard on Holman Road.

Honey Bear Bakery

Location: *Near Green Lake at 2106 N. 55th*
Phone: *206-545-7296*
Days/Hours: *6 a.m. to 11 p.m., daily.*
Wheelchair/Stroller Access: *Yes*
    You'll find both devoted sweet-lovers and health food addicts here. Nearly all 50 varieties of cakes offered are whipped up from scratch right on the premises. The bakers use whole wheat and

honey. This is a great place to visit with family and friends, or come alone with a newspaper or your favorite book. It's a popular stop for zoo and Green Lake visitors. There's indoor seating available in the nice weather.

Ivar's Salmon House on Lake Union

Location: *Near Wallingford at 401 N.E. Northlake Way*
Phone: *206-632-0767*
Days/Hours: *11 a.m. to 2 p.m. for lunch, Monday through Friday; 10 a.m. to 2 p.m., Sunday brunch; 4 p.m. to 10 p.m., Monday through Thursday; 4:30 p.m. to 11 p.m., Friday; 4 p.m. to 11 p.m., Saturday; and 4 p.m. to 10 p.m., Sunday.*
Wheelchair/Stroller Access: *Yes*

Ivar's is a Seattle landmark that is amazingly popular with both locals and tourists. Popular menu items are salmon broiled over an alder fire, fish and chips, and Ivar's famous clam nectar. Try some of Ivar's signature cornbread. This place is great for children because the atmosphere is relaxed and friendly. While waiting for their meals, kids can color their placemats and fold them into masks.

Some guests moor their vessels next to the restaurant and arrive in their boating clothes. Others dress up for an evening of dining on the water with a view of downtown Seattle.

Northeast Neighborhoods

From the University of Washington to Lake City, Seattle's northeast neighborhoods offer comfortable living for thousands of residents. The 22-mile Burke-Gilman Trail, the second most popular urban recreation trail in the country, connects many of the communities. The Burke-Gilman is a relatively flat, paved route for bicyclists, in-line skaters and pedestrians. Blackberry bushes dot either side, and late in the summer, kids enjoy picking these sweet treats. The trail officially begins in Ballard but has a smoother surface starting at Fremont's Gas Works Park. It then extends along the abandoned bed of the Burlington-Northern Railroad for 12.5 miles to Kenmore's Tracy Owen Station, previously named Log Boom Park. From here, the trail meanders another six miles along the Sammamish Slough to northeast of Bothell, where it meets the Sammamish River Trail.

Great Destinations

Civic Light Opera

Location: *South of Lake City neighborhood at Jane Addams Theatre, 11051 34th N.E.*
Phone: *206-363-2809*
Days/Hours: *Box office open 1 p.m. to 4 p.m., Monday & Wednesday.*
Wheelchair/Stroller Access: *Yes*

With three musical productions each year, this theatre leaves audiences humming. Local talent takes the stage for these performances that are geared toward families. Summer workshops for children 6 to 12 offer classes in acting, dancing and singing. Call for audition information and a list of classes.

Henry Art Gallery

Location: *University of Washington campus, 15th Avenue Northeast at Northeast Campus Parkway*
Phone: *206-543-2280*
Days/Hours: *11 a.m. to 5 p.m., Tuesday through Sunday; open until 9 p.m. on Thursday.*
Wheelchair/Stroller Access: *Yes*

The Henry Art Gallery specializes in fine art and features local artists, pieces from state collections, and important national exhibitions. American paintings and sculptures are emphasized here, and new exhibits appear monthly. A $13 million underground addition will display even more works of art when the museum reopens in early 1997.

Older children with an appreciation for fine art find this a great destination. Call ahead for group tours and ask about group discounts. Museum officials recommend one adult accompany each group of 10 children. Many visitors combine a stop here with one at the Thomas Burke Museum. Gallery admission is $3.50 for adults, $2 for ages 13 to 18, and free to those 12 or younger. U.W. staff and students are admitted free. Admission is by donation on Thursdays.

Northwest Puppet Center

Location: *9123 15th Ave. N.E.*
Phone: *206-523-2579*
Days/Hours: *Varies depending on scheduled weekend performances.*
Wheelchair/Stroller Access: *Yes*

Enchanting puppets and marionettes from all over the world seem to come alive on this stage. Some performances feature Seattle's own Carter Family Marionettes. If you stop at the center's puppet museum before or after a show, you'll see visiting exhibits from all over the world. Entertainment is designed for those 3 years or older. The first Saturday matinee in each series is signed for the hearing-impaired. Kids can have a unique birthday party here ($6.50 per child). Included in the price is admission to a play and a puppet to take home, and the birthday kid gets a crown. Regular ticket prices are $6.50 for adults and $4.50 for children younger than 10.

Seattle Youth Symphony

Location: *11065 5th Ave N.E, Suite E (box office)*
Phone: *206-362-2300*
Days/Hours: *9 a.m. to 5 p.m., Monday through Friday (box office).*
Wheelchair/Stroller Access: *Depends on location of concert*
These concerts are a great way for families to enjoy music together. Young musicians play a fairly sophisticated repertoire and have gained a reputation for very professional performances. Performers in the Debut Symphony are aged 8 to 18; the Junior Symphony includes those junior high to college age. Tickets can be ordered by phone and can either be mailed or picked up at the address listed above. Call for schedule information and admission prices.

Thomas Burke Memorial Washington State Museum

Location: *At the University of Washington, at Northeast 45th Street and 17th Avenue Northeast*
Phone: *206-543-5590 or 206-543-5591 (tours/education department), and 206-543-9762 (general programs)*
Days/Hours: *10 a.m. to 5 p.m., Friday through Wednesday; 10 a.m. to 8 p.m., Thursday.*
Wheelchair/Stroller Access: *Yes*
Natural history is the emphasis at this museum featuring Native American artifacts, zoological and insect collections, and geological exhibits. Ask about special exhibitions. Tours are self-guided, but group tours are available through the education department. Groups must make reservations one month in advance. There's no admission charge, but the following donations are suggested: $3.00 for adults, $2.00 for seniors and students, and $1.50 for students ages 6-18. Ask about traveling exhibits and classes for kids.

University of Washington Waterfront Activity Center

Location: *Behind Husky Football Stadium off Montlake Boulevard*
Phone: *206-543-9433*
Days/Hours: *10 a.m. to dusk, Monday through Friday; 9 a.m. to dusk, Saturday and Sunday, February through October.*
Wheelchair/Stroller Access: *Yes*

Many of Lake Washington's lovely inlets outline the Arboretum's shoreline, making this a popular facility for canoe and rowboat rentals. Paddle your way around lily pads and weeping willows on Foster Island. Rent by the hour or day. The facility requires valid I.D. for each boat rental. Fees for U.W. students are $1.60 per hour, $2.50 for U.W. staff, $3.10 for U.W. alumn,i and $3.50 for the general public. Rates are subject to change. All boats carry seat cushions and life vests. On sunny days, expect a long wait for a boat. It's smart to go early with a picnic lunch. Typically, no reservations are accepted but on some busy days, families of four may reserve special boats. For boats carrying passengers younger than 16, each boat must have at least one adult 18 or older on board.

Places to Play

Burke-Gilman Playground Park

Location: *North of Laurelhurst at Northeast 52nd Street and Sand Point Way Northeast*

This playground near Children's Hospital and Medical Center is totally accessible to the physically challenged. Look for the innovative water play equipment, picnic tables and restrooms. The park sits along the Burke-Gilman Trail.

Lake City Playground

Location: *Lake City Way at Northeast 125th Street*

This new playground assembled by local Lion's Club volunteers offers spring toys, embankment slides, climbing rocks, sand scoops and water play.

Laurelhurst Community Center

Location: *4554 N.E. 41st St.*

Kids are sure to have a barrel of fun on the big, new play structure here. It's equipped with tire swings, two slides, arch climbers, trapeze rings and climbing platforms installed over a safe bed of sand.

Magnuson Park

Location: *Northeast 65th Street at Sand Point Way Northeast*

Once part of the former Sand Point Naval Air Base, these park grounds offer paved trails for walking, biking, and skating. Tennis courts, softball fields, picnic tables, a boat launching area, wading pool, and a lifeguarded (during summer) swimming beach are some of its other features. At the north end of the park's beachfront walkway, walk through the gate to the adjacent National Oceanic and Atmospheric Administration (NOAA) property and explore the fine public art on-site. The Sound Garden, located just past the gate, is a sculpture of aluminum pipes that are "played" by the wind. Sit quietly, listen, and enjoy the views of Lake Washington.

Matthews Beach

Location: *Northeast 93rd Street at Sand Point Way Northeast*

Many north-end families consider this their favorite playground because of the innovative climbing equipment. There's plenty of room for a family picnic or birthday party. This park also boasts Seattle's largest freshwater beach. Lifeguards are on duty from Memorial Day through Labor Day. Be sure to bring along your stale bread because the ducks will line up for a snack. The Burke-Gilman Trail runs through the park.

Madison Park and Capitol Hill

These neighboring communities reflect an eclectic mix, from old mansions and urbane apartments to cosmopolitan shopping and the grunge music scene. Capitol Hill's Broadway district bustles with activity nearly round-the-clock, while the Arboretum near Madison Park offers a tranquil respite from the city's fast-paced activity.

Great Destinations

Cornish College of the Arts

Location: *On Capitol Hill at 710 E. Roy St.*
Phone: *206-323-1400 (ask for public affairs)*
Days/Hours: *9 a.m. to 4 p.m., Monday through Friday.*
Wheelchair/Stroller Access: *Yes*

At Cornish College for the Arts, student artists and performers offer wonderful presentations each year, attracting children interested in creative arts. The Cornish Junior Dance Company performs in December and June. Call for ticket prices and schedules.

Cornish's Fisher Gallery hosts visual art exhibits from noon to 5 p.m., Monday through Friday. Admission to this gallery is free. Works on display are by professional artists, with occasional student shows. Each semester there is an Exhibition and Performance Plus presentation. Every department holds an exhibit or performance, including a lecture by the department chair. Call for more details.

Museum of History and Industry

Location: *Between University District and Madison Park at 2700 24th Ave. E.*
Phone: *206-324-1125*
Days/Hours: *10 a.m. to 5 p.m., daily.*
Wheelchair/Stroller Access: *Yes*

This museum, dedicated to Seattle and King County's history, features a number of hands-on exhibits and weekend programs for families. Each December, the museum highlights Northwest holiday traditions with an exhibition and activities.

Outside, two nature trails belonging to the Arboretum offer pleasant places to picnic and observe nesting birds, ducks, geese and fish. Trail One winds under the Montlake Bridge and meanders before ending at the Seattle Yacht Club. Trail Two goes to little

Marsh Island, crosses a bridge and continues to Foster Island. The walk around Foster Island is rather long for small children. The trails have no restrooms. Museum admission is $5.50 for those 13 or older, $3 for seniors, disabled, or students 6 to 12, $1 for kids 2 to 5, and free for those children younger than 2. Call ahead to ask about "Family Funtivities" planned throughout the year.

Pioneer Cemetery

Location: *On Capitol Hill at 1554 15th Ave. E.*
Days/Hours: *8 a.m. to 8 p.m., Monday through Saturday; 9 a.m. to 8 p.m., Sunday.*
Wheelchair/Stroller Access: *Yes*

This is the final resting place for many of Seattle's pioneers. Reading the gravestones is a trip through the city's history — from the area's earliest white settlers to martial arts film star Bruce Lee, who was buried here in 1973.

Seattle Asian Art Museum

Location: *On Capitol Hill's north end in Volunteer Park at East Prospect Street*
Phone: *206-654-3100*
Days/Hours: *10 a.m. to 5 p.m., Tuesday, Wednesday, and Friday through Sunday; 10 a.m. to 9 p.m., Thursday.*
Wheelchair/Stroller Access: *Yes*

Formerly the site of the Seattle Art Museum, this beautiful facility has been remodeled to showcase some of the country's finest Asian art. Six galleries are devoted to Chinese works; another six feature Japanese pieces. Also look for masterpieces from the Himalayas, India, Korea and Southeast Asia. Admission is $6 for adults, $4 for seniors and students 13 to 19, and free to those 12 or younger. Admission includes entrance to the Seattle Art Museum downtown, if visited within two days.

Seattle Mime Theater

Location: *915 E. Pine, No. 419*
Phone: *206-324-8788*
Days/Hours: *Box office open 9 a.m. to 5 p.m., Monday through Friday.*
Wheelchair/Stroller Access: *Yes*

This small troop of mime performers produces several plays a year in the Seattle area. Many shows and workshops are scheduled at schools. Performances are geared to audiences of all ages, but kids seem especially excited about the unusual nature of mimes. Call for ticket prices and schedule information.

Volunteer Park Conservatory

Location: *On Capitol Hill in Volunteer Park at 15th Avenue East at East Galer*
Phone: *206-684-4743*
Days/Hours: *9 a.m. to 5 p.m., daily and holidays; tours available September through June.*
Wheelchair/Stroller Access: *Yes*

Kids love the warm, humid atmosphere, vivid colors and fragrant smells found here. Diverse exhibits of exuberant floral displays are part of the conservatory. The Bromeliad House (temperature 72 degrees) features just about every relative in the pineapple family — there are more than 2,000 species. In the Fern House, you'll see a Sago Palm, a small pond (no coins, please; metal kills the fish) and many tropical and sub-tropical flowers. The Palm House contains a permanent display of orchids blooming year-round. The Seasonal Display House, at 65 degrees, is slightly cooler. Here you'll recognize begonias, coleus, fuschias, geraniums, gardenias, and poinsettias. For warm days, there's a wading pool for young ones nearby in the park. Large groups require an appointment.

Volunteer Park Water Tower

Location: *Volunteer Park*
Days/Hours: *8 a.m. to 5:30 p.m., daily.*
Wheelchair/Stroller Access: *No*

If you're willing to climb 106 steps, the Observation Deck at Volunteer Park offers a beautiful view of the city and the grounds. The park is a great place to visit during the day, but should be avoided at night.

Washington Park Arboretum

Location: *Near Madison Park at Graham Visitors Center, 2300 Arboretum Dr. E.*
Phone: *206-543-8800*
Days/Hours: *Dawn to dusk, daily; Visitors Center 10 a.m. to 4 p.m., Monday through Friday; noon to 4 p.m., Saturday and Sunday, September through April, and 10 a.m. to 4 p.m., May through August.*
Wheelchair/Stroller Access: *Yes, at the Visitors Center, but limited on the trails*

The Arboretum is a popular year-round destination that features more than 5,000 trees, shrubs and vines. Families often picnic in this natural setting where there's plenty of space for kids to frolic.

Guided tours are managed by the University of Washington Center for Urban Horticulture and describe the areas that are most interesting at that particular time of year. After the tour, browse through the gift shop where you'll find a remarkable collection of garden-oriented gifts, books and accessories. Drop by for the free tour on Sundays at 1 p.m., except in December. It's important that children be able to walk the entire distance, since one- to two-hour tours may cover several acres.

Washington Park Arboretum Japanese Garden

Phone: *206-684-4725*
Days/Hours: *10 a.m. to 4 p.m., daily, March through May and September through November; 10 a.m. to 8 p.m., daily, June through August.*
Wheelchair/Stroller Access: *Yes*

The Arboretum's three-acre Japanese Tea Garden, founded in 1960, re-creates one of Japan's most beautiful assets. After a fire in the 1980s destroyed the teahouse, it was rebuilt with the help of a local Japanese architect and several artists. Great care has been taken to preserve the garden's authenticity. Different stones represent mountains, calm water, and fire, and shrubs must be pruned according to design. Visitors receive a brochure telling the garden's story and each feature's symbolism.

Best times to visit are in April and May, when shrubs are in bloom, or during the fall, when autumn turns the leaves into blazing yellows and reds. Summers, you'll find beautiful koi swimming in the lovely ponds and large turtles sunning themselves on the rocks. A 30-minute public tea ceremony is open for observation, but not participation, at 1:30 p.m. on the third Saturday of each month from April through October.

Appointments are required for groups of 25 or more. General garden admission is $2 for adults; $1 for seniors, the physically challenged, or students 6 to 18, and free those kids 5 or younger. Groups pay an additional $8.50 admission.

Places to Play

Peppi's Playground

Location: *32nd Avenue at East Spruce*

Named by Leschi schoolchildren for a first grader who was killed in an auto accident, Peppi's Playground offers a wading pool and excellent new play equipment.

Roanoke Park

Location: *Slightly north of Capitol Hill at 10th East and East Roanoke*
Here's a nice place to spread a picnic on a blanket and let kids romp in a small neighborhood playground. It's especially pretty in spring when the flowering trees are in bloom.

Places to Eat

Fran's

Location: *In Madison Park at 2805 E. Madison*
Phone: *206-322-6511*
Days/Hours: *10 a.m. to 6 p.m., Tuesday through Friday;*
10 a.m. to 5 p.m., Saturday.
Wheelchair/Stroller Access: *Yes*
Light, dark or milky, it's all chocolate at Fran's. From behind glass cases, exquisite dipped chocolates, tortes and truffles tempt visitors. Many don't consider it Easter or Christmas until they've made a stop for chocolate bunnies or Santas here. While you're shopping, treat yourself to a rich mug of hot chocolate.

South Seattle

The face of South Seattle has many shapes and colors — from residential neighborhoods to industrial areas. Visitors to Seafair's hydroplane races on Lake Washington most likely drive through the residential Mount Baker neighborhood. Those visiting Columbia City will find a 100-year-old business district. On Beacon Hill and in the Rainier Valley, the city is a blend of Asian, African-American and Hispanic families. Georgetown, near Boeing Field, is home to the Rainier Brewery plant.

Great Destinations

Goodwill Memory Lane Museum

Location: *1400 S. Lane Street*
Phone: *206-329-1000*
Days/Hours: *By appointment only, Monday through Friday.*
Schedule one week ahead.
Wheelchair/Stroller Access: *Yes*
The Memory Lane Museum is located at the back of Seattle's huge Goodwill store and features donated articles that reflect

Seattle's history from World War I through World War II. These items are not for sale and change periodically. Highlights include "Miss Bardahl," one of Seattle's favorite hydroplanes in the '60s, and an 11-foot-tall grizzly bear named Bruce, donated by Eddie Bauer. Tours last about 45 minutes.

Mount Baker Rowing and Sailing Center

Location: *3800 Lake Washington Blvd. S.*
Phone: *206-386-1913*
Days/Hours: *Call for information.*
Wheelchair/Stroller Access: *Yes*
A summer program here includes sailboarding and sailing camps for children 10 years or older. During the rest of the year, kids must be 13 to 18 to participate. The length of the rowing classes varies from season to season. Autumn rowing continues eight weeks; spring lasts 12; summer rowing is six weeks. Call for a brochure of class listings.

Museum of Flight

Location: *9404 E. Marginal Way S.*
Phone: *206-764-5720 or 206-764-5712 (tours)*
Days/Hours: *10 a.m. to 5 p.m., Friday through Wednesday; 10 a.m. to 9 p.m., Thursday.*
Wheelchair/Stroller Access: *Yes*
The Red Barn, Boeing's first manufacturing plant, houses the Museum of Flight. Its two floors of exhibits capture visitors' imaginations with flight displays dating back to a replica of the Wright Brothers' 1902 glider. Children let their imaginations run wild at The Hanger, where there's a plane they can climb into. Older kids especially enjoy this outing. Appointments are required for guided 90-minute tours; call two weeks ahead. Admission is $6 for adults, $3 for students 6 to 15 years, and free to those 5 years or younger. There's plenty of free parking available.

Pratt Fine Arts Center

Location: *1902 S. Main St.*
Phone: *206-328-2200*
Days/Hours: *9 a.m. to 5 p.m., Monday through Friday. Call for class and tour times.*
Wheelchair/Stroller Access: *Yes*
Almost hidden behind the Wonder Bread plant in Pratt Park is the Pratt Fine Arts Center. Teachers here are professional artists

who offer classes in printmaking, jewelry casting and all glass-making disciplines.

The school's goal is to emphasize the exchange between working artists and students. Pratt is one of the few non-academic visual arts facilities in the country offering beginning and advanced classes and studio space. The annual December show features some of the finest work created here. Call ahead for details. Ask about the free program, *Kids Artworks*, offered Saturdays each fall for elementary school-age youngsters.

Places to Play

Beer Sheva Park

Location: *Seward Park South at South Henderson*

The name mirrors Seattle's sister city in Israel, a site of great historical and religious significance. When strolling here, notice the park's chestnut trees — some are more than 100 years old.

Jose Rizal Park

Location: *South Judkins at 12th Avenue South*

This park honors the leader of the Philippines' fight for independence. It includes a play area, picnic shelter, viewpoint and a mural by Filipino artist Val Laigo.

Kubota Gardens

Location: *Renton Avenue South at 55th Street South*

This display garden is one of the newest additions to Seattle's park system and is more than the sum of its exquisite wildlife, waterfalls, ponds and prayer stones. It's an important historical and cultural resource for the city. Lovingly tended for 60 years by Fujitaro Kubota and his descendants, the garden is a memorial to the man, as well as a fulfillment of his dream of helping Americans understand Japanese culture.

Powell Barnett

Location: *East Jefferson at Martin Luther King Jr. Way*

Here, a new PipeLine play structure competes for attention with a wading pool and brightly painted castle-like restrooms.

Seward Park

Location: *South Juneau at Lake Washington Boulevard*

The vast grounds of Seward Park support many activities. The amphitheater is a great place for summer Sunday concerts. Others prefer this park for its playground, picnic facilities, public beach and bathhouse, and walking and bicycle paths along the lake. The lovely flowering cherry trees at the entrance were a gift from Seattle's Japanese community. The fish hatchery run by the University of Washington College of Fisheries offers tours by appointment. Call 206-723-3883 for information.

Places to Eat

Ezell's Fried Chicken

Location: *501 23rd Ave.*
Phone: *206-324-4141*
Days/Hours: *10 a.m. to 10 p.m., Monday through Thursday;*
10 a.m. to 11 p.m., Friday and Saturday; 11 a.m. to 10 p.m., Sunday.
Wheelchair/Stroller Access: *Yes*

The fried chicken here is so good, TV talk show host Oprah Winfrey sometimes breaks her diet and has it shipped cross-country to her! Kids may want to select two drumsticks and a melt-in-your-mouth roll for less than $4. For a real treat, give the sweet potato pie a try.

West Seattle

One of West Seattle's best-kept secrets is the picture postcard view of downtown Seattle it offers from the end of a gravel road off West Marginal Way at Dakota Street. No secret at all is the popularity of Alki Beach, where thousands come to walk the sandy shore, play in the water, munch a lunch or fly a kite. With all the activity going on here year-round, it's hard to imagine that the beach was nearly desolate until 1851, when the Arthur Denny party arrived to settle the area with some of the first white women.

Great Destinations

Alki Beach Park

Location: *Alki Avenue Southwest.*
Wheelchair/Stroller Access: *Yes*

Alki extends more than two miles along Elliott Bay, with a gently sloping beach pleasant for family outings. Teens hang out here in the evenings, especially during spring and summer. The waters aren't clean, so don't eat any fish caught here. The annual sand-sculpting contest held each August is one of the park's highlights. Teams of sculptors of any age pay an entry fee which goes to children's programs at Alki Community Center. Call 206-684-7430 for details.

Camp Long

Location: *In West Seattle's Delridge neighborhood at*
5200 35th Ave. S.W.
Phone: *206-684-7434*
Days/Hours: *8:30 a.m. to 5 p.m., Tuesday through Sunday, except holidays.*
Wheelchair/Stroller Access: *Yes*

Camp Long is a wilderness experience within the city limits. It's especially good for families who love the outdoors and don't want to travel far to enjoy it. This place has a self-guided trail, but if you want a tour, Camp Long naturalists lead free 90-minute nature hikes starting at 2 p.m. Saturdays. There's no age limit, but children should be accompanied by an adult.

Ten cabins provide overnight accommodations. Each has six double beds and can sleep as many as 12 people. Three cabins are wheelchair accessible. Cabin rentals are $20 per night. Ask about the once-a-month rock climbing program for those 7 or older. Students learn how to scale a 25-foot artificial rock.

Seacrest Boat House

Location: *1660 Harbor Ave. S.W.*
Phone: *206-932-1050*
Days/Hours: *5:30 a.m. to 6 p.m., Monday through Friday and 4:30 a.m. to 7 p.m., Saturday and Sunday; closed Monday and Tuesday during the winter.*
Wheelchair/Stroller Access: *Yes*

Here's a grand opportunity to go boating on Elliott Bay. Boaters must be 18 or older to rent a boat at Seacrest, but children accompanied by adults are welcome. The 16-foot boats are available for $11 per hour with a $50 deposit, three hours minimum. Life jackets and cushions are provided. Kayak rental is $10 per hour; rowboat rental is $15 per day. All boats are available on a first-come, first-served basis except during fishing derbies, when pay-in-advance reservations are required. Off the water, kids can help feed salmon in outdoor holding pens.

Places to Eat

Husky Deli and Ice Cream

Location: *4721 California S.W.*
Phone: *206-937-2810*
Days/Hours: *9 a.m. to 7 p.m., Monday; 9 a.m. to 10 p.m., Tuesday through Friday; 9 a.m. to 10 p.m., Saturday; 10 a.m. to 9 p.m., Sunday.*
Wheelchair/Stroller Access: *Yes*
  This take-out only sandwich, deli and ice cream shop is so popular, people have been known to drive all the way from the University District for the ice cream and the name recognition. There are more than a dozen flavors to choose from and all are homemade.

Pegasus Pizza

Location: *2758 Alki S.W.*
Phone: *206-932-4849*
Days/Hours: *4 p.m. to 11 p.m., Monday through Friday; noon to 11 p.m., Saturday and Sunday.*
Wheelchair/Stroller Access: *Yes*
  Pegasus Pizza, across the street from Alki Park beach, offers a delectable Greek pizza topped with feta cheese, spinach, diced mushrooms, green peppers, olives, fresh garlic and sunflower seeds. There are several more traditional Italian varieties, too. Order take-out or dine at the restaurant.

Spud Fish and Chips

Location: *In West Seattle at 2666 Alki S.W.*
Phone: *206-938-0606*
Days/Hours: *11 a.m. to 10 p.m., daily.*
Wheelchair/Stroller Access: *First floor only*
  Another longtime Seattle favorite, Spud makes some of the best fish 'n' chips around. The food is prepared in cholesterol-free oil, and the potatoes used to make the chips are fresh. You can order

one of the single "fish with fries," or prawns, oysters, scallops or clams. Sit at the second-floor window tables for a great view of the water. Highchairs and booster seats are available for little ones. If you have any leftovers, take them outside to feed the seagulls. Other locations are at 6860 E. Green Lake Way N. and 9702 N.E. Juanita Drive in Kirkland.

Places to Play

Ed Munro-Seahurst Park

Location: *12th Southwest at Southwest 144th. Turn west off Ambaum Boulevard to Southwest 144th. Turn north on 13th Southwest. Access road leads to beach.*

At Seahurst, you'll find 185 acres of saltwater park land and plenty of outdoor activities. The south end of the park has great beachcombing. The north end is both sand and grass and offers fire pits on the beach, picnic tables with individual grills, a Marine Skills Center, freshwater holding ponds, and a fish ladder. All pets must be leashed within the park. Parking near the beach is restricted to the physically challenged.

Lincoln Park

Location: *Fauntleroy Southwest at Southwest Webster*

This beautiful beachfront park stretches along the coast from Southwest Webster to Trenton Street. Playgrounds, a restroom, picnic tables and a few picnic shelters are located throughout the area. Paths wind through groves of madrona, fir and redwoods.

The park's most unique feature is Colman Pool at Point Williams, a heated seawater swimming pool (open summers only). Other recreationalists will enjoy the tennis courts, 11 acres of playfields and horseshoe pitching pits. The beach has no lifeguard, but offers beach-side barbecues, an Olympic Mountains view and a vantage point for watching the Vashon-Southworth ferries.

Helpful Phone Numbers:

Seattle City Libraries Quick Information, 386-4636

Seattle Parks and Recreation Department information and recreation scheduling, 206-684-4075

Seattle Parks and Recreation Department Youth Sports Information, 206-684-7091

Seattle Parks and Recreation Summer Beach Program, 684-7185

Puyallup is home to the popular Western Washington State Fair
each September.

Greater King County
North King County

Three predominantly residential communities rest in the wooded area between Seattle and the Snohomish County line: Shoreline, Lake Forest Park and Kenmore. At one time, many of the homes in this area were summer or weekend houses for Seattle residents. Many of these homeowners once sailed their boats to Lake Washington's north end or along Puget Sound's shoreline to docks near their vacation getaways. After World War II, when veterans with growing families began looking for new homes, North King County's population soared.

Today, families predominate in this area with numerous parks and playgrounds. The recreational Burke-Gilman Trail winds through the east side of Lake Forest Park and Kenmore.

Great Destinations

Families at Play

Location: *In Lake Forest Park at 17711 Ballinger Way N.E.*
Phone: *206-363-4844*
Days/Hours: *Noon to 8:30 p.m., Monday; 9:30 a.m. to 8:30 p.m., Tuesday through Friday; 9 a.m. to 8:30 p.m., Saturday; 11 a.m. to 6:30 p.m., Sunday.*
Wheelchair/Stroller Access: *Yes*

Families at Play started out as Discovery Zone, one of the original indoor play centers in the Puget Sound area. The owners have changed, but the colorful climbing tubes, slides and padded romping areas are the same. Designed for children 12 months to 12 years, this place is popular when the weather is cold and wet. For $5.25 kids get unlimited play time and parents can always "play" for free. This is a popular place for birthday parties too. Guests play for an hour, then move into nearby party rooms where the birthday kid can open gifts and everyone can enjoy cake, ice cream and pop, all supplied as part of the party package. There's also a Families at Play indoor playground in Bellevue at 14506 N.E. 20th. Call 206-643-2550 for more details or to reserve a birthday party.

Highland Ice Arena

Location: *In Shoreline at 18005 Aurora Ave. N.*
Phone: *206-546-2431*
Days/Hours: *10:30 a.m. to 12:30 p.m. and 3 p.m. to 5:15 p.m., Monday through Friday; 8 p.m. to 10 p.m., Wednesday; 7:30 p.m. to midnight, Friday; 10 a.m. to noon, 1:30 p.m. to 4:45 p.m. and 8 p.m. to 11 p.m., Saturday; 10 a.m. to noon and 2 p.m. to 5 p.m., and 7 p.m. to 9 p.m., Sunday.*
Wheelchair/Stroller Access: *Yes*

Sunday rates make this an ideal afternoon outing for the family. Lessons are available for beginning and advanced skaters. There's a class for kids 6 and younger at 2:30 p.m. Mondays and 10:30 a.m. Tuesdays. Some late evening sessions can be reserved for parties. After a skating session, you can snack on goodies from the vending machines or bring your own munchies. Call for lesson schedules, rink reservations and admission prices.

Shoreline Historical Museum

Location: *In Shoreline at 749 N. 175th St.*
Phone: *206-542-7111*
Days/Hours: *1 p.m. to 4 p.m., Thursday through Saturday; tours by appointment Monday through Saturday.*
Wheelchair/Stroller Access: *No*

At this museum you can take a free, self-guided tour and learn about the history of one of the state's newest cities. Special exhibits, ranging from dolls to military themes, change regularly. Some are for display only; others encourage hands-on activity. There's no age limit for the 45-minute tours, but guides recommend visitors be 5 years or older. Museum curators suggest one adult accompany every five children. Donations are accepted.

Places to Play

Richmond Beach Park

Location: *At Richmond Beach Road and 20th Avenue Northwest.
From Aurora Avenue North and Northeast 185th Street, turn west on
Northeast 185th Street until it becomes Richmond Beach Road. At
20th Avenue Northwest, turn south for three blocks to park entrance.*
Phone: *206-296-2976*
Days/Hours: *Dawn to dusk, daily.*
Wheelchair/Stroller Access: *Yes*

Richmond Beach Park is popular with beachcombers, picnickers
and kids who enjoy the upper playground. It was recently remodeled
to handle more people. A new picnic plaza on the upper level can be
reserved for gatherings, and a newly paved path makes it easy for
strollers and wheelchairs to travel from the parking lot to the beach.
King County parks officials plan events here throughout the year,
including a sunset tide pool walk where children are invited to bring
their flashlights. After the walk, families sit around a bonfire and a
storyteller weaves tales guaranteed to enthrall listeners.

Places to Eat

Great Harvest Bread Company

Location: *On the lower level of the Lake Forest Park Towne Centre
at 17171 Bothell Way N.E.*
Phone: *206-365-4778*
Days/Hours: *6 a.m. to 9 p.m., Monday through Friday; 6 a.m. to
6 p.m., Saturday and Sunday.*
Wheelchair/Stroller Access: *Yes*

Some of the healthiest baked goods around are fired up in the
ovens at Great Harvest. Soft oatmeal cookies and giant, melt-in-your-
mouth cinnamon rolls are favorites among young visitors. There are
always bowls of butter and slices of the day's specialty breads on
the counter for sampling. Bakers here knead the dough and pop
loaves into ovens right behind the counter, and kids really enjoy
watching them work. This is a popular stop for bicyclists using the
nearby Burke-Gilman Trail. There are also Great Harvest Bakerys at
5408 Sand Point Way N.E., north of Laurelhurst (206-524-4873), and
at 17192 Redmond Way in Redmond (206-883-6909).

East King County
Bellevue

From strawberry fields to a metropolitan technology and business corridor, Bellevue has changed dramatically in the past half century. When the Highway 520 and Interstate 90 floating bridges made commuting between Bellevue and Seattle easier, families flocked to this Eastside city. Now Bellevue boasts parks and dozens of other cultural and entertainment activities for families.

Great Destinations

Bellevue Art Museum

Location: *Third floor of Bellevue Square*
Phone: *206-454-3322*
Days/Hours: *10 a.m. to 6 p.m., Monday, Wednesday, Thursday and Saturday; 10 a.m. to 8 p.m., Tuesday and Friday; 11 a.m. to 5 p.m., Sunday.*
Wheelchair/Stroller Access: *Yes*

Bellevue Art Museum is an exciting way to introduce children to the visual arts. A six-week "Celebration Especially for Children" each winter features displays aimed at kids. This museum is conveniently located on the third floor of Bellevue Square, and has a number of rotating exhibits. Be sure to call for exact dates, guided tours and future exhibits. Admission is $3 for adults, $2 for seniors and students 13 years or older, and free to those 12 years or younger. Admission is free on Tuesdays.

Geer Planetarium

Location: *Bellevue Community College's Science Building, Room B-244, 3000 Landerholm Circle S.E.*
Phone: *206-641-2321*
Days/Hours: *One autumn and one spring show each year; dates vary so call ahead.*
Wheelchair/Stroller Access: Yes

Stars millions of miles away seem very close to those visiting Geer Planetarium. Twice each year the doors are opened to audiences for a study of the night sky. Children will understand the earth's small role in our giant galaxy after they listen to experts talk about the constellations, planets and black holes of outer space. Call ahead to find out when shows are scheduled. Geer Planetarium is the silver dome at the north end of the main cluster of buildings at Bellevue Community College. Admission is $2 per person.

Rosalie Whyel Museum of Doll Art

Location: *1116 108th Ave. N.E.*
Phone: *206-455-1116*
Days/Hours: *10 a.m. to 5 p.m., Monday through Wednesday, Friday and Saturday; 10 a.m. to 8 p.m., Thursday; 1 p.m. to 5 p.m. Sunday.*
Wheelchair/Stroller Access: *Yes*

Viewing the memorabilia on display here is like discovering treasures in your attic. More than 1,200 dolls, teddy bears and other childhood favorites are exhibited in a museum with wonderful Victorian architecture. A rotating exhibit gallery features four shows each year. Admission is $5 for adults, $4.50 for seniors, $4 for kids 5 to 17, and free to those 4 or younger.

Places to Shop

F.A.O. Schwartz

Location: *2070 Bellevue Square*
Phone: *206-646-9500*
Days/Hours: *10 a.m. to 9:30 p.m., Monday through Saturday; 11:00 a.m. to 6:00 p.m., Sunday.*
Wheelchair/Stroller Access: *Yes*

More than just a shop to browse, this is a shop to experience! A giant bear marks the entrance to this incredible toy store. Inside, visitors are greeted by animated creatures (roaring lion, talking dinosaur, moving birds) and a talking tree. If that's not enough to grab your attention, stop for a look at the talking clock, complete with an animated Humpty Dumpty and dancing ruby slippers. If this gets to be a bit over-stimulating for young children, head them back to the preschool section for some hands-on play. Customers are encouraged to play with toys on display and the staff members are often seen playing too — throwing boomerangs, riding floor toys, and demonstrating the latest toy fad.

Pets 'N Things

Location: *14310 N.E. 20th*
Phone: *206-746-9782*
Days/Hours: *10 a.m. to 7 p.m., Monday through Friday; 10 a.m. to 6 p.m., Saturday; 1 p.m. to 5 p.m., Sunday.*
Wheelchair/Stroller Access: *Yes*

It's the "things" that make this shop so different. Owner Bob Mackin is a python breeder, and he usually has a family of snakes at the back of the shop. You may also see a pocket mouse, a red-foot tortoise, African spiny mice, iguanas, exotic birds, lizards of all sizes, tarantulas and scorpions. Kids love it here.

Places to Eat

Brenner Brothers Bakery and Deli

Location: *12000 N.E. Bellevue-Redmond Rd.*
Phone: *206-454-0600*
Days/Hours: *6 a.m. to 7 p.m., Monday through Saturday; 8 a.m. to 6 p.m., Sunday.*
Wheelchair/Stroller Access: *Yes*

Brenner Brothers Bakery and Deli is one of the area's oldest family-owned bakeries and a great lunch stop. Kids love to peer into the cases chock-full of cookies, cakes and pastries. At 9 a.m. Wednesdays, they offer a 20- to 30-minute tour for children. Appointments for these casual events are a good idea, but not necessary. Come by yourself or with a group. Your guide leads you around the butcher blocks where bagel dough is rolled. Kids can peek into the walk-in ovens and watch large mixers kneading the dough. You might even see one of the decorators transform frosting into sculpture.

Kamon of Kobe

Location: *2444 N.E. Bellevue-Redmond Rd.*
Phone: *206-644-1970*
Days/Hours: *11:30 a.m. to 2 p.m., and 5 p.m. to 10 p.m., Monday through Friday; 5 p.m. to 10 p.m., Saturday; 5 p.m. to 9:30 p.m., Sunday.*
Wheelchair/Stroller Access: *Yes*

Kamon is located just across the street from Uwajimaya's. Colorful Japanese art adorns this place, and the Teppanyaki Room is especially popular with families. In the Tao dining room, a special children's dish is geared to younger appetites and served in a toy fire engine, and a special surprise is included with the meal. For birthdays, consider the $2.50 package which includes a song performed by the staff, a photograph of the birthday guest and a pineapple dessert. Parents will enjoy the Japanese garden outside the restaurant.

The Pancake Corral

Location: *1606 Bellevue Way S.E.*
Phone: *206-454-8888*
Days/Hours: *6:45 a.m. to 2:30 p.m., Monday through Friday; 6 a.m. to 3 p.m., Saturday and Sunday.*
Wheelchair/Stroller Access: *Yes*
   The Pancake Corral is a Bellevue fixture so popular that on some Sunday mornings it's standing room only. Little has changed on the breakfast menu in nearly 30 years. The pancakes are great, as are the eggs and waffles. Parking is limited.

Twelve Baskets Restaurant

Location: *201 106th S.E.*
Phone: *206-455-3684*
Days/Hours: *11 a.m. to 3 p.m., daily.*
Wheelchair/Stroller Access: *Yes*
   Twelve Baskets has special items on the menu for children such as whole-wheat teddy bears. This restaurant is known for its emphasis on nutrition. Twelve Baskets offers fireside or outdoor patio dining during the appropriate season.

Places to Play

Bellevue Nature Park

Location: *1905 118th S.E. Take I-405's Richards Road exit. Drive west to Southeast 118th; park is about a mile south of SE 118th.*
Wheelchair/Stroller Access: *Yes*
   When the Montlake Cut lowered the level of Lake Washington the lake receded, leaving the huge peat bog that serves as the base for this park. The peat can be as soft as butter, so wear sturdy boots or old tennies and stay on the wide, beautiful wood chip paths. Hikers should sign in and out of the park. In the center near the channel the peat bog is six feet deep: that's another reason to stay on the trails. Look for water birch in the swampy areas which early pioneers used to made their brooms.

Downtown Park

Location: *Downtown Bellevue, just south of Bellevue Square*
Wheelchair/Stroller Access: *Yes*
This park at the south end of Bellevue Square is easily accessible. Special features include a 12-foot-wide canal and a play structure at the south side sporting unusual wooden domes. Kids love to play on the swings, slides and climbing fort. Great times to visit this seven-acre site are during spring and summer, when the park's gardens are in bloom.

Kelsey Creek Park

Location: *13204 S.E. Eighth Place. Call for directions; it can be challenging to find*
Phone: *206-455-6885 and 206-455-7688*
Days/Hours: *Vary, so call ahead*
Wheelchair/Stroller Access: *Yes*
This animal park is open 8 a.m. and 4 p.m., daily, but the best time to visit is between 10 a.m. and 2 p.m., when the critters are most active. Cows and goats are milked daily at 7 a.m. and 3 p.m. Young children seem attracted to the goats, horses, rabbits and chickens living here. Expect new babies each spring. Keep in touch with Kelsey Creek Farm through its delightful newsletter. To get on the mailing list, call the Bellevue Parks and Recreation Department. Kelsey Creek also offers children's pottery parties ($7 per child) for six to 20 kids. The Barn Room is a great place for parties. It rents for $17 per hour and accommodates 30 to 40 small bodies. For groups of 50 guests or more, you can reserve the entire park for three hours. Cost is $50.

Playspace

Location: *At Crossroads Mall, 156th Avenue Northeast and Northeast Eighth Street*
Phone: *206-644-4500*
Days/Hours: *9 a.m. to 9 p.m., Monday through Thursday; 9 a.m. to 10:30 p.m., Friday and Saturday; 10 a.m. to 6 p.m., Sunday.*
Wheelchair/Stroller Access: *Yes*
"Let's get physical!" this child-care center tells kids ages 3 to 12. After parents drop their children off here, licensed supervisors watch them burn off energy at the indoor playground. They must wear socks to play. Drop-off care costs $5.95 per hour, plus $1 for pager rental, or parents can stay on-site and pay $5.95 for unlimited play. Fridays and Saturdays feature "Parents Night Out" between 5:30 p.m. and 10:30 p.m. During these sessions kids have free time, watch PG-

rated videos, create crafts and eat dinner. This session is $16.50 per child.

Robinswood Community Park

Location: *2340 148th Ave. S.E.; Take I-90 Exit to Bellevue Community College/148th Avenue Southeast. Drive north on 148th Avenue Southeast; turn right/east on Southeast 22nd Street.*
Phone: *206-455-6803; 206-455-7690 (tennis center information).*
Wheelchair/Stroller Access: *Yes*
  A log cabin homestead in 1882, Robinswood is now a multi-use park. There are 13 acres of bridle trails and a public horse show ring south of the park's meadow. North of the meadow are a climbing area for tiny tots and ball fields with bleachers, as well as two lighted soccer fields and tennis courts. A cabana, swimming pool and main house great for entertaining also can be found here. They're all available for private gatherings.

Sherwood Forest Park

Location: *At Bellevue's Sherwood Forest Elementary School, 16411 N.E. 24th*
Days/Hours: *After school and weekends, dawn to dusk.*
Wheelchair/Stroller Access: *Yes*
  This popular and innovative playground features equipment accessible to physically challenged youngsters. Sand and water tables, textured paths, a sensory maze and embankment slides make this a fun place for children of all abilities.

Tube Town

Location: *4051 Factoria Square Mall S.E.*
Phone: *206-747-2020*
Days/Hours: *10 a.m. to 7 p.m., weekdays; 10 a.m. to 6 p.m., Saturday; noon to 5 p.m., Sunday.*
Wheelchair/Stroller Access: *Yes*
  This indoor play and child care center features an assortment of tubes, tunnels, balls and slides to entertain and occupy kids. Their rates are the lowest in the area: $3.70 for unlimited play when parents stay on-site. For drop-off care, it's $3.70 per hour for ages 6 years or older and $5.50 per hour for ages 3 to 5 (available Friday through Sunday only). Tube Town also offers an evening "Parents Paradise" option — four hours of care that includes a movie, play time, and dinner for $20 per child and $10 for siblings. This option is available for ages 6 and over every night and for ages 3 to 5 on Thursday through Saturday nights.

Kirkland

Named after Peter Kirk, an English millionaire who settled the town in the 1800's, Bellevue's northern neighbor has a small-town feel. A welcoming downtown offers art galleries, eateries, and window shopping. The city has some of the finest playgrounds in King County, with inventive and colorful climbing and play equipment. Kirkland can be reached from Interstate 405 but a more scenic route is via Lake Washington Boulevard from Highway 520. Besides great views of Lake Washington, the lake route offers the upscale Woodmark Hotel and Carillon Point shopping development and several waterfront parks along the way.

Places to Eat

Kidd Valley Hamburgers

Location: *5910 Lake Washington Blvd. E.*
Phone: *206-827-5858*
Days/Hours: *10:30 a.m. to 9 p.m., Monday through Saturday; 11 a.m. to 9 p.m. Sunday.*
Wheelchair/Stroller Access: *Yes*

Big burgers, great fries, deep-fried zucchini and mushrooms, thick shakes, and ice cream cones are the items of choice here. This is a popular chain (there are also restaurants in Seattle's U-District, Greenlake, Kenmore/Bothell and North Seattle). There is both indoor and outdoor seating at this location — Or cross the street to the beach park on the lake and enjoy your snack or meal there.

Places to Play

Juanita Beach Park

Location: *9703 Juanita Dr. N.E.*
Hours: *Dawn to dusk.*
Wheelchair/Stroller Access: *Yes*

Located north of the downtown Kirkland area, Juanita Beach has a large swimming area with lifeguards in summer. The park also participates in the Children's Hospital's life-jacket loan program during the swimming season; visitors can borrow one while swimming. Picnic areas and a playground invite visitors to stay awhile. For exercise, walk the boardwalk.

Marina Park

Location: *Downtown Kirkland on Lake Washington at the foot of Central Way*
Hours: *Dawn to dusk.*
Wheelchair/Stroller Access: *Yes*
   This prime city park has a fishing dock, boat moorage pier, ducks and geese (which the shop owners nearby hope you won't feed!), a grassy area and a pleasant beach for sunning, wading and swimming.

Mercer Island

   Once only a summer vacation destination from Seattle, Mercer Island began changing in the 1940s when the original I-90 floating bridge was erected. A storm in 1990 sank the concrete pontoons connecting the island to Seattle, but luckily construction was already under way on a new bridge. Mercer Island is primarily a residential community, and its residents take great pride in their recreational programs.

Places to Play

Children's Park

Location: *Island Crest Way and 54th Southeast. From I-90, take Island Crest Way Exit south to just beyond Island Park School at about 54th Southeast*
Wheelchair/Stroller Access: *Yes*
   This park's unique climbing equipment was conceived and designed by the Mercer Island Preschool Association and is specifically for young children — but everyone enjoys it. Two tennis courts and small trails make the park especially appealing during the summer. A fence around the perimeter keeps little ones from roaming too far, but most kids are too busy climbing on the dinosaur, scrambling through the forts, and crawling around the oversized drain tiles to wander off.

First Hill Lid

Location: *West Mercer Way and Interstate 90*
   This park atop an interstate freeway features soccer, baseball and other play fields, two children's playgrounds, basketball and

tennis courts, restrooms and a picnic shelter. It's also a great place to enjoy views of Seattle, the Eastside and Mount Rainier. Seattle has a Lid Park, too. Look for it at 23rd Avenue South and Yakima Street.

Luther Burbank Park

Location: *2040 84th S.E. (north end)*
Phone: *206-296-4438*
Wheelchair/Stroller Access: *Yes*
Originally a private estate, Luther Burbank Park now is one of the Eastside's very special parks. There are 77 acres of lake front, three tennis courts, a grass amphitheater and outstanding playgrounds with balance beams, climbing nets and other play equipment for kids. Skateboard enthusiasts can cruise a downhill trail to the water's edge. With moorage for 80 craft, those with boats may motor or sail to picnic here. Picnic tables are complete with hibachis which overlook the swimming beach. Large groups must make reservations for weekends and holidays.

Youth Theatre Northwest

Location: *Southeast 40th Street and 88th Avenue Southeast*
Phone: *206-232-2202*
Days/Hours: *Noon to 5 p.m., Monday, Wednesday, Thursday and Friday (box office).*
Wheelchair/Stroller Access: *Yes*
Entertainment blends with education at this theater where young people are trained in dramatic arts. Children learn acting, construction, lighting and other theater skills in weekly classes and special summer workshops. The company puts on five productions every year, one of them written, produced and adapted by the members of the ensemble. Call for schedules, ticket information and audition announcements.

Redmond

Would you believe that high-tech Redmond was originally named Salmonberg? The name came from the abundant quantities of dog salmon swimming in the Sammamish River. Today this burgeoning city is home to the computer software giant Microsoft, and every kid's favorite company, Nintendo Corporation. The newly-built suburban neighborhoods are filled with families.

Great Destinations

Balloon Depot

Location: *16138 N.E. 87th St.*
Phone: *206-881-9699*
Days/Hours: *Only by appointment made several days in advance; daily morning and evening flights, weather permitting.*
Wheelchair/Stroller Access: *No*
Want to see the countryside from hundreds of feet up? Take a ride in a hot air balloon. Children 6 years or older may join in groups of four to six people per balloon. For adults, this company offers deluxe weekend flights with champagne brunch. Kids 10 or younger ride for half-price. Call for details.

Marymoor Museum

Location: *In Marymoor Park. From the Evergreen Point Bridge/ Highway 520 or Interstate 405, drive east to the Marymoor Park exit. Inside the park, follow signs to Marymoor Museum.*
Phone: *206-885-3684*
Days/Hours: *11 a.m. to 4 p.m., Tuesday through Thursday, year-round; 1 p.m. to 4 p.m., Saturday and Sunday, Memorial Day through Labor Day; 1 p.m. to 4 p.m., Sunday the rest of the year.*
Wheelchair/Stroller Access: *Yes*
A long-time favorite on the Eastside, Marymoor Museum occupies the north half of the Clise Mansion. Five exhibit rooms feature history of the Eastside, the park and the mansion. Included are logging, farming and mining displays, and information about current silicon chip-based industries. Admission is free, but donations are encouraged. One-hour group tours are available by appointment. Call during the summer or check local newspapers for special events for families. Part of the mansion is available for rentals, and summer parties are popular here.

Redmond Children's Playhouse

Location: *At the Redmond Senior Center, 8703 160th N.E.*
Phone: *206-882-6401*
Days/Hours: *9 a.m. to 5 p.m., Monday through Friday.*
Wheelchair/Stroller Access: *Yes*
This facility is part of the Redmond "Arts in the Parks" summer series featuring children's arts, mimes and puppeteers, but it makes a great contribution to performing arts for children year-round. An

autumn series includes four or five different shows on consecutive Saturdays. Popular entertainers including Tickle Tune Typhoon, Tim Noah and the Missoula Children's Theater have performed here. Tickets go on sale in mid-August. Call for prices and information.

Zones

Location: *2207 N.E. Bel-Red Rd., in the Ethan Allen Building*
Phone: *206-746-9411*
Days/Hours: *11 a.m. to 10 p.m., Sunday through Thursday, 11 a.m. to midnight, Friday and Saturday.*
Wheelchair/Stroller Access: *Yes*

High-tech, state-of-the-art and just plain fun video games are part of the appeal of this indoor amusement center. A 19-hole miniature golf course tests your putting skills. The pool tables are fun for families with older children.

Places to Eat

British Pantry

Location: *8125 161st Ave. N.E.*
Phone: *206-883-7511*
Days/Hours: *10 a.m. to 5:30 p.m., Monday and Tuesday; 10 a.m. to 8:30 p.m., Wednesday through Saturday.*
Wheelchair/Stroller Access: *Yes*

This truly English restaurant is divided into two parts. One half is a perfectly authentic bakery featuring remarkable scones, shelves of English teas, candies and other goodies. On the other side, a lovely little tea room is set with cozies and all other appropriate accessories for tea-time. Stop here for an afternoon respite or just to pick up some excellent baked goods. The owners say grandparents enjoy bringing their young company here.

Places to Play

Farrell-McWhirter Park

Location: *19545 Redmond Road*
Phone: *206-556-2300*
Days/Hours: *Varies depending on programs.*
Wheelchair/Stroller Access: *Yes*

This lovely and uncrowded park is perfect for young children. A big field to run in, an orchard, trails to walk (including one that is asphalt-paved and accessible to wheelchairs and strollers) and a children's farm are some of its many features. The Redmond Parks Department offers special programs for kids here throughout the year, including pony riding classes and summer day camps.

Marymoor Park

Location: *6064 W. Lake Sammamish Parkway N.E.*
Phone: *206-296-2966*
Days/Hours: *8 a.m. to dusk, daily.*
Wheelchair/Stroller Access: *Yes*

If parkgoers want space, this is the place to come. Marymoor features acres of picnic grounds, baseball and soccer fields, swing sets, places to stroll and the Clise Mansion, home of Marymoor Museum. Dog trainers come to work their dogs and let them play at the doggie playground. Model airplane fanciers fly their planes here in good weather. Marymoor is the starting point for people drifting down the Sammamish Slough in rafts or innertubes. Four tennis courts, a concession stand and the jogging track are popular, too.

In another section of the park, a large covered picnic area is frequently reserved for family reunions and birthday parties. The park also features a Velodrome — one of a handful in the country — and special bicycling activities that go with it. There are 18 different park stations with facilities for wheelchairs and other equipment for the physically challenged.

New to the park is the man-made climbing rock south of the Velodrome. This 35-foot-high concrete structure is 40 feet wide at the base, making it one of the largest free-standing climbing structures in the country. A series of intersecting walls with fixed hand holds gives climbers different avenues to the top. There's also a special climb for the physically challenged.

The Parcourse, an exercise route for both able-bodied and physically-challenged athletes, can be completed in about an hour. Call for details about any park facility or the various concerts and festivals scheduled here throughout the year.

Sammamish River Park

Location: *Northeast 116th at the Sammamish River*
Wheelchair/Stroller Access: *Yes*

With 60 acres bordering the river, this park is a sports-oriented site that includes picnic facilities.

Sammamish River Trail

Wheelchair/Stroller Access: *Yes*

The Sammamish River Trail is a 10-foot-wide asphalt path starting in Redmond and connecting with the Burke-Gilman Trail. This is a mecca for bicyclists, joggers, skaters and pedestrians, and continues to grow in popularity. No motor vehicles or horses are allowed, but horseback riders do frequent the riverbanks alongside the trail. Oft-used access points are near Redmond City Hall and off Leary Way in Redmond.

Bothell and Woodinville

Around the turn of the century, river traffic between Lakes Washington and Sammamish boosted the growth of Bothell and Woodinville. Both areas changed from quiet hamlets to important logging towns. In 1917, the completion of the ship canal lowered Lake Washington and left the Sammamish too shallow to navigate. As a result, the logging business slowed. Farming, however, has always been excellent here, and both towns cling to their rural roots even in the face of encroaching suburbia.

Great Destinations

Bothell Landing Park

Location: *In Bothell at Bothell Way and Northeast 80th Avenue.*
Wheelchair/Stroller Access: *Yes*

What do a Swedish immigrant's cabin, the town doctor's home, and the Hannan House (now a historical museum) have in common? All were moved to this park to commemorate the pioneer families who settled the area. A trip through the buildings brings history to life for kids and adults. Summer weekends bring outdoor evening concerts. You'll enjoy listening as you relax on the sloped and terraced hillsides beside the river. Children enjoy the climbing toys and swings nearby. Active families will enjoy crossing the bridge to the Sammamish River Trail and walking, jogging or biking along the riverside. The exercise stations along the trail are also fun to try out.

Chateau Ste. Michelle

Location: *In Woodinville at 14111 N.E. 145th. Take I-405 Exit 23/ Monroe-Wenatchee and follow Highway 522 to Woodinville-Redmond Road exit. In Woodinville, turn west at Route 202; cross the railroad tracks. Turn south on Route 202/Woodinville-Redmond Road. In about two miles the road curves toward the east and the winery is on the south side.*
Phone: *206-488-1133 and 206-488-4633 (tour information)*
Days/Hours: *10 a.m. to 4:30 p.m., daily.*
Wheelchair/Stroller Access: *Yes*

One of Washington's most recognized wineries, Chateau Ste. Michelle is modeled after a French country chateau. Its vast grounds are often used for special events and concerts. Tours are available year-round and last about 45 minutes. Call for times. Tours are popular, so it's smart to arrive early, especially on weekends. Appointments are required for groups of 10 or more. You'll learn about the art of making wine and see the 6,000-gallon tanks the winery uses for curing. Tours end in the tasting room where visitors may sample a variety of wines. Children receive grape juice and may not sample wine, even from a parent's glass. Cyclists who arrive via the Sammamish River Trail may park their bicycles at the rack near the winery's front door. Call for details about summer outdoor concerts.

Columbia Winery

Location: *In Woodinville at 14030 N.E. 145th St. From I-405, take Exit 23/Monroe-Wenatchee east to Highway 522. Take the Woodinville/Redmond exit. In Woodinville turn west on Route 202; cross the railroad tracks. Turn south of Route 202/Woodinville-Redmond Road. Drive about two miles until road curves east. Columbia Winery in on the road's north side.*
Phone: *206-488-2776*
Days/Hours: *10 a.m. to 5 p.m., daily.*
Wheelchair/Stroller Access: *Yes*

This winery is in a blue Victorian manor house. Tours are available by request between 10 a.m. and 4:30 p.m., Saturday and Sunday. Wine tasting is available on a drop-in basis. Children will be offered only non-alcoholic beverages.

Gold Creek Trout Farm

Location: *In Woodinville at 15844 148th N.E. Take I-405 Exit 23 to Highway 522/Monroe-Wenatchee. Follow Highway 522 into Woodinville. Turn west at 175th and right at 140th. Drive about a mile before turning left on 148th. Go two more blocks.*
Phone: *206-483-1415*
Days/Hours: *10 a.m. to 5 p.m., daily.*
Wheelchair/Stroller Access: *Yes*

Imagine the proud look on your child's face as he or she pulls in a rainbow trout after fishing at Gold Creek Trout Farm. If your group is small, you might talk your guide into telling some entertaining fish stories. Charges for fish vary according to length — call for costs. Gold Creek supplies poles, bait, cleaning and bagging at no extra charge. Appointments are required for school and birthday party groups, but families can just drop in.

Places to Shop

Country Village

Location: *In Bothell at 23730 Bothell-Everett Highway. Take I-405 to exit 26 and head south one mile on the Bothell-Everett Highway.*
Phone: *206-483-2250*
Days/Hours: *10 a.m. to 6 p.m., Monday through Saturday; 11 a.m. to 5 p.m., Sunday.*
Wheelchair/Stroller Access: *Yes*

Brick pathways and flower-lined boardwalks guide you through this shopping center's blooming garden setting. Kids will enjoy the Doll Palace General Hospital, Toys that Teach and The Whistle Stop. And they'll delight at feeding the chickens and ducks, watching the goldfish, peacocks and albino doves, and chasing after the roosters. There's a merry-go-round in the courtyard and an inviting play area with swings, slides and a play house

The 50 individually-owned shops are unique— many featuring a variety of crafts from woodworking and pottery to fine arts and stained glass. There are shops offering kitchenware, baskets, collectibles, linens, furniture and home accessories, apparel, fabrics, antiques, and much more. For a sweet treat to take home, there's Linda B's Pies, etc. and MM Fudge Tug. Stop at Gramma's Restaurant and Sweet Shoppe or the Country Cafe for a relaxing meal.

Special festivals throughout the year, including the holiday open house (usually the second weekend in November) bring crowds to Country Village — where you can see Santa "fly" through the sky on his sleigh and land in a country courtyard where he's serenaded by carolers.

Molbak's Greenhouse & Nursery

Location: *In Woodinville at 13625 N.E. 175th. Take I-405 to Monroe-Wenatchee exit. Follow State Route 522 to Woodinville and into town. Turn left at 175th. Drive two blocks and Molbak's is on your right.*
Phone: *206-483-5000*
Days/Hours: *9:30 a.m. to 6 p.m., Saturday through Thursday; 9:30 a.m. to 9 p.m., Friday.*
Wheelchair/Stroller Access: *Yes*

You couldn't miss Molbak's if you tried, and you wouldn't want to. One of Puget Sound's most popular and energizing places to visit, Molbak's grows more than 2,000 varieties of plants and beautiful flowers inside and out. Children love watching the birds in the tropical bird cage. Inside, there are two acres of tropical foliage and several outstanding gift shops, including a festive Christmas shop. The exterior landscaping is wonderful, especially in the spring and summer. Call for details about October Floral Fairyland, which offers free live performances of a selected fairytale.

Duvall and Carnation

Carnation gained fame after Elbridge Amos Stuart established his Carnation Milk Farm in 1909. Today it's still going strong, providing milk and milk products for the whole family. These bucolic communities are home to other dairies, ranches, berry, and vegetable farms.

Great Destinations

Carnation Research and Dairy Farm

Location: *28901 N.E. Carnation Farm Rd., off Highway 203. Take I-90 to Preston-Fall City exit. Drive through Fall City to Carnation. Watch for signs just outside Carnation.*
Phone: *206-788-1511*
Days/Hours: *10 a.m. to 3 p.m., Monday through Saturday, April through October.*
Wheelchair/Stroller Access: *Yes*

Kids' eyes will pop at the statue of "Possum Sweetheart" standing at the entrance to this farm. She was an actual Carnation cow who produced a record 37,381 gallons of milk in 1920. Here, too, are special homes for cats and dogs who were once taste-testers for Friskies brand pet food (a division of Carnation). This dairy offers 45-minute self-guided tours, featuring calves children can pet, mama cows being milked, and beautiful grounds with exquisite flowers. Group tours are available by appointment.

Remlinger Farms

Location: *One mile south of Carnation on Highway 203*
Phone: *206-333-4135*
Days/Hours: *9 a.m. to 7 p.m., daily, mid-March through December.*
Wheelchair/Stroller Access: *Yes*

More than just a U-Pick farm, Remlinger has become a destination farm for city dwellers seeking a taste of the country. Festivals are held throughout the year. The Harvest Festival in the fall is perhaps the most popular, with a pumpkin patch, hay maze, pony rides, and more. There's plenty to do here even when no special event is scheduled.Visit the General Store for fresh produce, homemade jams, soups, and other specialties; stop by the bakery or restaurant for a treat or lunch; select some new plants in the large nursery; and visit the barnyard animals in their petting area.

U-Pick Farms

Carnation and Duvall offer several U-Pick farms. A complete list is available from the Washington State/King County Extension Service at 206-296-3986. It's a good idea to call before you leave to pick. Here are two farms to consider:

Lydon's "Berry Patch"

Location: *In Duvall at 14510 Kelly Road N.E., Duvall*
Phone: *206-788-1395*
Days/Hours: *9 a.m. to dusk, Wednesday through Sunday, late July through Labor Day*

Harvold Berry Farm

Location: *North of Carnation on the Carnation-Duvall Road*
Phone: *206-333-4185*
Days/Hours: *8 a.m. to 8 p.m., daily, for raspberries, July through mid-August*

Issaquah

Things started snowballing in this rural community more than a century ago, after a settler discovered coal on his property. Daniel Gilman had dreams of wealth and a bustling city when he established the Seattle, Lake Shore and Eastern railroad to carry coal to national markets via Spokane. But the railroad was never completed. The old depot built in 1888 still stands at the corner of Front and Sunset as an architectural remnant of the era. New homes and shopping centers now cover much of the city's past.

Great Destinations

Boehm's

Location: *255 N.E. Gilman Blvd.*
Phone: *206-392-6652*
Days/Hours: *9 a.m. to 6 p.m., daily, November through Memorial Day; 9 a.m. to 6 p.m., Monday through Thursday and 9 a.m. to 7 p.m., Friday through Sunday the rest of the year.*
Wheelchair/Stroller Access: *Yes*

Boehm's is one of Issaquah's oldest, most charming and delicious attractions. Candy makers here concoct more than 150 kinds of European and American sweets. Tours are offered weekdays (except Wednesdays) at 10:30 a.m. and 1 p.m., weekends at 1 p.m. During these visits you'll see manufacturing areas with huge copper tubs and three-inch-thick marble slabs used to make individual candies, plus Julius Boehm's authentic Swiss chalet — the first one built in the Pacific Northwest. The chalet is filled with Boehm's collection of European art and mementos of a very unique and active life. Sample some candy and you and the kids will be hooked. Boehm's also has stores in the Green Lake area (559 NE Ravenna Blvd., 206-523-9380), Lynnwood (18411 Alderwood Mall Blvd., 206-329-6869), and Seattle (140 S.W. 148th, 206-243-2027).

Geology Adventures

Phone: *206-255-6635.*
Wheelchair/Stroller Access: *No*

Parent-child field trips are the specialty here and you can look for amber, pan for gold, or search for fossils. All ages are welcome and most hikes are ok for beginners. You'll learn that the only amber deposits on the West Coast are located on Tiger Mountain. A child on one expedition found a piece the size of a walnut! The owner is the author of "Washington Geology for Kids." Call for current prices and schedules and ask about the new Crystal Kid and Hallelujah Junction tours. Younger kids may enjoy the marine fossils class. Some visitors are surprised to learn that marine fossils dating back 32 million years are just under your feet in Issaquah.

High Country Outfitters/Camp Wahoo, Inc.

Location: *3020 Issaquah-Pine Lake Rd., Suite 544*
Phone: *206-392-0111*
Days/Hours: *Vary; call for schedule and required reservations.*
Wheelchair/Stroller Access: *Depends on location*

If you and your kids love horses, stop at Cle Elum in the Wenatchee National Forest. There are summer trail rides and overnight and extended pack trips. This means fresh air, sunshine, scenery and solitude in the High Cascades. It's a great way for families with children age 8 or older to test their skills and endurance.

Camp Wahoo, a summer horse camp in the wilderness, is for boys and girls ages 9 to 16. Each camper is assigned a horse to care for and ride for the week. Campers handle, saddle and bridle horses. This is a wonderful way for children to learn about responsibility, as well as have a great time. Advanced work is available for those with experience. Kids can try half-day, whole-day and/or overnight pack trips. They'll learn how to build shelters, use compasses, read maps, build cooking fires, and prepare meals on the trail.

Village Theater

Location: *120 Front St. N.*
Phone: *206-392-2202*
Days/Hours: *Noon to 7 p.m., Tuesday through Saturday (box office).*
Wheelchair/Stroller Access: *Yes*

Fast becoming one of the Eastside's most popular entertainment attractions, the Village Theater offers consistently good productions of Broadway musicals. Teenagers and pre-teens interested in the stage or music will likely enjoy a show here. Call for schedules and prices for the upcoming season. Season tickets go quickly, but there are singles available for individual performances.

Washington Zoological Park

Location: *5410 194th Ave. S.E., just south of I-90*
Phone: *206-391-5508*
Days/Hours: *April through September, 10 a.m. to 5 p.m., Tuesday through Saturday; 11 a.m. to 5 p.m., Sunday; October through March, closes at 4 p.m. daily.*
Wheelchair/Stroller Access: *Limited*

This small zoo is a teaching facility that specializes in threatened or endangered animals and birds. Visitors get an up-close and personal look at the residents here, and zoo docents will gladly answer questions and give guided tours. Some of the animals include alpacas, emus, sheep, reindeer and cougars. Admission is $2 to $4.

Places to Eat

Cascade Garden

Location: *In Meadows Shopping Center at 1580 N.W. Gilman Blvd.*
Phone: *206-391-9597*
Days/Hours: *11 a.m. to 2:30 p.m. for lunch, Monday through Friday; 5 p.m. to 9:45 p.m. for dinner, Monday through Friday, and 5 p.m. to 11 p.m., Saturday and Sunday.*
Wheelchair/Stroller Access: *Yes*

This place serves great Chinese food at affordable prices. Children get a kick out of the noodle-making demonstrations on Friday and Saturday nights. A Seattle restaurant is at 96 Union in the Pike Place Market.

Places to Shop

All For Kids

Location: *170 Front St. N.*
Phone: *206-391-4089*
Days/Hours: *10 a.m. to 6 p.m., Monday through Saturday;*
noon to 5 p.m., Sunday.
Wheelchair/Stroller Access: *Yes*

Hundreds of children get their introduction to books and music at this store featuring more than 1,500 titles for kids ages 12 years or younger. Music lovers come from all over to buy song books for children. Story times typically are on Wednesday or Thursday, in the morning and afternoon. All for Kids occasionally sponsors concerts, too. There's also a store in Seattle just north of University Village on Blakeley Street (call 206-526-2768 for information).

Gilman Village

Location: *In downtown Issaquah. Take I-90 Exit 17 to Front Street. Turn south on Gilman Boulevard. Turn right to cross the railroad tracks and turn left into Gilman Village.*
Phone: *206-392-6802 (office)*
Days/Hours: *10 a.m. to 6 p.m., Monday through Saturday; 11 a.m. to 5 p.m., Sunday; some stores have extended hours.*
Wheelchair/Stroller Access: *Yes*

Gilman Village is a collection of old houses transported from their original sites and refurbished to form a delightful cluster of nearly 40 specialty shops and restaurants. The area is especially appealing during spring and summer, when bright, sweet-smelling flowers and outdoor accessories make it a browsing delight. Call ahead for special events geared for kids and families. Those shops especially geared for children are listed below:

Cottontail Corner

Location: *Suite 48 in Gilman Village*
Phone: *206-392-3818*

A real bunny often comes to visit this Beatrix Potter gift and collector's shop. The store is filled with bunny stories, bunny buttons, bunny pictures and many of Peter Rabbit's favorite friends, as well as linens, Wedgwood dishes and Royal Albert figurines.

Country Mouse

Location: *Suite 1 in Gilman Village*
Phone: *206-392-1050*
This consignment-based shop for handmade gifts has an old-fashioned country image with its incredible variety of lovely handcrafted pieces in all sizes, shapes and materials. It's appealing to kids, moms and grandmas.

Gilman Village Books

Location: *Suite 42 in Gilman Village*
Phone: *206-392-3766*
You'll find lots of books and personal service here. The whole second floor is children's books. If you can't climb the stairs, they'll bring volumes down for you.

Myken's

Location: *Suite 3 in Gilman Village*
Phone: *206-392-5672*
A distinctive shop for pet supplies and gifts, Myken's gift items cover over a hundred different breeds of dogs and cats. Find books, jewelry, and even matching clothes for you and your dog.

The Paper Place

Location: *Suite 25 in Gilman Village*
Phone: *206-392-3666*
Besides a huge party selection, you'll discover unusual memo pads, wild erasers, rubber stamps and stickers by the hundreds — all the things children enjoy.

Places to Play

Lake Sammamish State Park

Location: *Off I-90 Exit 15 or 17, turn north to Lake Sammamish*
Phone: *206-455-7010 (reservations).*
Wheelchair/Stroller Access: *Yes*
This marvelous park offers an expansive beach and swimming area, plus several places to play. Climbing equipment is made from rustic logs. A pagoda-covered eating area includes a central barbecue, hot plates and running water. Come here for birthday parties, barbecues or other large group events. Reservations are required for large groups.

Snoqualmie Valley

Snoqualmie developed in the 1880s around a hops farm so busy it had its own hotel. The little mountain town of North Bend was named by the railroad for the northerly turn that the nearby Snoqualmie River takes here. Farming and mining induced people to settle the valley, but the spectacular Snoqualmie Falls is what attracts visitors.

Great Destinations

The Herbfarm

Location: *In Fall City at 32804 Issaquah-Fall City Rd. Take I-90 to Exit 22/Preston-Fall City. Follow the road three miles. At the green bridge at 328th Street, turn left, cross the bridge and drive another half mile.*
Phone: *206-784-2222*
Days/Hours: *10 a.m. to 7 p.m., Sunday through Friday; 10 a.m. to 6 p.m., Saturday. Closes at 5 p.m. in January and February.*
Wheelchair/Stroller Access: *Yes*

One of the most irresistible places on the Eastside, the Herbfarm sells plants by the thousands, with 160 varieties of succulents and 600 varieties of herbs. You'll find at least 15 kinds of mint, including pineapple, licorice, basil and creme de menthe. Older kids may want to join adults in classes for gardening, crafts and basket weaving. Call for a brochure. The restaurant is so popular you need to make reservations early in the season. Equally popular is a special event with horse-drawn wagons, llamas and more. Look for the small aviary filled with cooing doves. The Herbfarm also has a smaller Seattle store at 1629 Queen Anne Ave. N., 206-284-5667.

Puget Sound & Snoqualmie Valley Railroad

Location: *In Snoqualmie at Route 202*
Phone: *206-746-4025 and 206-888-3030*
Days/Hours: *Seasonal; call for information.*
Wheelchair/Stroller Access: *No*

Families love riding these vintage trains on a beautiful 10-mile journey through scenic Snoqualmie Valley. Board at North Bend or Snoqualmie for one-way or round-trip rides. The Snoqualmie Depot, built in 1890 by the Seattle, Lake Shore and Eastern Railways, is now on the National Register of Historic Places. Tickets for December's Santa Train are often sold out by October, so call early. Admission is

$6 for adults, $5 for seniors, $4 for children 3 to 12, and free to those 2 or younger. Add a 5 percent tax for tickets purchased at the Snoqualmie Depot.

Snoqualmie Falls

Location: *Snoqualmie.*
Wheelchair/Stroller Access: *Yes*

Snoqualmie Falls, some 26 miles east of Seattle, plunges 268 feet — 100 feet further than Niagara Falls — into a 65-foot deep pool. Tourists and locals are often elbow-to-elbow at this gorgeous waterfall. The roar of the spray, the gentle mist and the fascination of the falling water attract thousands each year. The falls are especially dramatic when the spring snow melts into the river, creating huge swells and currents. Impressive views of the falls from nearby Salish Lodge make dining here a treat. The food is terrific too. A breakfast, lunch or dinner table often requires early reservations. A little known fact: this is the site of the first major electric plant in the Northwest to use falling water as a power source.

Snoqualmie Falls Forest Theater

Location: *Near Fall City at David Powell Road. Take I-90 Exit 22. Follow signs to Fall City for four miles. Turn right on David Powell Road and go three miles to the gate.*
Phone: *206-222-7044*
Days/Hours: *Performances June through August; box office open 10 a.m. to 5 p.m., Monday through Friday.*
Wheelchair/Stroller Access: *Yes*

Hike down the wooded trail to the outdoor amphitheater and watch a summer production from the terraced seats. The peaceful pounding of Snoqualmie Falls is the backdrop to the stage. Shows are scheduled June through August. The group performs at least one children's production each year; most shows are scheduled for Saturdays. Before or after the show, stroll through the peaceful woods. Call for schedules and ticket prices.

Snoqualmie Historical Museum

Location: *In North Bend at 222 North Bend Blvd.*
Phone: *206-888-3200 or 206-888-0062*
Days/Hours: *1 p.m. to 5 p.m., Saturday and Sunday, April through October.*
Wheelchair/Stroller Access: *Yes*

This museum, sponsored by the Snoqualmie Valley Historical Society, features both permanent and changing exhibits of Indian and pioneer life. The kitchen and parlor include furnishings and models in authentic costumes. They've recently completed a Farm Shed with equipment and tools dating back to the early 1900s. Special groups may make appointments to visit at nonscheduled times. There's no admission charge, but donations are welcome.

Snoqualmie Pass Skiing

Alpental/Ski Acres/Snoqualmie Summit

Location: *Just off I-90 Exit 52*
Phone: *206-236-1600*

Snoqualmie Pass is one of the region's most popular downhill and cross-country skiing destinations, offering three slopes for snow-lovers. Parents with young children will appreciate the child-care services provided here. Snowboarding continues to grow in popularity, too. Ask about guided hikes for young teenagers. Advanced skiers may want to explore the guided tours to the back country.

Kids love nearby Snowflake Inner Tubing. Children of all ages flop onto inflated tire tubes or sleds and sail down the snow for a fun ride. The rope tow at the bottom hoists tubers back to the top for another ride.

East King County Hikes

Asahel Curtis Nature Walk

Location: *Snoqualmie Pass at I-90 Exit 47*

This trail on the south side of I-90 just past Denny Creek begins at Asahel Curtis Picnic Area; there you'll walk through a quarter-mile of old fir, cedar and hemlock. The Eastlake District of Federated Garden Clubs has identified more than 40 plants for novice botanists. Four of the 28 picnic tables here are on the Snoqualmie River. There are fire pits to cook over. Kids enjoy collecting water from the hand pump.

Denny Creek Campground

Location: *Snoqualmie Pass area*

About 17 miles east of North Bend along I-90, this campground serves as a base for several short hikes. In spring, the rushing water in this creek can pose a hazard to children. In the summer, many shallow spots offer safe wading and water play. The Franklin Falls Trail, about a mile off the Denny Creek Trail, leads to a cliff face where water falls more than 70 feet to a pool. Children love the feel of the spray on their faces as they watch for rainbows.

High Point Trail

Location: *West Tiger Mountain*

To find the most popular way up Tiger Mountain, leave I-90 at Exit 20/High Point Road. Turn right at the stop sign. At the frontage road, turn left and park on the shoulder. From here, the high rises of downtown Seattle, Bellevue's urban sprawl, and the streets and fields of Issaquah are laid at your feet.

Snoqualmie Tunnel

Location: *At I-90 Exit 54/Hyak*

This 2.3-mile-long abandoned railroad tunnel is the longest one in the country open to hikers. The tunnel links the west and east sections of the John Wayne Iron Horse Trail, which begins at Rattlesnake Lake near North Bend. The tunnel is unlighted at Snoqualmie Pass, so be sure to bring a flashlight. It's wise to bring good walking shoes and a warm jacket, too.

South King County
Renton, Kent, Tukwila and Federal Way

Once an industrial coal mining town, Renton is now a leader in the aerospace industry. The Boeing Company is the lifeblood of many jobs in Renton and neighboring Kent, Tukwila and Federal Way. Population growth in this area has been rapid in the past decade, so cities are hurriedly working to create activities for families. Call the local parks and recreation departments or chambers of commerce to learn about the newest programs for kids and adults.

Great Destinations

Aqua Barn Ranch

Location: *In Renton at 15227 S.E. Renton-Maple Valley Highway*
Phone: *206-255-4618*
Days/Hours: *8 a.m. to 9 p.m., daily, by appointment only.*
Wheelchair/Stroller Access: *Yes*
Aqua Barn offers a variety of activities centered around horses and swimming. Children 8 or older can enjoy trail rides or day camp activities. There's a horse camp for kids 7 to 10 years and another for those 10 to 14. Horseback riding is $19.50 hourly. If you prefer swimming, the pool is open 1 p.m. to 3 p.m. daily with additional 7 p.m. to 9 p.m. hours on Friday and Saturday. Call for admission prices.

City Park

Location: *In Kent at Panther Lake Center, 20510 S.E. 108th*
Phone: *206-850-PLAY*
Days/Hours: *10 a.m. to 8 p.m., Monday through Thursday;*
10 a.m. to 8:30 p.m., Friday and Saturday; 11 a.m. to 7 p.m., Sunday.
Wheelchair/Stroller Access: *Yes*
What child doesn't love climbing, crawling and sliding? Kids 12 months to 12 years will enjoy these activities and more at this indoor playground. Children must wear their socks to romp here. Admission is $4.99 for children 3 years or older; $2.99 for ages 2 years or younger.

Enchanted Village/Wild Waves Water Park

Location: *In Federal Way at 36201 Enchanted Parkway S. Take I-5 Exit 142B*
Phone: *206-661-8000 and 206-661-8001 (for groups and birthday parties)*
Days/Hours: *11 a.m. to 7 p.m., Memorial Day through Labor Day; 10 a.m. to 6 p.m., weekends during the spring and fall. Call for specific dates.*
Wheelchair/Stroller Access: *Yes, at Enchanted Village; not at Wild Waves*

A fantasy land next door to a water park — who could ask for more? At Enchanted Village, furry animals greet children at a small zoo. Set aside enough time to ride the carousel, pet the animals and have a picnic before visiting the children's museum, bird aviary, and putting course. Activities are geared to younger children. Admission includes all rides and entry to on-stage entertainment featuring costumed animals.

Wild Waves tends to draw people of all ages. A river ride, slides and fountains attract little ones, and older kids go for the Raging River, Cannonball ride, and a giant wave pool. This place is popular with teenagers and pre-teens, too. Admission to Enchanted Village is $11 for those 10 to 50; $9 for children 3 to 9 and adults older than 50. A passport to Enchanted Village and Wild Waves costs $8.50 for those 10 to 50, $16.50 for kids 3 to 9, and $10 for adults older than 50. Admission for children younger than 2 is free in both places. Prices are subject to change. Ask about season passes, group rates and birthday party packages.

The Fish Gallery (three locations)

Location: *Renton Village, Renton; 3710 128th E., Factoria; Easthill Plaza, Kent*
Phone: *206-226-3215 (Renton); 206-641-9240 (Factoria); 206-852-9240 (Kent)*
Days/Hours: *9 a.m. to 9 p.m., Monday through Friday; 9 a.m. to 6 p.m., Saturday; 11 a.m. to 6 p.m., Sunday.*
Wheelchair/Stroller Access: *Yes*

Tropical fish collections here are extraordinary. Kids love watching the fish, and the squawking parrots with vivid plumage are sure to capture everyone's attention. Some of these tropical birds have life spans so great, they'll likely outlive you! Pet choices range from the exotic to the traditional. Families are welcome to

Young children delight in a train ride through Enchanted Village
in Federal Way.

drop in and handle the animals or talk to the birds. The owners are
happy to give group tours, but need plenty of warning and prefer
morning hours.

Pacific Rim Bonsai Collection

Location: *In Federal Way at 33663 Weyerhaeuser Way S. Take I-5
Exit 143/Federal Way-South 320th St. to east side of freeway onto
Weyerhaeuser Way South. Continue to road's Y, following to the left.*
Phone: *206-924-3153*
Days/Hours: *11 a.m. to 4 p.m., Saturday through Wednesday; public
tours at noon on Sundays in summer.*
Wheelchair/Stroller Access: *Yes*

Created in 1989 as Weyerhaeuser's tribute to the Washington
State Centennial, this collection displays more than 50 examples of
this ancient art. In honor of the company's trade relations, the plants
come from Taiwan, Japan, China, Canada and the United States. Tours
are conducted by people who actually tend the trees. They provide
a wealth of information about the grounds.

Renton Civic Theatre

Location: *507 South Third*
Phone: *206-226-5529*
Days/Hours: *10 a.m. to 5 p.m., Monday through Wednesday; noon to 6 p.m., Thursday, Friday and Saturday (box office).*
Wheelchair/Stroller Access: *Yes*
  Renton Civic Theatre puts whimsy on the stage with six shows during each September-to-June season. Musicals are a favorite at this 311-seat theater. Matinees are slated on some Sundays. This group has more than 2,000 season ticket holders, but it's possible to find a seat by arriving at the box office 30 minutes before show time. Tickets are $16 for adults and $12 for students and seniors.

Rhododendron Species Botanical Garden

Location: *In Federal Way at 33663 Weyerhaeuser Way S.*
Phone: *206-661-9377 (general information); 206-838-4646 (tours and classes)*
Days/Hours: *11 a.m. to 4 p.m., Saturday through Wednesday, June through February.*
Wheelchair/Stroller Access: *Partial*
  Weyerhaeuser Company provided the Rhododendron Species Foundation 24 acres to display their plants, which include over 500 species with 2,000 types of shrubs from around the world. Although spring is the peak season, one variety or another is in bloom from January until late summer. Companion plants lend color throughout the year. It's a breathtaking stroll and children are welcome. Admission is $3.50 for adults, $2.50 for seniors and students 12 or older, and free for those younger than 12.

River Bend Mini Putt

Location: *In Kent at 2020 W. Meeker*
Phone: *206-859-4000 and 854-3673*
Days/Hours: *7 a.m. to 10 p.m., daily, mid-spring through Labor Day; 8 a.m. to 9 p.m., Monday through Saturday and 8 a.m. to 6 p.m., Sunday during the rest of the year.*
Wheelchair/Stroller Access: *Yes*
  This mini-putt course is next to a larger driving range so you can try out both styles of golf shots. Seniors and kids 16 or younger may play an 18-hole round for $2; those 17 or older pay $3 a round. A bucket of balls at the driving range runs $2.

Springbrook Trout Farm

Location: *In Renton at 19225 Talbot Rd. Take I-405 to Exit Highway 167 South. Take Southwest 43rd Exit off Highway 167 to Valley General Hospital, which is one block east. Trout Farm is a mile south of the hospital.*
Phone: *206-852-0360*
Days/Hours: *10 a.m. to dusk, Monday through Saturday and 10 a.m. to 6 p.m., Sunday, March through October.*
Wheelchair/Stroller Access: *Yes, but ground can be soft in wet weather*

Three ponds await young anglers at Springbrook. Admission depends on the size of the catch. Pull in a 10-inch fish and pay about $1.95; reel in an 11-incher and pay $2.75. Those hoisting a big lunker fish will pay $4 to $12, depending on the length of the fish. Tackle and bait are furnished. Cleaning and bagging are free. Wear jeans and walking shoes. There are picnic facilities and a playground with a tree fort, swings and a slide for before or after the fishing session. Call for reservations with groups of 10 or more.

Places to Shop

Imaginarium

Location: *In Tukwila at Southcenter Mall*
Phone: *206-439-8980*
Days/Hours: *9:30 a.m. to 9:30 p.m., Monday through Saturday; 11 a.m. to 6 p.m., Sunday.*
Wheelchair/Stroller Access: *Yes*

Imagine a store sporting signs on the toys reading, "Please Touch." You'll find it at Imaginarium. Toys here are sturdy and incite creativity without being unduly expensive. There's an incredible array of stuffed animals and a nice book department. The staff will help schools and day-care centers set up their libraries and materials. Children enter through a separate tot-sized door. Other Imaginariums are in Bellevue Square, Tacoma Mall and Lynnwood's Alderwood Mall.

Places to Eat

Cascade Cookies

Location: *In Kent at 22435 68th Ave. S.*
Phone: *206-872-7773*
Days/Hours: *8 a.m. to 5 p.m., Monday through Friday, by appointment only.*
Wheelchair/Stroller Access: *Yes*

Kids and cookies are a natural combination; and when you combine them, you have a winner. Cascade Cookies does a lot of institutional baking for stores in the Puget Sound area. They make five kinds of frozen dough and 20 varieties of cookies. Tours are available for children 7 or older and must be reserved a week in advance. Tour-goers leave with a tasty treat.

Zoopa

Location: *In Tukwila at 393 Strander Blvd.*
Phone: *206-575-0500*
Days/Hours: *11 a.m. to 9:30 p.m., Sunday through Thursday; 11 a.m. to 10 p.m., Friday and Saturday.*
Wheelchair/Stroller Access: *Yes*

The huge salad, pasta and soup buffets here aren't only colorful and tasty, they're affordable. Children 5 or younger eat free. Those 6 to 11 pay half. Look for the Kidstall filled with raisins, trail mix, assorted crackers and other snacks. Paper placemats and crayons make the seating area especially fun for kids. A new Zoopa recently opened at Bellevue Square; call 453-7887 for more information.

Places to Play

Dash Point State Park

Location: *Southwest of Federal Way via Southwest Dash Point Road (Highway 509)*
Phone: *206-593-2206*
Days/Hours: *Daily, 6 a.m. to dusk*

A fine beach park on the Puget Sound, Dash Point offers camping and picnicking sites. There's a nice beach for wading, sunning, playing and exploring the intertidal life. For a break from the water, six miles of forested trails can also be explored.

Gene Coulon Memorial Park

Location: *In Renton at Lake Washington's south end. From I-405, take Sunset Highway exit. Follow to Puget Power Shuffleton Plant.*
Days/Hours: *6 a.m. to 9 p.m., daily.*
Wheelchair/Stroller Access: *Yes*

Formerly known as Lake Washington Park, this area offers a delightful public beach. Lifeguards are on duty only during the summer. This park has it all, including plenty of parking, a good boat launch site and excellent picnic facilities, especially the covered pavilion with cooking areas. There are also bike racks, volleyball and tennis courts, shuffleboard, horseshoe pits, concession stands and a complete first-aid station. The playground has tiny swings for tiny folks. A wooden bridge takes you to a small, grassy island with a sturdy climbing tower and fort donated by the Renton Lions.

You may rent canoes, sailboards and rowboats, picnic, listen to summer concerts, ride bikes or take a stroll. The park prohibits kite flying because of nearby power lines. No animals or alcohol allowed, however, hungry ducks are plentiful, so bring your stale bread.

Saltwater State Park

Location: *25205 Eighth Place South, Kent. Take exit 149 (Highway 516, Kent-Des Moines) and proceed west and drive south on Pacific Highway South to 240th Street. Turn south on Marine View Drive and follow signs to the park.*
Phone: *206-764-4128*
Days/Hours: *Daily, 6 a.m. to dusk*

With 88 forested acres, 1,500 feet of waterfront, overnight camping, picnicking facilities, and much more, this is the most-used state park in the Seattle area. It's popular with divers, who come to explore the marine life residing at an artificial reef 150 yards from the shoreline. The sandy swimming beach is especially nice for toddlers, who will find a sun-warmed wading spot located over the park's tidelands.

Black Diamond and Enumclaw

Many families on their way to Mount Rainier discover great side excursions in southeast King County's Black Diamond and Enumclaw. The area once lured miners hoping to strike it rich. Now the area is home to horse farms and increasing numbers of young families looking for homes in a rural setting.

Great Destinations

Black Diamond Historical Museum

Location: *At Baker Street and Railroad Avenue. From I-405 in Renton, take the Enumclaw exit and follow Highway 169*
Phone: *206-886-1168*
Days/Hours: *9 a.m. to 4 p.m., Thursday; noon to 3 p.m., Saturday and Sunday.*
Wheelchair/Stroller Access: *Yes*

This museum is housed in an old train depot, now restored and refurbished. You'll find some little-known and fascinating information about this old coal-mining community. Admission is free, but donations are happily accepted. Families can drop in to visit; special groups should make arrangements. The small museum can accommodate between 50 and 75 people. Look for the 1920s caboose at the museum's depot entrance. Next door is the old Black Diamond Jail, built in 1910.

The Sales Pavilion

Location: *In Enumclaw at 22712 S.E. 436th St. Take I-5 exit to Auburn. Drive five miles on Highway 18 to Auburn/Enumclaw exit. Turn east and drive another 12 miles on Highway 164.*
Phone: *206-825-3151*
Days/Hours: *Doors open at 8 a.m., sales start at 10 a.m., the first Saturday and Sunday of every month.*
Wheelchair/Stroller Access: *Yes*

If you're searching for a "Western" experience, bring your family to the Sales Pavilion. This is the place where pigs, sheep, goats, poultry and horses are auctioned off. Much of the countryside near Enumclaw and Black Diamond is farmland, and farming families make it a special day when they come to buy or sell here. The Barn really *is* a barn, and the atmosphere inside is bursting with animal sounds and smells and the staccato rhythm of the auctioneer's voice. Rows of old theater seats surround a center stage for those wanting to sit back and watch the auction action. There's a snack bar and some gift-type items nearby. In the lobby near the entrance to the auction, you'll often find vendors displaying hand-knit sweaters, hand-tooled leather goods and more. Admission is free.

Places to Eat

Black Diamond Bakery and Restaurant

Location: *32805 Railroad Ave.*
Phone: *206-886-2741*
Days/Hours: *7 a.m. to 5 p.m., Tuesday through Sunday (bakery);
7 a.m. to 4 p.m., Tuesday through Friday, and 7 a.m. to 5 p.m.,
Saturday and Sunday (restaurant).*
Wheelchair/Stroller Access: *Yes*

   Candies, jams, jellies and syrups line the shelves at this wonderful
bakery and deli. If your group is fewer than 20, call ahead and arrange
a 15-minute tour. Visit early in the morning when the bakers are
working and you'll find a fresh assortment of goodies. They'll show
you the original brick ovens, which use a half-cord of alder wood
daily. Fresh doughnuts are the house specialty and are popular with
skiers, hikers and other fresh-air enthusiasts who drop in. This place
also features a new gourmet coffee, candy and ice cream shop.

Helpful Phone Numbers:

   Bellevue Parks and Recreation Department, 206-455-6885 or
   206-462-6046

   Enumclaw/Black Diamond District, 206-825-4400 or
   206-296-0909

   Federal Way Chamber of Commerce, 206-838-2605

   Federal Way/Des Moines District, 206-941-0655 or 206-296-4279

   Kent Chamber of Commerce, 206-854-1770

   King County Library System, 206-462-9600 (the "answer line") ;
   206-684-4494 (TDD)

   King County Library System, 206-462-9600 (the "answer line");
   206-684-4494 (TDD)

   King County Parks Department, 206-296-4232
      Enumclaw/Black Diamond District
      Federal Way/Des Moines District
      Marymoor/Eastside District
      North Highline/Vashon District
      Northshore/Shoreline District
      Southeast District

Kirkland Parks and Recreation Department, 206-828-1218
Marymoor/Eastside District, 206-296-2966
Mercer Island Parks and Recreation Department, 206-236-3545
North Highline/Vashon District, 206-296-2956
Northshore/Shoreline District, 206-296-2976
Northshore/Shoreline District, 206-296-2976
Renton Chamber of Commerce, 206-226-4560
Snoqualmie Pass Visitor Information Center, 206-434-6111
(Thursday through Sunday only)
Southeast District, 206-296-4281

Polar Bear watching is a main attraction at the Point Defiance Zoo and Aquarium.

Southwest Washington
South Puget Sound

There are plenty of family activities awaiting in the South Puget Sound area. Tacoma, Washington's second largest city, is the gateway to many family attractions. Magestic Mount Rainier is a short drive away, as is Olympia, the state capital.

Greater Pierce County

Great Destinations

Fort Lewis Military Museum

Location: *At I-5 Exit 120 at Dupont, just west of the freeway*
Phone: *206-967-7206*
Days/Hours: *Noon to 4 p.m., Wednesday through Sunday; closed federal holidays.*
Wheelchair/Stroller Access: *Yes*

Three galleries filled with nearly 2,000 Northwest military exhibits ranging from the mid-1850s to the present are displayed here. Tour guides say school-age children — especially boys of 8 years and older — enjoy looking at the tanks, jeeps, armored cars, missiles, and rockets. The presentation of uniforms and weapons is interesting as well. Family members who served in the military make great guides here. Admission is free. One-hour guided tours are available for school-age groups of 15 to 35 students by calling ahead.

Northwest Trek

Location: *11610 Trek Dr. E., Eatonville. Take I-5 Exit 127 east to Highway 512. Turn on South Hill Mall/Eatonville exit to Highway 161.*
Phone: *800-433-TREK, 360-832-6117 or 206-847-1901*
Days/Hours: *9:30 a.m. to dusk, daily mid-February through October; 9:30 to dusk Friday, Saturday, Sunday and some holidays the rest of the year. Call ahead for current hours.*
Wheelchair/Stroller Access: *Yes*

This 600-acre wildlife park is located at the foothills of Mount Rainier, 17 miles south of Puyallup. Northwest Trek is home to hundreds of Pacific Northwest creatures living in the area's natural wetlands, forests, and grasslands. Grizzlies and black bears are the newest residents here. Hop on an hour-long Trek Tram inside the park and visit a forested region of big-horn mountain sheep and shaggy goats. In the wetlands, you'll see beavers, otters, wolverines, and herons splashing as they build homes, hunt, and play. The setting is more natural and spacious than most zoos, making it easy to forget this is an animal enclosure.

One of the best times to tour is on rainy days, when most visitors shy away and the animals are active. No matter when you come, take time to catch the 14-minute show at the new Forest Theater. Make sure the kids try the hands-on exhibits in the Cheney Discovery Center.

A picnic area, restaurant, and covered outdoor eating area make this park an all-day destination. Park admission is $7.75 for adults, $6.75 for seniors, $5.25 for students 5 to 17, $3.25 for 3- and 4-year-olds and free to those younger. Ask about discount rates for groups of 12 or more. Call for a listing of special events.

Pioneer Farm

Location: *7716 Ohop Valley Rd., Eatonville (Between State Route 7 from Tacoma and State route 161 from Puyallup, four miles west of Eatonville)*
Phone: *360-832-6300*
Days/Hours: *Varies with programs; call for specific information.*
Wheelchair/Stroller Access: *Yes*

Learn what life was like in the Pacific Northwest 100 years ago, with a hands-on farm experience on this re-created pioneer farm.

grain, milking cows, scrubbing clothes, sawing wood, and churning butter. A 90-minute tour includes visits to a trading post, barn, blacksmith shop, wood shop, 1880s log cabin and more. Admission is $5 for adults and $4 for children and seniors.

Western Washington State Fair - The Puyallup Fair

Location: *Puyallup Fairgrounds at 110 Ninth S.W. Take I-5 Exit 127/ Highway 512 east to Puyallup*
Phone: *206-841-5045*
Days/Hours: *Gates open 8 a.m. to 11 p.m., daily for 17 days beginning the first Friday after Labor Day.*
Wheelchair/Stroller Access: *Yes*

Everybody and their hog finds something to enjoy at the Western Washington State Fair, dubbed "the Puyallup Fair" by locals. When you're "doin' the Puyallup," you'll see the 4-H animal blue-ribbon winners, take a stomach-turning carnival ride and snack on chicken grilled on an open spit. Children can milk cows and pet some smaller barnyard critters. Few visitors leave here without at least one of the locally renowned scones topped with sweet preserves. Children younger than 5 are admitted free every day. Other daily admission prices vary with special discounts available. Grandstand entertainment is not included in the admission price, but performances are typically geared more toward adults. At least one day is designated for discounted kiddie carnival rides. Stroller rental is available.

Places to Play

Parkland Putters

Location: *10636 Sales Rd., Parkland. Take I-5 Exit 127/Highway 512 to Steele Street exit. Turn at the first right.*
Phone: *206-588-2977*
Days/Hours: *10 a.m. to 11 p.m., daily, Memorial Day through Labor Day; 1 p.m. to midnight, Friday, 11 a.m. to midnight, Saturday, and 11 a.m. to 9 p.m., Sunday, the rest of the year.*
Wheelchair/Stroller Access: *One of the four courses is suited for wheelchairs; strollers can be maneuvered on all four*

Kids feel like real champs at this miniature golf center. Four 18-hole courses with varying difficulty are spread out around the grounds. Sinking a putt on the 18th hole earns a trophy. Top scores earn blue and red ribbons and the honor of having the staff read a player's name over the loud speaker. The courses are well-lit and landscaping is carefully tended. Want a break from golf? A small building on the premises sells concessions and offers video games.

Tacoma

Nicknamed "The City of Destiny," Tacoma is a favorite for families who are eager to discover world-class sporting events, cultural arts, and hours of indoor and outdoor recreation. Concert-goers and fans of amateur and professional sports teams regularly pack the Tacoma Dome. Outdoor recreationalists frequent Point Defiance Park — the largest of the city's leisure spots. And historic Pantages Theater, restored in 1983 (65 years after it first opened), hosts family theater productions by traveling troupes. Call the Pantages Theater at 206-591-5894 for schedules and tickets.

A great time to visit Tacoma is during the annual Daffodil Festival in April. The week-long event features floral displays, parades and other community events. Call 206-627-6176 for exact dates and more details. Another fun celebration for families is Tacoma's Ethnic Fest in late July. Folks gather at Wright Park to sample different cultural foods, and watch musical and dance performances from a variety of ethnic heritages. Call 206-305-1036 for details.

Great Destinations

Children's Museum of Tacoma

Location: *925 Court "C"*
Phone: *206-627-2436*
Days/Hours: *10 a.m. to 5 p.m., Tuesday through Friday; 10 a.m. to 4 p.m., Saturday; noon to 4 p.m. Sunday.*
Wheelchair/Stroller Access: *Yes; find the ramp between 9th and 11th at Court street*

Exhibits here cater to children. Curators introduce new offerings about once every 18 months and kids can play with the hands-on displays. One of the displays is "Body Basic," with information about healthy nutrition and personal safety choices. Kids love stuff about their "innards." Call ahead to find out when new exhibits are planned.

Nature Center at Snake Lake

Location: *1919 S. Tyler St.*
Phone: *206-591-6439*
Days/Hours: *Park open 8 a.m. to dusk, daily; interpretive center open 8 a.m. to 5 p.m., Monday through Saturday.*
Wheelchair/Stroller Access: *Yes*

If you're squeamish about reptiles, you'll be happy to know that Snake Lake is named for its shape, not for its slithery creatures. This 54-acre wildlife preserve has nearly 36 educational stops along three miles of wooded paths. From these spots, kids and adults can observe the birds and waterfowl living here.

Children love crawling through the small-size beaver lodge at the new Interpretive Center, which is just one of many features at the center. On-site forest creature puppets give younger children lots of incentive to role play as animals. Other kids will get a kick out of the myriad of hands-on exhibits and the wetlands diorama. Admission is free. Call ahead for details about classes and school tours. Guided tours are available for groups of 12 to 60.

Port of Tacoma Public Observation Tower

Location: *Just off East 11th St. Take I-5 Exit to Port of Tacoma Road*
Phone: *206-383-5841*
Days/Hours: *Round-the-clock.*
Wheelchair/Stroller Access: *No*

If you climb the three flights of stairs to the top of the Port of Tacoma's Public Observation Tower, you'll get a free look at the Olympic Mountains. From here you can watch the small boats and large industrial ships flowing in and out of the Northwest through this port city. Go at sunset, and you can snap some great photographs. There's no charge to use the tower's telescope.

Tacoma Art Museum

Location: *1123 Pacific Ave.*
Phone: *206-272-4258*
Days/Hours: *10 a.m. to 5 p.m., Tuesday through Saturday; noon to 5 p.m. Sunday.*
Wheelchair/Stroller Access: *Yes*

This museum offers something for people of all ages. Parallel displays for kids give younger museum visitors a chance to appreciate what adults see on a grander level. While adults enjoy works by such famed Northwest artists as Jacob Lawrence, children can pose for portraits and test their art skills with water colors. Look for displays created by local children in one section of the museum. Groups must schedule tours two weeks in advance. Admission is $3 for adults, $2 for seniors, and free for those 12 or younger. Tuesdays, everyone gets in free.

Tacoma Dome

Location: *West of I-5 at Exit 133 and 134*
Phone: *206-572-DOME, 206-272-3663, and TDD/TDY 206-591-5559*
Days/Hours: *Varies with event.*
Wheelchair/Stroller Access: *Yes*

The world's largest wood-domed arena, the Tacoma Dome is home to the Tacoma Rockets of the World Hockey League, ice skating competitions, world-class concerts and more. The newest addition here is the Shanaman Sports Museum, next to the Dome near the lower level entrance. This gallery is dedicated to city and county athletes from amateur and professional sports, and covers the history of sports in Tacoma and Pierce Counties. Accomplishments by outstanding local athletes, coaches, referees, sports broadcasters, and sports writers are profiled in 22 display cases. The museum opens one hour before all sporting events and stays open throughout the event. Admission is free. Call 206-537-2600 for more details.

Tacoma Rainiers

Location: *Cheney Stadium; take I-5 Exit 132. Drive west two miles to South 19th Street.*
Phone: *206-752-7707*
Days/Hours: *Early April through Labor Day.*
Wheelchair/Stroller Access: *Yes*

The Tacoma Rainiers (formerly the Tacoma Tigers) took their name from the original minor league Seattle baseball club. Today they're a Seattle Mariners farm club. The boys of summer take the field for Triple A baseball here. It's a great place to get autographs of soon-to-be big league players. Willie McCovey, Gaylord Perry and José Canseco all played with this club before their major league careers. The best time to collect signatures is at least one hour before the game, as players warm up at hitting practice. Little League teams and other groups can reserve blocks of seats if they call ahead.

Wapato Park at Wapato Lake

Location: *South 68th Street at Sheridan Avenue in south Tacoma*
Phone: *206-305-1070*
Days/Hours: *Daylight hours.*
Wheelchair/Stroller Access: *Yes*

Wapato Lake is a great place for kids to fish, because only those 13 or younger may dip their lines into the waters. The State Department of Fisheries regularly stocks this freshwater lake with wily trout. Adults and older children can rent paddle boats and canoes here, or stroll the great paths around nice picnic areas. Lifeguards are on hand to watch summer swimmers.

W.W. Seymour Botanical Conservatory at Wright Park

Location: *316 S. "G" St.; park entrance is at Sixth Avenue and "I" Street*
Phone: *206-591-5330*
Days/Hours: *8 a.m. to 4:30 p.m. daily; closed Thanksgiving and Christmas Day.*
Wheelchair/Stroller Access: *Yes*

Kids can't help creating jungle adventures among the more than 200 species of exotic plants and flowers growing in this Victorian-style domed conservatory. Twelve thousand panes of glass let in plenty of light. Another 700 trees grow outside, including a lemon tree with fruit the size of grapefruit, and a Sago Palm which grew when dinosaurs roamed the earth. Special presentations are available for groups of up to 25; call at least one week ahead.

Point Defiance Park

Location: *North 54th at Pearl Street. Take I-5 Exit 132 and follow to Highway 16. Take the Sixth Avenue exit and turn left. Drive to the next right onto Pearl Street and follow this all the way to the park.*
Phone: *206-305-1070*
Days/Hours: *Dawn to dusk daily.*
Wheelchair/Stroller Access: *Yes*

This 698-acre gem is full of amenities guaranteed to delight the whole family. No wonder more than two million people play here each year! Few parks offer so much for so many.

Pack your own meal and warm up the fixins in one of the kitchen areas dotting the park. Spend time exploring the gardens and wooded areas. Rent a go-cart and race around the track at the park's east entrance — it's open daily in the summer and weekends much of the rest of the year. Call 206-752-6413 for details.

Then take the kids to Owen Beach to swim or climb over the driftwood. It's a great spot to watch the Tacoma-Vashon ferry and other boats.

Theme gardens throughout the park are especially well kept. Lanterns and a little tea house give the Japanese garden an authentic flavor. Sweet-smelling flowers with eye-popping colors adorn the Herb Garden in the warmer months. There also are gardens dedicated to rhododendrons, roses, irises, dahlias and Northwest native plants.

Sound, nearby Vashon Island, Gig Harbor and the Cascade and Olympic mountains. This loop is closed to motorized vehicles until 1 p.m. Saturdays, so runners, bicyclists and walkers can exercise.

After circling the loop, visit any of the other featured destinations that make this park one of the 20 largest urban parks in the country. Admission into the park is free, but fees and hours vary at attractions within the park.

Boathouse Marina *(in Point Defiance Park)*

Location: *Park's northeast corner near Vashon Island ferry terminal*
Phone: *206-591-5325*
Days/Hours: *5 a.m. to 9 p.m., daily, Memorial Day through Labor Day; sunrise to about 7 p.m. the rest of the year.*
Wheelchair/Stroller Access: *Yes*
Anglers of all ages enjoy dropping a line in the waters of Commencement Bay at the Boathouse Marina. You can rent a small boat with or without a motor, buy bait in the Tackle Shop, or check out the boats moored at nearby Old Town Dock. The ferry to Vashon Island leaves from here, too.

Boathouse Grill Restaurant *(in Point Defiance Park)*

Location: *5910 N. Waterfront Dr., in park's northeast corner at Boathouse Marina, just west of ferry dock*
Phone: *206-756-7336*
Days/Hours: *6:30 a.m. to 9 p.m., Sunday through Thursday; 6:30 a.m. to 10 p.m., Friday and Saturday.*
Wheelchair/Stroller Access: *Yes*
Most Tacomans wouldn't think of letting an out-of-towner leave the city without dining at this six-sided restaurant with views of the Olympic Mountains, Commencement Bay, Mount Rainier and more. Open for breakfast, lunch and dinner, this casual-style eatery offers everything from steak and seafood to burgers and fish-and-chips. There's a kids' menu with nothing more expensive than $3. Take-out orders for eating on the nearby beach are also available.

Camp 6 Logging Museum *(in Point Defiance Park)*

Location: *Park's southwest corner*
Phone: *206-752-0047*
Days/Hours: *10 a.m. to 4 p.m., Wednesday through Sunday, January through October.*
Wheelchair/Stroller Access: *Yes*
There's no need to fell a mighty tree to get a feel for the old logging days. Just visit Camp 6, modeled after an authentic logging

camp. Steam-powered locomotives and equipment used between the 1880s and 1940s are displayed. Children love trains and here's the place to catch a ride behind an authentic locomotive. The train operates spring and summer weekends and on some holiday afternoons. The first three weekends in December, families can board the special Santa Claus train for a trip through the park.

Fort Nisqually Historic Site *(in Point Defiance Park)*

Location: *Park's southwest corner*
Phone: *206-591-5339*
Days/Hours: *11 a.m. to 6 p.m., daily, June through Labor Day; 1 p.m. to 5 p.m., Tuesday through Sunday, the rest of the year.*
Wheelchair/Stroller Access: *Yes*

More than 160 years ago, this Hudson Bay Company fur trading and farming post was located just south of Tacoma. In the early 1930s, historians reconstructed it at Point Defiance Park. This is the place to come if you want an idea of what blacksmithing, spinning, beadwork and trading was like in the 1850s. The Montgomery House shows what housing was like for a pioneer family, while the laborers' dwelling gives an idea of the home life for a worker. Fort staff clad in authentic clothing from this era give visitors a flavor of old Fort Nisqually days. Especially fun are the candlelight tours offered during the fall. Admission is $1 for adults and 50 cents for students, Wednesday through Sunday. Admission is free Monday and Tuesday because only the museum is open on those days.

Never Never Land *(in Point Defiance Park)*

Location: *Park's southwest corner*
Phone: *206-591-5845*
Days/Hours: *11 a.m. to 5 p.m., daily, in May; 11 a.m. to 7 p.m., daily, June through August; 11 a.m. to 5 p.m., weekends, April and September.*
Wheelchair/Stroller Access: *Yes, but paths are rough with wood chips*

Luckily for visitors to this fantasy land, Humpty Dumpty never had a great fall here. The legendary egg greets guests from atop the entrance arch to this 10-acre Mother Goose nursery rhyme and fairy tale village. The wooded setting offers nearly three dozen exhibits based on favorite children's stories. If adults can't remember the entire tale, no problem. Boards with rhymes and stories are printed next to each scene. Call ahead for special events and puppet shows. Little ones should visit a restroom outside Never Never Land before they begin their adventure because there is only one portable toilet inside. Admission is $2.00 for adults, $1.50 for teens and seniors, $1.00 for children ages 3 to 12 and free for ages 2 and under.

Point Defiance Zoo & Aquarium *(in Point Defiance Park)*

Location: *Near park's east entrance*
Phone: *206-591-5337*
Days/Hours: *10 a.m. to 7 p.m., daily, Memorial Day through Labor Day; 10 a.m. to 4 p.m., daily, the rest of the year. Closed Thanksgiving and Christmas.*
Wheelchair/Stroller Access: *Yes*

Wet, dry, or slimy animals and fish are on display at this combination zoo-and-aquarium complex. It's just a short stroll from the outdoor elephant exhibit to the indoor shark tank. Point Defiance is actually home to two aquariums, the North Pacific Aquarium and the Discovery Reef Aquarium. The North Pacific Aquarium houses hundreds of Puget Sound cold water fishes and invertebrates. Ask about feeding times, because when they're fed, fish are especially active and splash at the surface to get their share.

The newer Discovery Reef Aquarium has a South Pacific feel. A jungle trail leads to the beach, where young sharks and vibrantly-colored tropical fish swim. Look for the Blue Hole, where fish and eels are safe from the large predatory sharks at the coral reef's edge. Kids press their faces up against the tank's floor-to-ceiling window so they can bravely go nose-to-nose with these fearsome creatures.

Nearby, at the Rocky Shores exhibits, there's always some kind of activity with the larger-than-life beluga whales, walruses, harbor seals, and comical sea otters. Tiny tots will appreciate the underwater viewing windows just two feet off the ground.

Don't leave before you've observed the polar bears, monkeys, apes and more at other indoor or outdoor settings. Some play up to the crowd. Kids will want to take home one of the huggable pygmy marmosets.

Many locals make a pilgrimage here during December, when the zoo sparkles with half a million strung holiday lights. Admission to the zoo and aquarium is $6.25 for adults, $5.75 for seniors and disabled adults, $4.50 for ages 5 to 17, $2.25 for ages 3 to 4 and free for ages 2 or younger.

Places to Eat

Antique Sandwich Company

Location: *5102 N. Pearl, two blocks south of Point Defiance Park*
Phone: *206-752-4069*
Days/Hours: *8:30 a.m. to 7 p.m., Sunday; 7 a.m. to 8 p.m., Monday, Wednesday, Thursday and Saturday; 7 a.m. to 10 p.m., Tuesday; 7 a.m. to 9 p.m., Friday.*
Wheelchair/Stroller Access: *Yes*

Tots love this place, with its crates of toys on the carpet-covered stage — adults love it for the healthy food and family atmosphere. On Tuesday night the owners host open microphone entertainment, so the atmosphere is better for adults. Most other times, you'll find kids eating peanut butter and jelly sandwiches or spooning the thick, fresh-fruit milkshakes here, while parents dine on spinach lasagna, black bean burritos and quiches.

Flakey Jake's

Location: *6409 Sixth Ave. Take I-5 Exit 132/Highway 16 west to Sixth Avenue exit. Turn left on Sixth Avenue and drive a half block*
Phone: *206-565-5911*
Days/Hours: *11 a.m. to 10 p.m., Sunday through Thursday; 11 a.m. to 11 p.m. Friday and Saturday.*
Wheelchair/Stroller Access: *Yes*

This design-your-own burger restaurant invites guests to personally dress up their beef-and-buns from a varied condiment bar. That means kids can slop on the ketchup and don't have to scrape the pickles off their meat patty. Four kids' meals appear on the menu and all come with French fries.

Places to Shop

The Children's Bookstore

Location: *6615 South 12th, at 12th and Mildred streets*
Phone: *206-565-3039*
Days/Hours: *10 a.m. to 8 p.m., Monday through Friday; 10 a.m. to 6 p.m., Saturday; noon to 4 p.m., Sunday.*
Wheelchair/Stroller Access: *Yes, except for a few narrow aisles*

This store is a young bookworm's dream. There are more than 23,000 titles for children to choose from. A play area for little ones gives adults some time to browse for new releases. School groups and other organizations will find great discounts here. Ask about the Birthday Club and frequent customer discounts.

Freighthouse Square

Location: *25th Avenue and East "D" Street, one block north of the Tacoma Dome*
Phone: *206-272-6178*
Days/Hours: *10 a.m. to 7 p.m., Monday through Saturday; noon to 5 p.m., Sunday.*
Wheelchair/Stroller Access: *Yes*

More than a dozen fun shops pack this public market within the former Milwaukee/St. Paul Railroad freighthouse. Older kids like the adventure games and comic books at Lady Jayne's, while the younger set is fascinated by the myriad of inflatables at Ba'loonnie Toone Lane. Children who enjoy crafts will find ornamental beads for jewelry and other creations at The Bead Factory. Nibble at some of the snack stops here, including Mrs. M's Popcorn and Freighthouse Fudge Factory.

Mount Rainier National Park

Mount Rainier is a dormant volcano and the highest volcanic peak in the Cascade Mountains. But don't worry. Scientists say this 14,411-foot mountain last blew about 2,500 years ago and shouldn't erupt again for several hundred years. Only in the past century has the peak been a destination for tourists. In 1884, settlers James and Martha Longmire opened Mineral Springs Resort, now the park's headquarters. It's also home to Longmire Museum, packed with natural, human, and geologic history. The park is open daily. Admission is $5 per vehicle; bicyclists and walk-in visitors pay $2.

At Paradise, a few miles east of Longmire on Highway 706, there are 300 miles of back country trails winding over the mountain. During the summer, kids old enough to endure two weeks of hiking will enjoy the 93-mile Wonderland Trail encircling the mountain. For those less rugged, try the half-mile Life Systems Trail around the hot springs at Ohanapecosh or the three-quarter mile Trail of the Shadows from Longmire.

Paradise Inn, just above the visitors center, offers overnight accommodations from late May through October. Exposed-beam ceilings and log furniture give this 1917 lodge a rustic feel. Even if ceilings and log furniture give this 1917 lodge a rustic feel. Even if you're not staying in one of the 125 guest rooms, you'll want to warm yourself by one of the two stone fireplaces before stepping out to the nearby hiking and cross-country skiing trails. For more information call 360-569-2275.

Winters, you can see the park on snowshoes, cross country skis, sleds or innertubes. Most of these activities originate at the Ski Touring Center at Longmire, open daily from about mid-December through April. Sledding and innertubing is allowed at Paradise, but there are no rentals, so bring your own equipment. For snowshoe rental, call 360-569-2411.

Off Highway 410, west of Chinook Pass, there's a visitors' center at Sunrise (elevation 6,400 feet). The lodge here offers concessions, but no overnight accommodations. Outdoor tables give visitors a great place to enjoy a summer picnic.

Summer evenings, families can huddle around a campfire at Carbon River, White River, Paradise, Longmire or Ohanapecosh to study the stars or listen to cozy educational programs hosted by park service naturalists. Summer is also the time of year for kids 6 to 11 to take part in Junior Ranger activities at White River, Ohanapecosh, Cougar Rock and Ipsut Creek. Most are 90 minutes to two hours long and involve short educational hikes led by park naturalists. Children who don't yet read may need some help from a parent or older child.

If you're looking for old growth forest, try Ohanapecosh at the park's southeast corner. Many of the Douglas fir, western hemlock and red cedar here are 500 to 1,000 years old. Walk the self-guided Grove of the Patriarchs Trail to gain an appreciation for these immense aged trees.

Great Destinations

Crystal Mountain Resort

Location: *Just off Highway 410 on Crystal Mountain Boulevard. Take I-5 Exit 142A. Follow Highway 164 through Enumclaw to Highway 410 and drive 33 miles east to Crystal Mountain turnoff just before entering Mount Rainier National Park. Or follow Highway 410 from Yakima west over Chinook Pass; turn onto Crystal Mountain Boulevard just after leaving national park. The Yakima route is closed during the winter.*
Phone: *360-663-2265 and 360-634-3771*
Days/Hours: *Year-round overnight accommodations and recreational activities.*

Wheelchair/Stroller Access: *Yes*

Mount Rainier is so close to this resort, you can almost reach out and touch the peak. Summers attract mountain bicyclists, hikers, anglers, and swimmers. There are more than 35 miles of trails and access roads to explore. Don't have a mountain bike? You can rent one. Winters here are meant for downhill skiing. The high-speed "Rainier Express" quad chair lift whisks riders to the summit in 13 minutes. (It runs summers, too.) A family rate is $24, adults and older children pay $7 and youngsters 6 years and younger ride free.

Mount Rainier Scenic Railroad

Location: *In Elbe. Take I-5 Exit 127 to Highway 512. Turn on Mount Rainier exit to Pacific Avenue/Highway 7. Turn right and follow for 33 miles.*
Phone: *360-569-2588*
Days/Hours: *11 a.m., 1:15 p.m. and 3:30 p.m., daily, June 15 through Labor Day, plus weekends Memorial Day through September.*
Wheelchair/Stroller Access: *Yes*

This locomotive offers 90-minutes of fun as it totes passengers 14 miles across bridges and through emerald forests to Mineral Lake, and back again. Kids and adults alike will tap their toes to the live music on board. Admission is $7.50 for adults, $6.50 for seniors, $5.50 for students 12 to 17, $4.50 for kids 2 to 11, and free to those younger. Telephone reservations are accepted only for groups of 25 or more. Another trip features a 40-mile, four-hour excursion on the 1920s Cascadian Dinner Train, and includes a five-course prime rib dinner. Pre-paid reservations for this $55 trip are required.

Places to Eat

Sweet Peaks Bakery and Ski Mountaineering

Location: *In Ashford at 38104 Highway 706 E.*
Phone: *360-569-2720*
Days/Hours: *7:30 a.m. to 8 p.m., Monday through Thursday; 7 a.m. to 8 p.m., Friday, Saturday and Sunday.*
Wheelchair/Stroller Access: *Yes, except for one small step outside to the main floor bakery and shop*

After a day on the mountain, the huckleberry pie here tops off your visit. In the morning, if you're stopping here to rent or buy ski or mountain equipment (they have everything from sunscreen to ice axes) treat everybody in the family to their own gooey cinnamon roll.

Wild Berry Restaurant

Location: *37721 Highway 706 E., Ashford*
Phone: *360-569-2628*
Days/Hours: *11 a.m. to 9 p.m., daily, April through September;*
11:30 a.m. to 8 p.m., daily, October through March.
Wheelchair/Stroller Access: *Yes*

This lunch-and-dinner place serves up mountain trout so fresh you can almost see it being reeled in. The tangy wild blackberry pie is made daily. A children's menu features ham, roast beef, turkey, grilled cheese and peanut butter and jelly sandwiches. Wild Berry offers comfortable dining for the whole family, with highchairs for the smaller set.

Thurston County/Olympia

Thurston County is home to Olympia, Washington's capital and the hotbed of the state's political activities. Children who visit the 35-acre capitol campus during the legislative session, typically the first four months of the year, will find a mix of rural and metropolitan leaders of all ages and ethnic backgrounds. There are a variety of educational tours geared toward adults and school-age children.

Thurston County is at the southern, protected tip of Puget Sound. To the north, Nisqually Reach Nature Center attracts visitors to what some consider the state's major natural estuary. Seabirds, shellfish and other fish call this region home. Call 360-459-0387 for visitor information.

Great Destinations

Capitol Tours

Location: *Olympia State Capitol. Take I-5 Exit 105; follow signs west*
Phone: *360-586-8687*
Days/Hours: *10 a.m. to 4 p.m. daily, except holidays.*
Wheelchair/Stroller Access: *Yes*

While state lawmakers haggle over the current issues of the day under the hallowed dome, kids are busy running up and down the Capitol's interior marble steps and testing the building's echo. Free guided tours leave on the hour and loop through the senate and house chambers, stopping in the balconies if the Legislature is in session (typically January through early spring). Guides will explain the history behind "Ulcer Gulch," where lobbyists cajole and sometimes twist arms for their causes.

Watch for the teenagers clad in blue or red blazers scurrying through the Capitol, delivering packages and messages. They are House and Senate pages sponsored by their local lawmakers. Interested high schoolers should call their district representative or senator and ask about a week-long assignment.

There are 262 steps to the top of the dome. Children must be at least 10 years old to attempt the climb up the narrow, winding staircase. Tour reservations are not required for groups of fewer than 15.

First Gallery

The Chattery Down, Gnomes World and Buck's Fifth Avenue

Location: *209 Fifth Ave. E.*
Phone: *360-352-9301*
Days/Hours: *9 a.m. to 5 p.m., Monday through Friday;*
8 a.m. to 5 p.m., Saturday.
Wheelchair/Stroller Access: *Yes*

There are three fun stops under one roof in downtown Olympia's First Gallery. At *Chattery Down*, kids point their pinkie fingers up as they sip from china cups and nibble on scones during the traditional children's tea parties on Wednesday and Saturday afternoons. It's wise to call ahead for reservations, though drop-ins may find openings. Children who need to brush up on their table manners will appreciate the etiquette parties coordinated by a proper English nanny. Call ahead for class registration. Breakfast, lunch and dessert are served throughout the week, when classes aren't in session. At *Gnomes World*, fanciful art workshops draw youngsters from about age 3 to 13 years to sewing, puppet-making, knitting, bees wax molding and sidewalk chalk design courses. This shop is open 10 a.m. to 5 p.m., Monday through Saturday. Nearby, *Buck's Fifth Avenue* shop carries a myriad of hand-crafted items designed for children.

Governor's Mansion

Location: *Walking distance north of the Capitol*
Phone: *360-586-8687*
Days/Hours: *Appointment required for eight tours leaving between 1 p.m. and 2:45 p.m. Wednesdays.*
Wheelchair/Stroller Access: *No*

Get a glimpse of how the mansion's current governor lives during a 45-minute tour. Kids who have studied state government in school get the most out of this tour. Guides point out furniture and accessories added over the years by former governors. The library, sitting room, dining room and ballroom are featured in the tour. Private quarters are off limits.

Japanese Garden

Location: *Ninth and Plum streets, Olympia*
Phone: *360-753-8380*
Days/Hours: *10 a.m. to dusk, daily.*
Wheelchair/Stroller Access: *Yes*
　　Japanese lanterns give this small park an international feel. A delightful waterfall adds to the pristine nature. Most park goers come here for quiet strolls or to sit and enjoy the landscape. Spring is a favorite time for families because the flowering cherry trees are in full bloom.

Millersylvania Memorial State Park at Deep Lake

Location: *10 miles south of Olympia and three miles east of I-5 at Exit 95 on Tilley Road Southwest*
Phone: *360-753-1519*
Days/Hours: *Overnight camping year-round; day use dawn to dusk.*
Wheelchair/Stroller Access: *In most places*
　　Most campers like to keep this special park a well-guarded secret, but there's enough lake here for everyone. Many public school district students and graduates will recognize Millersylvania as the first place they attended outdoors camp. One end of the park has cabins with bunks, its own swimming beach and acres of well-groomed open fields for ball games and other group activities. The other end is for tent and RV campers. It features a gradually sloping sandy swimming beach and leisurely fishing from a dock with several benches. Within walking distance is Deep Lake Resort, a commercial campground where visitors can rent paddle boats and bicycles, or play a round of miniature golf.

Olympia Brewery/Pabst

Location: *In Tumwater; take I-5 Exit 103 east a few blocks*
Phone: *360-754-5000*
Days/Hours: *8 a.m. to 4:30 p.m., daily, year-round.*
Wheelchair/Stroller Access: *Yes*
　　The big, lighted sign over the brick brewery still reads, "Olympia," but Pabst makes the beer here now. Free guided 40-minute tours depart at least every half hour. Tours move through the brew house, where the beer is flavored, to the cellars, where it ages, and on to the

packing room, where it's funneled into cans and bottles. Visitors are always impressed with how spotless this place is. Even the floors are immaculate. At the tour's end, adults may sample free beer while children quench their thirsts with Pepsi.

Taylor United

Location: *S.E. 130 Lynch Rd., Shelton. Take I-5 Exit 104 onto Highway 101 to Taylor Farm, three miles south of Shelton*
Phone: *360-426-6178*
Days/Hours: *Appointment required; open 8 a.m. to 5 p.m., Monday through Friday, 9 a.m. to 4 p.m. Saturday, and noon to 4 p.m., Sunday.*
Wheelchair/Stroller Access: *Yes*

Taylor United is located northeast of Thurston County, in neighboring Mason County. Take the free guided tour and you'll see workers nimbly shuck thousands of oyster shells each day. Shuckers prepare these slippery shellfish for packing into tiny jars and hefty containers. The tour also includes a 15-minute video about oysters and their mollusk cousin, the clam. Floors here can be slippery, so wear shoes with good traction.

Tumwater Falls Park

Location: *Just north of the Olympia Brewery. Take I-5 Exit 102/ Deschutes Way. Cross the bridge over the freeway then turn right down the hill. Turn right again to cross another bridge and past Falls Terrace Restaurant to park entrance.*
Phone: *360-943-2550*
Days/Hours: *8 a.m. to 8 p.m., daily, Memorial Day through Labor Day; 8 a.m. to dusk the rest of the year.*
Wheelchair/Stroller Access: *In some areas; the gravel trail leading to the park is steep with no barriers separating it from the Deschutes River*

Children who see this park just east of the freeway can't wait to get down to the concrete gunboats and pirate ships planted firmly in the sand. Once there, they'll discover even more playground equipment at adjacent Tumwater Historical Park. A private playground-equipment company convinced the Tumwater Park Department to let them display their designs here so kids could romp on them. Children enjoy feeding the geese and ducks, who somehow know this is a prime picnic place and gladly accept handouts.

Wolf Haven International

Location: *3111 Offut Lake Rd., Tenino. At I-5 Exit 99, just south of Olympia, go east about three miles. Turn right on Highway 99. Drive another four miles through a short tunnel. Offut Lake Road is another quarter-mile ahead on your left.*
Phone: *800-448-9653 or 360-264-4695*
Days/Hours: *10 a.m. to 5 p.m., Wednesday through Monday, May through September; 10 a.m. to 4 p.m., Wednesday through Monday, the rest of the year. Gates open at 6 p.m. for 6:30 p.m. "Howl Ins," May through September.*
Wheelchair/Stroller Access: *Not too good*

Who's afraid of the big bad wolf? Nobody, once they've visited this sanctuary where these animals are revered and respected. There are more than three dozen wolves, coyotes and foxes living here. You can't touch the fenced-in creatures, but guides will share stories about the wolves' relationships and behavior. Call ahead to find out about special mini tours for kids. Children may have their faces painted with paw prints and can also learn how to make an origami paper wolf or decorate a wolf cookie.

The best time to come here is Friday and Saturday evening, May through September. That's when "howl-in" visitors sit on bleachers around a campfire. Storytellers weave legends about wolves while kids from the audience beat drums or dance wearing an animal headdress. After the story, audience members are invited to call out to the nearby canines with a hearty howl. It's both eerie and exciting when the wolves howl back. Admission is $6 for adults, $4 for children age 5 to 12, and free to kids 4 or younger. Group rate discounts are available.

Southwest Counties

Washington's southwest corner is perhaps best known for Mount St. Helens, the volcano that blew off its snowcone-shaped cap in 1980. Hundreds of families discover parks, hiking trails, historic sites and shopping while visiting this region. The most convenient driving route to Mount St. Helens National Monument is along Interstate 5. From Seattle, travelers pass through Lewis County, named for famed explorer Meriwether Lewis. Visitors looking for a good buy on childrens' and adults' clothes, toys, and household items often stop at the factory outlet stores in Centralia.

Continuing south along I-5 you'll find Cowlitz County, where more than a decade after the eruption's devastation, much of the area is now blanketed by pristine forests. Most of the population here lives in the neighboring towns of Kelso and Longview. For a quiet afternoon, stroll Longview's Lake Sacajawea Park, a ring of ponds and grassy fields with a children's playground. Older children may prefer skateboarding or in-line skating at Cloney Park.

Farther south, in Clark County, is a historic city which residents call "Vancouver, U.S.A." or " the other Vancouver." This is where you'll find the re-created Fort Vancouver, home of the Hudson's Bay Trading Company from the 1820s to the 1860s. It's separated from metropolitan Portland, Oregon, by the Columbia River.

Outdoors, boating and fishing on Clark County's numerous rivers and lakes are popular year-round. Vancouver's Marshall Community Center, on West McLoughlin Boulevard off Fort Vancouver Way, features an indoor swimming pool and recreation facilities for all ages.

Lewis County

Great Destinations

Chehalis-Centralia Railroad

Location: *On Main Street near Dairy Queen in Centralia; just south of Main Street in Chehalis near Dairy Bar*
Phone: *360-748-9593*
Days/Hours: *1 p.m. to 5 p.m., weekends, Memorial Day through Labor Day.*
Wheelchair/Stroller Access: *Yes, for strollers; limited for wheelchairs*

This vintage 90-ton locomotive no longer hauls logs; it now hauls people. While aboard this 12-mile roundtrip leisure ride between Chehalis and Centralia, boys and girls may pretend they're part of the old-time rail crews which brought logs to the mill. The train leaves at 1 p.m. and 3 p.m. from Chehalis, and 2 p.m. and 4 p.m. from Centralia. Fares are $6.50 for adults, $4.50 for children 4 to 16 years, and free to those 3 or younger. One-way tickets are half price.

Places to Eat

Burgerville U.S.A.

Location: *In Centralia at 818 Harrison Ave., (plus several other restaurants in the Vancouver area)*
Phone: *360-736-5212*
Days/Hours: *10 a.m. to 11 p.m., Saturday through Thursday, 10 a.m. to midnight, Friday.*
Wheelchair/Stroller Access: *Yes*
   This Southwest Washington hamburger chain is tops in the region. Sundae flavors vary depending on the season or upcoming holiday (mint green shamrock milkshakes on St. Patrick's Day!). Best of all, this Centralia establishment has a fenced-in outdoor playground for toddlers and young children with a slide, merry-go-round, and bouncing rides.

Places to Shop

Centralia Antiques

Location: *In downtown Centralia between Maple and Locust streets and Railroad and Pearl Avenues*
Phone: *360-748-8885*
Days/Hours: *Hours vary; most close by 5:30 p.m.*
Wheelchair/Stroller Access: *Depends on the shop*
   Most children aren't big antique hunters, but those over the age of 7 often enjoy browsing through these shops looking at old books, toys and other items from their parents' or their grandparents' childhood days. Dozens of stores line these streets. A red trolley which runs Wednesdays and Saturdays takes visitors from several downtown stops to the factory outlets across town.

Centralia Factory Outlet Stores

Location: *East and west side of I-5 at Exit 82*
Phone: *800-831-5334*
Days/Hours: *9 a.m. to 8 p.m., Monday through Saturday; 10 a.m. to 6 p.m., Sunday.*
Wheelchair/Stroller Access: *Yes*
   You'll find some sturdy and affordable children's clothes at a half dozen of the retail stores here. Look for garb for newborns and toddlers at Carter's, or the V.S. Factory Store featuring Healthtex clothes. Genuine Kids features Osh Kosh clothing up to size 14.

Young teens may prefer contemporary styles of jeans at Quik Silver and Lee Jeans, which also have clothes for younger children. The kids can browse through Toy Liquidators for a fun plaything costing as much as 30 to 70 percent less than what most retail stores charge.

Mount St. Helens National Volcanic Monument/Cowlitz County

With the fury of 30 million tons of TNT, the once sleepy Mount St. Helens erupted 75,000 feet into the air on the morning of May 18, 1980, taking with it 8.8 billion cubic yards of ice, rock and dirt. The blast blew 1,300 feet off from the mountain's original 9,667-foot peak. Its aftermath left 57 people dead and 300 homes demolished and created a mushroom cloud seen throughout most of the state. Today, new life has returned to the mighty mountain and visitors can get a first-hand look. Before taking a trip up to the mountain, stop in Kelso at I-5 Exit 39 to collect maps at the Mount St. Helens Visitors Center.

There are several ways to reach the monument. The most accessible is from the west, via I-5 exit 49 at Castle Rock. Drive five miles to the Visitors Center at Silver Lake. Another 40 miles east on Highway 504 is Coldwater Ridge. From the north, via Morton and Randle to Windy Ridge on the crater's east side, take Highway 131 south from Randle.

Great Destinations

Coldwater Ridge Visitors Center
Location: *On Highway 504. Take I-5 Exit 49 at Castle Rock; drive 43 miles east*
Phone: *360-274-2131*
Days/Hours: *9 a.m. to 6 p.m., daily, April through September; 9 a.m. to 5 p.m. the rest of the year.*
Wheelchair/Stroller Access: *Yes, on some trails, too*
On clear days, the Highway 504 route to Mount St. Helens offers eye-popping views of the crater which is less than eight miles away. Bridge designers and engineers deserve a prize for the spectacular

spans on this drive. At the route's end, Coldwater Ridge Visitors Center gives children and adults a hands-on geology lesson with colorful displays.

If Mount St. Helens were divided into a before and after history lesson, Coldwater Ridge would be the "after" portion. Take the free tour and learn how life returned to the area after the eruption. Be sure to watch the life-like but mechanical National Forest Service ranger describe how wildlife and wild flowers have brought new life to the blast zone. Outside, The Winds of Change Trail is a paved path with a moderate grade in some places. It leaves from the visitors center and leads to crater views. The Birth of a Lake Trail leaves from the Coldwater Lake Picnic Area parking lot about three miles down the hill. Both are leisurely hikes for children and their families.

Mount St. Helens Forest Learning Center

Location: *About 34 miles east of I-5 at Exit 49 on the North Fork Ridge of Spirit Lake Memorial Highway 504*
Phone: *360-414-3439*
Days/Hours: *10 a.m. to 7 p.m., daily, mid-May to mid-October.*
Wheelchair/Stroller Access: *Yes*

The mountain's newest visitors site offers the only designated playground for children. Outside, there's a volcano-shaped playset where tots can climb inside the "crater" or slide down a "mudflow." Families may picnic nearby at one of three tables or grassy spots. Others may hike the trails — which vary from easy to challenging. Constructed of recycled rubber tires, the trail is soft enough so that children can't get hurt.

Inside the center, the emphasis is on forestry. Families will discover a miniature working railroad — a smaller version of the trains which used to work around the mountain. Youngsters can sit inside a one-seat helicopter like the ones which tracked the mountain's activity before the blast. Videos in the "destruction chamber" depict the May 18, 1980 eruption, mud flows, cloud plume and blowing ash. The eruption wiped out thousands of acres of trees, but much of this land has been replanted by Weyerhaeuser, which operates the forestry center with the state Department of Transportation. Another partner, the Rocky Mountain Elk Foundation, provides telescopes for viewing the Toutle Valley. Admission is free.

Silver Lake Visitors Center

Location: *Five miles east of I-5 Exit 49*
Phone: *360-274-2100 and TDD 360-274-2102*
Days/Hours: *9 a.m. to 6 p.m. daily, April through September; 9 a.m. to 5 p.m. the rest of the year.*
Wheelchair/Stroller Access: *Yes*

The Silver Lake Visitors Center offers visitors a lesson in pre-eruption history dating back centuries when Native Americans were the region's only human inhabitants. The Center presents a 22-minute video describing how volcanos form. Children who are beginning to study geology are often fascinated. Colorful dioramas describe the region's cultural history of early settlers, miners and loggers. Families who visit here often have a greater appreciation for the new life that has returned to this region. Admission is free.

Windy Ridge

Location: *A drive-up lookout overlooking the crater on the monument's east side off Highway 131*
Phone: *None*
Days/Hours: *Daylight hours year-round unless heavy snows prevent it.*
Wheelchair/Stroller Access: *Yes, but it's a little rustic*

If the weather is clear, this is a scenic place to park off the road, pull out the camera and take family snapshots near the crater. There are no trails or restrooms, but there's plenty of fresh air.

Places to Eat

Izzy's

Location: *In Kelso at Three Rivers Mall, 1001 Grade St.*
Phone: *360-578-1626*
Days/Hours: *11 a.m. to 10:30 p.m., Sunday through Thursday; 11 a.m. to 11 p.m., Friday and Saturday.*
Wheelchair/Stroller Access: *Yes*

This pizza chain offers some of the best pies in town and the affordable prices are appealing to parents. The "great pizza feed and salad bar" equals one trip through the salad bar plus all-you-can-eat pizza and cinnamon rolls. This costs 30 cents for each year in a child's age, but is limited to those 12 or younger.

Clark County

Great Destinations

Ape Cave

Location: *From I-5 Exit 21 at Woodland, drive 27 miles east to Cougar, then eight miles beyond. Turn left on 83 Road, go two miles to 8303 Road. Ape Cave is a mile ahead on the right.*
Phone: *None at cave sites; call 360-274-2100 in Cougar*
Days/Hours: *Year-round, but parking lot is open dawn to 9 p.m. in winter. Lantern rental available daily 10 a.m. to 5 p.m. during summer, but last rental available at 4 p.m.*
Wheelchair/Stroller Access: *No*

Junior spelunkers, ready with hard hats and flashlights or lanterns, may explore the longest intact lava tube in the continental United States. This neighbor to Mount St. Helens was created by the volcano's eruption 1,900 years ago. Despite its name, there are no apes here. The tube was named decades ago after a young band of adventurers calling themselves the St. Helens Apes. The tube is actually two caves. The 4,000-foot lower cave is the better choice for amateur explorers. Inside, it's chilly and dark year-round, and the floor is sharp in some places, so it's not recommended for children younger than 5. It's smart to bring a warm sweater or jacket, sturdy shoes and a lantern or flashlight. Lantern rentals are $3. On summer weekends only, a forest interpreter leads 30-minute tours on the half hour between 11:30 a.m. and 4:30 p.m. Non-guided tours of the cave take at least an hour, so arrive before 5 p.m. if you plan to rent a light. Though it's not a tight fit, the cave is not the place for claustrophic children or adults. On the map, the Ape Caves are in Skamania County, but the best access is through Clark and Cowlitz counties.

Fort Vancouver National Historic Site

Location: *In Vancouver at 1501 E. Evergreen Blvd.*
Phone: *360-696-7655*
Days/Hours: *9 a.m. to 4 p.m., daily, Labor Day through Memorial Day; 9 a.m. to 5 p.m. during the summer.*
Wheelchair/Stroller Access: *Yes, at the visitors center; limited at the fort*

For adults, it's an early example of a multinational corporation. For kids, it's a cool fort from the 1840s with a blacksmith shop,

Photo courtesy of the National Park Service and Rick Edwards
Kids watch volunteer Tom Medema reenact pioneer-style bread-making at the Fort Vancouver Historical Site.

kitchen, bake house, fur warehouse and a bastion tower from which to watch for intruders. Begin a trip to the re-created Fort Vancouver with a 15-minute video at the historic site's visitors' center. Hear about the Hudson Bay's Trading Company and its fur trade headquarters. After a walk down the hill or a 90-second drive to Fifth Street, just east of Fort Vancouver Way, you'll find the encampment. During the summer, guides take groups through the fort's working exhibits every half hour. Visitors 6 years or older are most likely to enjoy this attraction.

A favorite for agile kids is climbing into the bastion high above the fort to scan outside the walls. In early October, on the only two days the fort is open after dark, costumed guides perform historical re-enactments by candlelight. These days change each year, so call ahead. Admission is free mid-September through mid-May. Summer admission is free to those 16 years or younger, and $2 for adults with a maximum of $4 per family.

Pendleton Woolen Mills

Location: *In Washougal off Highway 14 along Columbia River*
Phone: *360-835-1118*
Days/Hours: *Tours begin at 9 a.m., 10 a.m., 11 a.m. and 1:30 p.m. weekdays, September through July.*
Wheelchair/Stroller Access: *Wheelchairs permitted, strollers not*
Anyone who has cuddled up under a warm wool blanket will appreciate the way machines process raw wool into cozy creations during a free tour through this mill. In 45 minutes, visitors can see the wool spun, colored and eventually finished in large rolls. This tour gives students who like to wear Pendleton sweaters a sense of where some of their back-to-school clothes come from. Pendleton wool clothing is sold in the adjacent gift shop.

Pomeroy House/Living History Farm

Location: *In Yacolt, 30 miles northeast of Vancouver at 20902 N.E. Lucia Falls Rd.*
Phone: *360-686-3537*
Days/Hours: *House and farm displays open the first full weekend of each month, June through October, 11 a.m. to 4 p.m., Saturdays, and 1 to 4 p.m., Sundays. The Tea Room is open 11 a.m. to 3 p.m., Thursday, Friday and Saturday year-round except Thanksgiving, Christmas, New Year's Day and Easter.*
Wheelchair/Stroller Access: *Possible, but rough*
The hard work of turn-of-the-century farmwork becomes fun for children when they try their hands at grinding coffee, churning butter, and spinning and weaving wool. With a little muscle, boys and girls can use a cross-cut saw, make rope and pump water. Younger children may get a kick out of feeding the chickens. Just try to get them this excited about chores at home! Weekend events change monthly, but puppet shows, crafts exhibits and a Laura Ingalls Wilder presentation about the pioneer author's "Little House on the Prairie" series return annually. Each fall, look for cider pressing, hay rides and harvest fun on weekends. Admission is $3 for adults, $1.50 for children 3 to 11 years, and free to those 2 or younger.

Sip tea and dine off pretty china in the Tea Room anytime during the year. It's open to all ages, but owner Lil Freese says her grandchildren began enjoying these more formal lunches when they were 4 years old. The special Tea Plate is a favorite here. It varies seasonally, but typically comes with finger sandwiches, scones, soup, and fruit, sorbet and dessert for $6.50.

Susie's Country Inn: Bed and Breakfast for Dogs & Cats

Location: *North of Vancouver at 7418 N.E. 159th St.*
Phone: *360-576-K9K9*
Days/Hours: *11 a.m. to 5 p.m., daily.*
Wheelchair/Stroller Access: *Available through half the grounds*

It's a dog's life (and cat's, too, for that matter) at this canine and feline home-away-from-home. Human visitors to this overnight hostel may watch animals relax in the TV room decorated with "101 Dalmations" designs; dog videos play on the TV here. There are other theme rooms for dogs and a kitty condo for cats. A free walk-through tour is short but young children get a kick out of seeing household pets in such a people-like setting.

Tears of Joy Theatre

Location: *In downtown Vancouver at Columbia Arts Center, 400 W. Evergreen Blvd.*
Phone: *360-695-3050*
Days/Hours: *Season runs November through April; call ahead for performance schedule.*
Wheelchair/Stroller Access: *Yes*

This award-winning puppetry theater group tours throughout the state but makes its home in Vancouver. Children as young as 3 years are won over to the stage by the lively multicultural stories showcased by Tears of Joy using shadow, stick and hand puppets. The troupe divides its local performances between the Columbia Arts Center in Vancouver and a stage in Portland. Tickets are $8.50 for adults and $6.50 for students.

Places to Eat

Uncle Milt's Pipe Organ and Pizza

Location: *In Vancouver near Fourth Plain at 2410 Grand Blvd.*
Phone: *360-695-6895*
Days/Hours: *11 a.m. to 10 p.m., Sunday through Thursday; 11 a.m. to 11 p.m., Friday and Saturday.*
Wheelchair/Stroller Access: *Yes, on the main floor (one step outside from curb into restaurant)*

When the music starts pumping out of this vintage pipe organ it can get loud here, but children are having so much fun in this festive pizza restaurant that they hardly notice. Bouncy tunes begin at 1 p.m. weekends and 6 p.m. weekdays. Vegetarians or those on a diet may prefer selecting from the salad bar.

Who-Song and Larry's Cantina

Location: *In Vancouver at 111 E. Columbia Way, one mile east of I-5 Exit 1A to Camas*
Phone: *360-695-1198*
Days/Hours: *10 a.m. to 10 p.m., Sunday; 11 a.m. to 10 p.m., Monday through Thursday; 11 a.m. to 11 p.m., Friday and Saturday.*
Wheelchair/Stroller Access: *Yes*

Hungry children may devour the free tortilla chips and salsa served to your table before adults have had a chance to consider this Mexican menu. Noisy? Yeah. Fun? What else would you expect from a place that answers its phone, "You're calling the place where the party never ends?" If you grab a window seat you can watch tugs, barges and other boats on the Columbia River while you eat lunch or dinner. Margaritas flow here, so some parents don't think it's appropriate for younger children.

Places to Shop

Story Station

Location: *In east Clark County at 14415 S.E. Mill Plain Blvd.*
Phone: *360-896-6784*
Days/Hours: *10 a.m. to 7 p.m., Monday through Saturday, September through June; 10 a.m. to 6 p.m., Monday through Friday, and 10 a.m. to 5 p.m., Saturday, July and August.*
Wheelchair/Stroller Access: *Yes*

Chug along to this brightly colored children's bookstore featuring hundreds of titles and a toy train that runs overhead on tracks around the inside perimeter of the store. Inside, you'll also find educational computer software and videos at a smaller shop, Knowledge Emporium.

Places to Play

Hazel Dell Golf-O-Rama

Location: *7120 N.E. Highway 99, Vancouver's Hazel Dell community. Take I-5 Exit 4 at Northeast 78th Street*
Phone: *360-694-4719*
Days/Hours: *7 a.m. to 11 p.m., daily, June through August; 9 a.m. to 9 p.m., the rest of the year.*
Wheelchair/Stroller Access: *Yes*

Visible on the east side of I-5, this "paragon of putting" awaits families with its miniature golf obstacles on two lighted and well-maintained 18-hole courses. Sink a hole-in-one on the 18th hole and win a prize. If you don't win a prize, buy yourself a dairy treat inside at *The Steakburger* restaurant featuring ice cream sundaes heaped with toppings. Children 13 or younger play 18 holes for $1.25 and 36 holes for $2; adults pay $2 and $3, respectively.

Clark County Parks

There are nearly 100 pristine, recreation-packed parks throughout Clark County. Here are some choices sure to please a variety of ages:

Carter Park

Location: *In Vancouver at Columbia and 33rd streets*
Although small, this park packs crawl-through toys, a merry-go-round, slides, and aim-for-the-sky swings best suited for children younger than 8, into half an acre in this downtown Vancouver neighborhood.

Elizabeth Park

Location: *In Washougal at 14th and "I" streets*
Local boys and girls can be found racing down any of the four slides at this new 1.2-acre park. A climbing toy with swinging rings, popular among 5- to 10-year-olds, is the centerpiece of this grassy site.

Homestead Park

Location: *In east Clark County's Cascade Park neighborhood near Southeast 158th Avenue Loop*
This six-acre gem features a new play area aimed at toddlers and young children. There's also a series of workout stations with instructions for exercise geared to teens and adults.

Lewisville Park

Location: *North of Battle Ground, 26411 N.E. Lewisville Highway*
Clark County's oldest park, this 154-acre favorite draws parkgoers with its Lewis River swimming and fishing. Others enjoy the hiking and sheltered picnic areas built during the Depression by the Works Progress Administration. Children of all ages can be found swinging and riding merry-go-rounds and slides throughout the park. Officials charge $2 for parking.

Marine Park

Location: *Southeast Marine Park Way, south of Highway 14, near Vancouver's Blandford Drive intersection*
Along the north edge of the Columbia River, Vancouver's largest park offers 90 acres of trails ideal for bicycling and in-line skating, plus playground equipment for young children. Those looking for a picnic site will find tables and restrooms here, too. Be prepared to pay a few dollars for parking.

Helpful Phone Numbers:

Battle Ground Chamber of Commerce, 360-687-1510

Camas-Washougal Chamber of Commerce, 360-834-2472

City of Olympia Visitor Information, 360-753-8262

Eatonville Visitors Information Center,, 360-832-4000

Gig Harbor/Peninsula Chamber of Commerce 206-851-6865

Lakewood Area Chamber of Commerce, 206-582-9400

Lewis County Visitors and Convention Information, 360-736-7132

Longview Chamber of Commerce, 360-423-8400

Mount Rainier National Park, 360-569-2211

Mount Rainier Disabled Visitor Information, 360-569-2211, ext. 2304

Mount Rainier TDD, 360-569-2177

Puyallup Area Chamber of Commerce, 800-634-2334 or 206-845-6755

State Capitol Visitor Services, 360-586-3460

Tacoma Visitor Information Center, 206-272-7801

Tacoma-Pierce County Visitors & Convention Bureau, 800-272-2662, ext. 1-B

Tumwater Chamber of Commerce, 360-357-5153

Vancouver/Clark County Visitors Services, 800-377-7084

Views of the Olympic Mountains attract thousands of visitors to Hurricane Ridge.

Olympic Peninsula, Ocean Beaches and Hood Canal

Nearly all of Washington's Pacific coastline will leave you with fresh sea air in your lungs and sand in your shoes. But the state's shoreline offers much more. What your familiy will enjoy depends on which section of the beach you visit. When planning a trip to the beach, consider separating the coastline into three parts: north, north-central and south. Each section has its own personality and activities for children. Before setting off for any part of the Washington coast with kids, it's smart to pack along three "must haves," a bucket and shovel for building super sand castles, a plastic bag for toting some favorite treasures home, and pairs of shoes and socks to warm up wet feet at the end of the day.

Olympic Peninsula

Because of Washington's mild climate, many visitors are surprised that much of the Olympic Peninsula is a rain forest. The gauge fills up with as much as 175 inches of precipitation annually at the Hoh River Rain Forest entrance to the peninsula's Olympic National Park. Rain here feeds majestic trees and monster mosses. Even in the summer, it's smart to pack along a raincoat. Not all stops on the Olympic Peninsula are waterlogged, however. From recreational resorts and Native American museums to aquariums and animal preserves, the region offers many stops for on-the-go families.

In the summer, National Park Service naturalists host nature programs designed for children and adults around the campfire at Mora, Kalaloch, Hoh, and Heart O' the Hills. Two guided rain forest walks suitable for children are offered daily at Hoh as well. On the Hall of Mosses Trail in the Hoh Rain Forest, let children touch the moist, furry and green plantlife along the non-guided three-quarter-mile hike. Throughout the park, 5- to 10-year-olds can earn their own "junior ranger" badge by completing a checklist that tests their understanding of plants, animals, and environmental protection. Check at a ranger station for more details.

There are several ways to reach the Olympic Peninsula. From Seattle, catch the Seattle-Winslow or Edmonds-Kingston ferry and drive to Highway 104, which crosses the Hood Canal Floating Bridge. Just a mile north of the bridge is Port Gamble. Encourage children who find unusual seashells to compare theirs with those at the town's Of Sea & Shore Museum, home of the largest privately-owned seashell collection in the country. This once booming sawmill town, done in the architectural style of 1850s New England, is still home to the Pope & Talbot mill. Grab a snack at the Port Gamble Country Store, open daily since 1853, then stroll streets lined by white picket fences and spiral-topped churches. About six miles farther, families heading to the Port Ludlow resort should take Highway 20 north. At least a dozen recreational activities await here.

In neighboring Port Townsend, the pace is relaxed and the setting romantic. Bed-and-breakfast getaways — many of them in Victorian homes — are more suited for adults, but attractions on the Strait of Juan de Fuca make this a nice stop for the younger set, as well. From Highway 104, take U.S. 101 for about three miles before turning onto Highway 20 North. Continue another 15 miles to Port Townsend. To the west, in the shadow of the Olympic Mountains, is Sequim. A game farm and wildlife preserve are two popular stops for families. From Highway 104, connect with U.S. 101 North and drive west about 30 miles.

The largest Olympic Peninsula city on the Strait of Juan de Fuca is Port Angeles, 18 miles west of Sequim on U.S. 101 North. Home to a marine life center and several destinations for families, Port Angeles is also a jump-off point to some of the peninsula's most beautiful and fascinating natural attractions. Consider combining a Port Angeles visit with a day trip to Victoria, B.C. The private Black Ball Ferry sails roundtrip between the two cities at least once daily. Call 360-457-4491 for details.

Port Ludlow Resort

Location: *9483 Oak Bay Rd.*
Phone: *800-732-1239*
Days/Hours: *Overnight accommodations available year-round.*
Wheelchair/Stroller Access: *Some units accessible*

By land or by water, this overnight resort has just about everything an outdoorsy family might want for relaxation and recreation. If you have a boat, cruise up to the 300-slip marina. On land, you'll find every possible recreation — from golf and tennis to bicyling the countryside. Stay in a guest room, or one of the one- to four-bedroom suites featuring furnished dining areas, kitchens and fireplaces. In the summer ask about the "Club Lud" program — planned recreation activities for guests age 4 to 12. Children younger than 12 stay free in a parent's room.

Port Townsend

Elevated Ice Cream Co.

Location: *In Port Townsend at 627 Water St.*
Phone: *360-385-1156*
Days/Hours: *9:30 to 10 p.m., daily, May through September;*
11 a.m. to 10 p.m., October through April.
Wheelchair/Stroller Access: *Yes*

It started nearly 20 years ago with three buckets of homemade ice cream and fresh fruit served from a shop so small that it fit in an unused Victorian elevator car. Now this Port Townsend shop is housed in a larger space and offers 16 different flavors. Elevated Ice Cream is still committed to homemade ice cream flavors, many of them created with local Sequim strawberries or Olympic Peninsula raspberries. There are specialty chocolates, candies and espresso drinks, too. A child's scoop is 95 cents. Single scoops for adults are $1.30 and double scoops are $2.30.

Fort Worden State Park

Location: *One mile north of Port Townsend*
Phone: *360-385-4730*
Days/Hours: *Overnight camping and rental home accommodations year-round; daylight hours for day visitors.*
Wheelchair/Stroller Access: *In most places, yes*

Even the tamest imagination can go wild in this old 330-acre park. Gunmounts and bunkers create a background for imaginative children to recreate make-believe battles. The beach outside the fort, which is still within the park, offers a great coastline for exploring and sand play.

Inside any of the 18 turn-of-the-century officers' quarters available for overnight rental, families are whisked back in time as they relax surrounded by ornate Victorian furnishings. Reservations can be hard to come by, so it's wise to call at least two months in advance. In fact, some popular summer and holiday dates require calling one year ahead.

The history of Fort Worden is depicted at the Commanding Officers' Quarters Museum, which is open daily from 1 p.m. to 5 p.m., and the 248 Coastal Artillery Museum, which is open noon to 5 p.m., Wednesday through Sunday. Here visitors can see World War II uniforms, guns and photographs.

Port Townsend Marine Science Center

Location: *Fort Worden State Park, at the end of the dock*
Phone: *360-385-5582*
Days/Hours: *Noon to 6 p.m., Tuesday through Sunday, June 15 through Labor Day; noon to 4 p.m., weekends, September 10 through October and April through June 14.*
Wheelchair/Stroller Access: *Yes*

Children are mesmerized by a live underwater video camera that captures action under the pier at this marine center. Stick your fingers into the indoor touch tanks to feel some underwater sea creatures. Outdoors, free interpretive beach walks are available on weekends, depending on the tide. Admission to the marine center is $2 for adults, $1 for students, and free to preschoolers.

Sequim

Dungeness Spit National Wildlife Refuge

Location: *North of U.S. 101, off Sequim Avenue and Marine Drive*
Phone: *360-683-5847*
Days/Hours: *Dawn to 10 p.m. during the summer; dawn to dusk the rest of the year.*
Wheelchair/Stroller Access: *In some areas*

Birds and kites fly overhead on six unobstructed miles of beach — the longest sandspit in the U.S. The water is chilly, but some daredevils wade in anyway because its so inviting. Clamdigging is popular here, too, but check ahead with Refuge or Clallam Bay Recreation Area rangers station to see if it's ok. Families who watch birds may try to keep track of the nearly 250 species which nest along this Strait of Juan de Fuca shoreline. Beach walkers may want to set aside about four hours for the 12-mile roundtrip route to the New Dungeness Lighthouse at the end of the spit. Volunteers from the U.S. Lighthouse Association lead daily tours between 10 a.m. and 4 p.m. Call 360-460-3259 for lighthouse information.

Hiway 101 Diner

Location: *In downtown Sequim on U.S.101 (look for the turquoise canopy out front)*
Phone: *360-683-3388*
Days/Hours: *6 a.m.to 9 p.m., daily.*
Wheelchair/Stroller Access: *Yes*
It may be noisy, but that's all part of the fun at this retro diner, complete with period decor. Spin a tune on the compact disc player tucked into the rear of a 1956 Thunderbird, and then order breakfast, lunch, or dinner any time of the day. Hamburgers and Chicago-style pizza are specialties here.

Olympic Game Farm

Location: *Near Sequim at 1423 Ward Rd.*
Phone: *800-778-4295 and 360-683-4295*
Days/Hours: *Driving tour open 9 a.m. to 6 p.m., daily, mid-May through mid-September, and 9 a.m. to 3 p.m. the rest of the year. Walking tour open 9 a.m. to 3 p.m., mid-May through mid-September, and closed the rest of the year.*
Wheelchair/Stroller Access: *On driving tour, but not on walking tour*
Lions and tigers and bears, oh my! This game farm has them all, plus several dozen other species of animals to delight kids and adults of all ages. You may spot them on separate walking and driving tours. Many of these creatures have starred in Walt Disney Studios' films.
The one-hour walking tour includes a visit to the movie set, fish ponds and an aquarium. Count your fingers after feeding creatures on the 45-minute driving tour, which is allowed as long as passengers stay in their vehicles. Bread loaves can be purchased for 50 cents before the trip.

Nearby, there's a special observation tower for aerial views of the cave- and den-dwellers below. During summer months, watch for little animals making their first appearance with the aid of their mothers; young children adore the small creatures in the animal petting area. Admission for separate driving or walking tours is $6 for those 13 or older, $5 for seniors and children 5 to 12, and free to those 4 or younger. Combination walk/drive tours are $8 for adults, $6 for seniors and children 3 or older, and free to those 2 or younger. Phone at least one week ahead to receive a discount available to groups of 10 or more.

The Three Crabs

Location: *In Sequim at 11 Three Crabs Rd.*
Phone: *360-683-4264*
Days/Hours: *11:30 a.m. to 10 p.m., daily; restaurant closes at 9 p.m. Sundays.*
Wheelchair/Stroller Access: *Yes*

For $4 or less, boys and girls can order the fish or clam basket, grilled cheese sandwich, or cheeseburger from the children's menu. Adults may prefer some of the delicious fresh-catch seafood; the Dungeness crab is always a good choice.

Port Angeles

Arthur D. Feiro Marine Laboratory

Location: *On the Port Angeles City Pier near Hollywood Beach off Railroad Avenue*
Phone: *360-452-9277, ext. 264*
Days/Hours: *10 a.m. to 8 p.m. daily, mid-June through mid-September; noon to 4 p.m. weekends during the rest of the year.*
Wheelchair/Stroller Access: *Yes*

Visitors may cuddle a sea cucumber or tickle a tube worm in the touch tank at this family-friendly marine lab. This is an ideal place for children to learn about the creatures who occupy the Washington coast — without getting all wet! Colorful, protected indoor tidepools exhibit barnacles, hermit crabs, and blossoming sea anenomes — all at a child's-eye level. Families can go face-totentacle with an octopus behind a window. Special risers allow kids a closer look into some of the tanks. Other viewing areas are just the right height for those in wheelchairs or strollers. Admission is $1 for adults, 50 cents for seniors and those 6 to 12, and free for those 5 or younger.

Frugals

Location: *In Port Angeles at 1520 East Front*
Phone: *360-452-4320*
Days/Hours: *10:30 a.m. to 11 p.m., Sunday through Thursday during the summer; closes at 11:30 p.m., Friday and Saturdays; closes at 10 p.m weeknights and 10:30 p.m. weekends the rest of the year.*
Wheelchair/Stroller Access: *Not needed; no inside dining*

This drive-up burger restaurant is a convenient place to stop with the whole family for something to eat. Readers of *Pacific Northwest Magazine* voted Frugal's the best "cheap eats" in the area. It's especially good for older children with large appetites because thick, juicy burgers are served on monster-sized buns.

Hurricane Ridge

Location: *17 miles south of Port Angeles*
Phone: *360-928-3211 and 360-452-4501*
Days/Hours: *Daily unless snow limits access; open 24 hours during the summer, and daylight hours the rest of the year.*
Wheelchair/Stroller Access: *In some places*

Olympic National Park offers more than two dozen day hikes in the summer, but some of the most panoramic are on Hurricane Ridge. A 17-mile drive up the ridge takes less than 30 minutes. Children may be amazed to learn that explorers spent a week making that same expedition for the first time in 1855. Now, day hikers can leisurely enjoy Hurricane Trail (first half mile is paved) and Meadow Loop Trail (half is paved, some steep hills); both are wheelchair/stroller accessible. It's best to check with a ranger about the trail's condition before starting a hike.

Those who make it to the top will be rewarded with breathtaking views of the Strait of Juan de Fuca and spectacular surrounding Olympic Mountain peaks. Encourage children to inhale the summer air, thick with the scent of wildflowers. If you are lucky, you will spot a blacktailed deer.

A few of the national park's trails have pit toilets; otherwise plan to make your own and cover it with soil when you're finished. And don't forget to pack out your garbage. Day hikes are free, but be prepared to pay the $5 vehicle fee charged daily, mid-May through September, and weekends, mid-December through March, at the Heart O' the Hills entrance. It's good for seven days.

On busy weekends, the National Park Service may close Hurricane Ridge Road to private vehicles carrying fewer than four passengers or those with a disabled driver/passenger designation. On these weekends, a bus takes visitors to the ridgetop. The ride is $3 per person 6 or older; those 5 or younger ride free. Bus passengers aren't charged the park's entrance fee. The buses leave every half-hour on the half-hour from the west end of the Peninsula College parking lot at East Lauridsen Boulevard and Ennis Street.

In the winter, the ridge attracts families who enjoy cross-country skiing, snow-shoeing, and innertubing. From mid-December through March, you can rent snowshoes for $6.50 a day at the Hurricane Ridge Shelter. The National Park Service leads guided trails on weekends as well. Bring your own sled, inner tube ,or disk to swoosh down a designated, but unsupervised hillside. Then tromp back up, because there's no rope tow.

Hurricane Ridge Lodge is open year-round. Its summer season offers a sandwich-and-salad restaurant; its winter doors are open to welcome those chilled to the bone inside for warming and restrooms.

Lake Crescent Cruise

Location: *Catch a free shuttle from Shadow Mountain General Store at mile post 233 on U.S. 101, 13 miles west of Port Angeles at the northern edge of Olympic National Park*
Phone: *360-452-4520*
Days/Hours: *Daily late May through September. First cruise sails at 11:30 a.m.; last cruise at 6 p.m. Arrive one hour ahead.*
Wheelchair/Stroller Access: *Yes*

Take to the water of ultra-blue Lake Crescent aboard the 149-passenger, double-decker M.V. Storm King paddlewheeler late May through September. Boys and girls will adore the Indian legends told by the shipboard ranger, including the story of a great white whale which brought good luck to the lake. Budding marine biologists will be fascinated to learn how the lake's depth (1,000 feet in some places), combined with certain sun-refractive water particles, gives Lake Crescent its deep color. The ranger also answers questions about the national park's environment and history. The 64-foot boat offers an open upper deck and a weather-protected lower deck for the 75-minute cruises which depart five times daily. A strong breeze can kick up on the lake, so bring a sweater or jacket for everyone. Boarding fees are $14 for adults and $10 for those 17 or younger. Arrive at the Shadow Mountain General Store (mile post 233 on U.S. 101) at least one hour before the cruise to catch the free shuttle to the paddlewheeler. After the cruise, you may buy the makings for a picnic lunch at the delicatessan in the General Store.

Olympic Park Institute

Location: *Port Angeles office at 111 Barnes Point Rd.; overnight stays at Rosemary Inn on Lake Crescent*
Phone: *800-775-3720 and 360-928-3720*
Days/Hours: *Two- and five-day camps, May through September.*
Wheelchair/Stroller Access: *No because some hiking is involved*
Tidepool table manners and tracking critter prints are part of the outdoor program for the whole family at this education center. A complete catalog from this private, non-profit organization details courses open to families with children, including, *Critters and Creatures* — following animal tracks in the forest, *Seashore Safari* — table manners in the tidepool, and *Exploring Nature Through Music and Art.* Youngsters must be at least 5 to take one of these classes. Participants stay overnight and dine at the Rosemary Inn on Lake Crescent. Course fees vary.

Sol Duc Hot Springs

Location: *On U.S. 101, a few miles past Lake Crescent, take Soleduck Road 12 miles to its end*
Phone: *360-327-3583*
Days/Hours: *Mineral pools open 9 a.m. to 9 p.m., daily, mid-May through October.*
Wheelchair/Stroller Access: *Yes, plus some cabins equipped with access*
For overnight or just a day visit, families can camp, soak, and swim at this park, which is the site of a natural hot springs. When pumped from beneath the ground, this bubbling mineral water is

Soleduck Trail is one of many hikes in Olympic National Park.

nearly 122 degrees! But by the time it reaches the three pools here, it's cooled to between100 and 107 degrees. One shallow, cooler pool is set aside for youngsters. There's also a large chlorinated swimming pool available for everyone. Admission for day visits run $5.50 for adults, $4.50 for those 52 or older, and free to youngsters 4 or younger. Families may stay overnight at any of the 84 campsites or 32 furnished cabins, which come either with or without kitchens.

North Beaches

From Cape Flattery to Queets, Washington's coast is rugged and its weather is often misty. Youngsters gain appreciation for the mighty Pacific's strength here. While beachcombing, even hard-to-impress teens are amazed at the effect the powerful surf has on driftwood. Encourage children to scoop up a handful of sand and sift through the myriad of colored grains pummeled by the seawater. Close your eyes and listen to the seagulls and osprey inhabiting the area.This is a good place to spot bald eagles.

Some of the north coast's best stops are within Olympic National Park (see Olympic Peninsula section). From the Seattle area, cross Puget Sound on the Edmonds-Kingston ferry. Drive over the Hood

Canal Floating Bridge via Highway 104 through Sequim and Port Angeles. Connect with the ocean beach on U.S. 101 or Highway 112. Return to the Seattle area on U.S. 101 south via Aberdeen. Merge onto Interstate 5 at Olympia.

Kalaloch Lodge

Location: *In Olympic National Park on U.S. 101, 36 miles south of Forks*
Phone: *360-962-2271*
Days/Hours: *Overnight accommodations year-round.*
Wheelchair/Stroller Access: *Yes, at the lodge; two of 40 cabins are accessible*

From its crest on the bluff overlooking the Pacific Ocean, Kalaloch Lodge offers different styles of overnight accommodations. Families may sleep in any of the 40 cabins on the bluff or in room at the 40-year-old lodge. During a winter storm, older children often watch transfixed at a window as the surf pounds the beach. Children 5 years or younger stay free here. The lodge dining room features a children's menu and highchairs. Some families find it more economical to cook their own meals; ask about units with kitchenettes. Eager beachcombers may walk the short distance to the beach for shellfish and driftwood treasures. Tidepools are filled with fascinating creatures, and are a favorite for kids to explore coastal sealife.

Lake Quinault Lodge

Location: *Southwest of Port Angeles, on U.S. 101 at mile post 125, turn onto South Shore Road*
Phone: *800-562-6672 in Washington state; 360-288-2571 out of state*
Days/Hours: *Overnight accommodations year-round.*
Wheelchair/Stroller Access: *Yes*

If there was ever a place to get away from it all, this is it. There are no televisions or telephones at this almost 70-year-old lodge. For entertainment, older children may join adults paddling canoes, playing badminton or croquet on a lake-view lawn, or reading in front of a cozy brick fireplace. Younger tykes may prefer swimming in a heated pool. Open for breakfast, lunch and dinner, the lodge dining room specializes in stuffed trout. Its homemade cheesecake is hard to resist as well. Room rates vary; children 5 or younger stay free. Ask about cribs and rooms with fireplaces.

Makah Museum

Location: *In Neah Bay, 75 miles west of Port Angeles*
Phone: *360-645-2711*
Days/Hours: *10 a.m. to 5 p.m., daily June through Sept. 16; closed Mondays and Tuesdays the remainder of the year.*
Wheelchair/Stroller Access: *Yes*

It's hard for many children to fathom, but some say the Makah Indians have lived on Washington's northwest coast since the beginning of time. Artifacts recovered nearby show what the tribe's way of life was like at least 500 years ago, before a mudslide covered the village. Three dioramas display tools and other items recovered after an 11-year excavation in the 1970s. A full-size longhouse gives visitors a look at what Makah life was like on land. Replicas of whaling and sealing canoes offer families a feel for Indian fishing and hunting on the water. Admission is $4 for adults, $3 for students and seniors, and free for those 5 or younger.

North Central Beaches

What kid (or kid at heart) can resist clam-digging? This 30-mile stretch of beach between Moclips and Ocean Shores is razor clam paradise. North of Moclips, waves crash into steep rock cliffs. To the south, however, the landscape becomes a gentle coastline beckoning beachcombers with miles of sandy coastline. All the way to Ocean Shores, visitors will find clam-digging beaches. This is a great activity for daring children with quick hands who don't mind grabbing something slimey. Check with local authorities about legal clam-digging seasons.

Tug on a pair of galoshes and carefully examine sea creatures in countless tidepools in this area. Then get crazy with sand-castle creations because the sand is great for packing. Frisbee fanatics will enjoy the challenge of tossing the disc in coastal winds; kite-flying is spectacular, too. Before dark, consider a sunset horseback ride. Later, marshmallow roasters will savor the ooey-gooey taste of a treat toasted over a driftwood fire.

In the winter, when the sea can turn mean, adventurous families may enjoy watching high winds create monster waves. Check with the Ocean Shores Police Department before getting too close to the beach. If it's safe, view the storm from the North Jetty at Ocean Shores' southern tip. For an overnight stay, consider one of the many motels or hotels (several have indoor swimming pools) or rent an overnight cabin in Ocean Shores, Copalis, Pacific Beach or Moclips. From I-5 near Olympia, reach the north-central coast by taking the Aberdeen/Ocean Beaches exit. Continue to Hoquiam and take Highway 109 to Ocean City. From Ocean City, drive south to Ocean Shores or north to Copalis, Pacific Beach and Moclips.

Kite Shops

Coastal winds around Ocean Shores make even a novice kite flier look like an expert. While strolling the beach, you'll see box kites, spinning tails, and kites of magnificent color flying overhead. Take children to any of these three shops to rent a kite. Many boys and girls younger than 8 may need an adult's help getting a kite to soar, but will soon be sailing them solo. Smaller children will likely need an adult partner. Kites are available to buy here as well, so bring your checkbook.

Cloud Nine Kite Shop
Location: *Just outside north gates of Ocean Shores entrance*
Phone: *360-289-2221*
Days/Hours: *9 a.m. to 6 p.m., weekends, year-round; 10 a.m. to 6 p.m. weekdays, March through October; select weekdays November through February.*
Wheelchair/Stroller Access: *Yes*

Cutting Edge Kites
Location: *Nantucket Mall on Ocean Shores Boulevard*
Phone: *360-289-0667*
Days/Hours: *10 a.m. to 6 p.m., year-round, Sunday through Thursday; 10 a.m. to 7 p.m., Friday and Saturday.*
Wheelchair/Stroller Access: *Yes*

Winds Northwest
Location: *Just west of Ocean Shores city entrance on Damon Road*
Phone: *360-289-4578*
Days/Hours: *10 a.m. to 5 p.m., Monday through Friday; 9 a.m. to 6 p.m., Saturday and Sunday.*
Wheelchair/Stroller Access: *Yes*

Miniature Golf

Even those as young as 5 years old can putt for glory on these two, separate 18-hole courses within a few miles of each other. Red's offers treats at the end for kids' scores — both high and low. Flipper's is next door to the Ocean Shores bowling alley — another recreational destination if the weather turns wet.

Flippers
Location: *Chance-A-La-Mer road near Ocean Shores Boulevard*
Phone: *360-289-4676*
Days/Hours: *10 a.m. to 6 p.m., daily, June through September. Open, if weather permits, the rest of the year.*
Wheelchair/Stroller Access: *Yes*

Red's Off-Course Mini Golf
Location: *Copalis Beach along Copalis River*
Phone: *360-289-4190*
Days/Hours: *9 a.m. to dark, daily, year-round.*
Wheelchair/Stroller Access: *Yes*

Mariah's

Location: *At the Polynesian Resort on the south end of Ocean Shores Boulevard*
Phone: *360-289-3315*
Days/Hours: *4 p.m. to 9:30 p.m., daily; Sunday brunch 8:30 a.m. to 1 p.m.*
Wheelchair/Stroller Access: *Yes*

Northwest cuisine attracts the older set while a $1.99 children's menu allows boys and girls to choose from chicken strips, corn dogs, hamburgers, or fish. All are served with French fries. Ask for a booster seat or highchair for little ones.

Nan-Sea Stables

Location: *At beach entrance off Chance-A-La-Mer road at Ocean Shores*
Phone: *360-289-0194*
Days/Hours: *10 a.m. to 5:30 p.m., daily, June through mid-September.*
Wheelchair/Stroller Access: *Not equipped for disabled riders*

First-timers and more experienced horseback riders alike can enjoy a jaunt along the beach high in the saddle of a horse from Nan-Sea Stables. Novice riders may be escorted by stable workers while those at ease with the reigns may ride at their leisure. Rides range from $11 for a 30-minute jaunt to $16 for a one-hour bay-to-woods ride. Another favorite is the 90-minute sunset ride ($27) which leaves from the beach at about 7:30 p.m. Those older than 6 may ride by themselves; younger children must ride with an adult. Discounts are available for groups of eight or more.

Playtime

Location: *Point Brown Avenue across from Ocean Shores City Hall*
Phone: *360-289-2702 (bumper cars and go-karts), and 360-289-3285 (bumper boats)*
Days/Hours: *10 a.m. to 10 p.m., daily, late March through September; closed the rest of the year.*
Wheelchair/Stroller Access: *OK for viewing the games*

Those too young for a driver's license may practice behind the wheel of a bumper car, bumper boat or go-kart at this Ocean Shores stop. Kids must be at least 3 years old and within the designated height range to ride. Ride admission prices range from $2.50 to $3.50.

South Beaches and Grays Harbor

The southern stretch from Grays Harbor to the mouth of the Columbia River is home to fishing charter boats and oyster and crab catchers. Though the timber industry has been hard hit in the past decade, the historic days of sawmilling and shipping live on in the museums and old homes in the area. In mid-July, the towns of Hoquiam, Aberdeen, and Cosmopolis host a *Family Fun Festival* with concerts, parades, and carnival attractions.

From Seattle, drive south on I-5 to Olympia. Take U.S. 12 exit to Aberdeen/Ocean Beaches, then it's about 50 miles to Aberdeen. Cut to South Beach on Highway 107 at Montesano; it connects with U.S. 101 to Raymond.

Visitors of all ages will find trinkets and souvenirs in the more than two dozen gift shops here. Listen to anglers tell of "the one that got away" as others weigh their prize catch at the public scale in Westport. The heaviest fish weighed here earn entries on the chalkboard. Another attraction are the great gray whales which migrate north along the Washington coast from Mexico, typically between late February and April. Sometimes you can see them with binoculars from the town's viewing tower, or get a closer look on a chartered whale-watching boat.

Drive farther south along Highway 105 to U.S. 101 to find the longest stretch of unbroken sand in the world: Long Beach Peninsula. Children may run along the elevated quarter-mile boardwalk in Long Beach. In the summer, stroll the boardwalk to see competitors in the town's annual sand-castle contest and kite-flying competition.

Grays Harbor, Aberdeen and Hoquiam

Friends Landing

Location: *South of Montesano on Chehalis River bank. Take Devonshire Road exit off U.S. 12. Turn south at Katon Road.*
Phone: *360-533-4453*
Days/Hours: *Round-the-clock daily.*
Wheelchair/Stroller Access: *Yes*

Snagging a fish becomes safer for all ages — especially the physically challenged — at this one-of-a-kind fishing hole. All docks are equipped with protective fences. Two covered shelters, a boat launch, and a picnic area are specifically designed with wheelchair riders in mind. Hydraulic lifts are planned to help wheelchair riders in and out of boats. Designs also include a pathway with fishing holes around a 32-acre man-made lake. Fishing tackle and bait are available in nearby Montesano.

Grays Harbor Historic Seaport and Lady Washington

Location: *On Aberdeen's Heron Street where Wishkah and Chehalis rivers meet*
Phone: *800-200-LADY*
Days/Hours: *Varies, so call ahead.*
Wheelchair/Stroller Access: *There's a special lift for wheelchairs which isn't available for strollers*

The majestic 18th century ship, Lady Washington, is docked here most of the year. Aboard, visitors can see what shipboard life was like for Capt. Robert Gray, who commanded the exploration of the Columbia River, as well as Grays Harbor (which was named after him). This is an educational stop for kids 8 years or older who study Washington state history in school. The Lady visits other seaports, so call ahead to ensure the ship is available for the 30-minute tours. Wheelchairs can be lifted onto the ship by crane, but since there are no ramps aboard, getting around is tough. Admission is $3 for adults, $2 for seniors and students, and $1 for those 11 years or younger. With reservations, visitors may enjoy a three-hour cruise on the Lady Washington for $45.

Hoquiam's Castle

Location: *In Hoquiam at 515 Chenault Ave.*
Phone: *360-533-2005*
Days/Hours: *10 a.m. to 5 p.m., daily, mid-June to Labor Day;*
11 a.m. to 5 p.m., Saturday and Sunday, the rest of the year.
Wheelchair/Stroller Access: *No*

Hoquiam's Castle is another educational stop for children studying Washington history. Adults with little ones may think twice about taking toddlers to see the antiques in this nearly 100-year-old estate built by a turn-of-the-century lumber baron. But grade-schoolers and teens may be interested to learn that there was plenty of wood to be harvested in this region in the 1800s. In fact, Hoquiam's name is derived from the Indian word meaning "hungry for wood." The half-hour guided tour here gives visitors a peek into what grand life was like in Grays Harbor during this period. Admission is $4 for adults, $1 for students 6 to 16, and free to kids 5 or younger.

South Beaches

Funland

Location: *In Long Beach at 200 Pacific Highway South*
Phone: *360-642-2223*
Days/Hours: *9 a.m. to 10 p.m., daily, May through August;*
10 a.m. to 10 p.m., daily, September to April.
Wheelchair/Stroller Access: *Yes*

This isn't just the latest new-fangled video-game and amusement arcade designed to eat quarters. This place has been around since the dark ages, when pinball was the only game in town. Popular among teens, Funland has both old favorites and new in the world of video games. Winners get tickets that can be redeemed for stuffed animals and other souvenir prizes.

Long Beach Go-Carts

Location: *In Long Beach at Pacific and 10th Street*
Phone: *360-642-2904*
Days/Hours: *10 a.m. to about 5 p.m., Monday through Friday; 9 a.m. to at least 5 p.m., Saturday and Sunday. Go-carts run as long as there are riders.*
Wheelchair/Stroller Access: *OK for viewing*
Touting itself as the area's largest go-cart track, this amusement center offers a senior track for those 12 or older, and a junior track for 5- to 11-year-olds. A three-minute blast around the course will cost you $3.

Long Beach World Kite Museum and Hall of Fame

Location: *In Long Beach at the corner of Third and North Pacific*
Phone: *360-642-4020*
Days/Hours: *11 a.m. to 5 p.m, daily.*
Wheelchair/Stroller Access: *Yes*
After visiting this growing museum, many families find it hard to resist an afternoon of kite-flying. Exhibits change regularly, but visitors can always count on seeing award-winning kites. Point out the children's kite display here. Admission is $3 for families, $1 for adults, and 50 cents for seniors and children 15 years or younger.

Pacific Salmon Charters

Location: *Port of Ilwaco*
Phone: *360-642-3466 and 800-831-2695*
Days/Hours: *January through October; call ahead for times and dates.*
Wheelchair/Stroller Access: *Three boats are equipped for wheelchairs*
Washington's southern coast offers several charter boats that take families fishing for sturgeon and bottomfish when salmon fishing is restricted. Pacific Salmon Charters also offers two-hour scenic cruises during the summer. Make sure little ones — or adults for that matter — are prepared for the rise and fall of ocean swells before committing to a trip. Boat operators say deep-sea fishing involves too much hard work for those 10 years or younger. Ask about less strenuous fishing trips for younger children, including a ride on a larger-size fishing boat designed to hold passengers.

Sandsations

Location: *On the shore of Long Beach*
Phone: *800-451-2542*
Days/Hours: *Last weekend of July.*
Wheelchair/Stroller Access: *Tough on sand, but viewing is great from the boardwalk*
Wild sand-castle creations come to life on the shores of Long Beach during the annual "Sandsations competition each July. Families can team together for competition entries ($15 to $35) or children can create their own ($1 per child). After prizes are awarded for these events, all sand engineers work side-by-side to build a behemoth sand sculpture in a "grain-to-grain" competition with castle-creators in another part of the country.

Twin Harbors State Park

Location: *Three miles south of Westport on Highway 105*
Phone: *360-268-9717*
Days/Hours: *Overnight camping year-round.*
Wheelchair/Stroller Access: *Yes*
Children become pirates hunting for buried treasure from the boat hull left for boys and girls to play on at this park. The saltwater shoreline provides razor clam digging, beachcombiing, and lookout sites for gray whales migrating north — typically in February and March. Horseback riders will find designated areas for riding on the park's north beach.
Pick up a brochure which describes plants and wildlife along the Shifting Sands Nature Trail. Tall beach grass sometimes keeps this one-mile trail from being clearly designated, so children should have an adult partner when hiking here. Nearly 320 campsites offer families a place to stay overnight. If campsites are full, try nearby Grayland Beach.

Washington State International Kite-Flying Festival

Location: *On the beach near the Long Beach Boardwalk*
Phone: *800-451-2542*
Days/Hours: *Third week of August; children's and seniors' days available.*
Wheelchair/Stroller Access: *Yes, on the boardwalk*
Kites fly to music, race down the beach, and light up at night during this competition open to novice fliers and expert kite masters alike. Even if nobody in your family is flying a kite, come to the

beach and vote for the most attractive one — audience votes determine the winner. A similar kite festival is held in September about 90 miles north on Highway 109 in Pacific Beach. Call Highfliers Kite Shop at 360-276-8377 for more details.

Westport Maritime Museum

Location: *In Westport at 2201 Westhaven Dr.*
Phone: *360-268-0078*
Days/Hours: *Noon to 4 p.m., Friday, 10 a.m. to 5 p.m., Saturday and Sunday, October through Mary; noon to 4 p.m., Monday through Friday, and 10 a.m. to 5 p.m., Saturday and Sunday, June through September.*
Wheelchair/Stroller Access: *No*

Big, thick whale bones resting outside this museum show visitors how immense the gray whales living off the Washington Coast actually are. Inside this former Coast Guard station there's an exhibit on whales with details about how these mammals were once hunted by fishermen. Children who know the fictional tale of Moby Dick will find real whaling stories here. A children's room features shell exhibits which teach boys and girls about different mollusks. There's also an exhibit showing how the surf pounds out different grains of sand from various rocks. Admission is free.

Helpful Phone Numbers:

Elma Chamber of Commerce, 360-482-2212

Forks Chamber of Commerce, 800-44-FORKS

Grays Harbor Chamber of Commerce, 800-321-1924

Grays Harbor Tourism, 800-621-9625

Hoh Visitor Center (west side), 360-374-6925

Hoodsport Ranger Station (east side), 360-877-5254

Long Beach Chamber of Commerce, 360-642-2400

Makah Tribal Council, 360-645-2201

Montesano Chamber of Commerce, 360-249-5522

National Park Service/U.S. Forest Outdoor Information Center (in Seattle), 206-220-7450

North Olympic Peninsula Visitor and Convention Bureau, 800-942-4042

Ocean Shores Chamber of Commerce, 360-289-2451

Olympic National Park Visitor Center (north side), 360-452-0330

Port Angeles Visitors Center, 360-452-2363

Port Townsend Chamber of Commerce, 360-385-2722

Raymond Chamber of Commerce, 360-942-5419

Sequim/Dungeness Valley Chamber of Commerce, 800-737-8462

Westport-Grayland Chamber of Commerce, 800-345-6223

Kids learn baseball drills from the Everett Giants during special pre-game programs.

North Puget Sound and the San Juan Islands

Kitsap Peninsula

From immense Navy ships to an authentic Native American village, the Kitsap Peninsula features a wide range of activities for families. Some visitors begin their Kitsap Peninsula trip aboard a Seattle-to-Bremerton ferry from Seattle's Colman Dock. Another route involves a 15-mile drive north of Seattle to Edmonds, where passengers take the Kingston ferry to Highway 104, which connects with Highway 3 South into Poulsbo. Others venture from Tacoma via Interstate 5 Exit 132 to Highway 16 which connects with Highway 3 North.

Those using the Seattle or Tacoma routes can make Bremerton their first stop. For more than 100 years, Bremerton has been home to the Puget Sound Naval Shipyard, whose workers take pride in building everything from aircraft carriers to guided missile-equipped frigates. Several of Bremerton's busiest visitor attractions are along the waterfront.

From the ferry terminal, stroll the four-block boardwalk built in the early 1990s to connect the ferry terminal to Waterfront Park. The park features the *USS Turner Joy* navy destroyer, the Northwest's only naval ship open for tours. Officials say children, especially those with parents or other family members who have served in the navy, are amazed at the ship's size as they walk the deck on self-guided tours. Look into berths, the bridge, and the engine room to get a sense of shipboard life.

Each year, thousands of passengers from Bremerton and Seattle depart on a short cruise to Blake Island, a re-created fishing camp of the Northwest Coast Native Americans at Tillicum Village. Children visiting this 475-acre island, with its Coastal Indian meal and pageant, feel as if they've traveled back in time. North of Bremerton along Highway 3 is Silverdale, where a marina and Waterfront Park offer prime picnic spots with playgrounds and a beach walkway.

Another route to the Kitsap Peninsula is via Bainbridge Island's Winslow ferry terminal. Just 30 minutes away from Seattle, the island offers rolling hills on roads with wide shoulders suited for families who enjoy challenging bike rides. If a leisurely walk through greenery sounds more like your pace, try Bainbridge Gardens. Each garden section has its own theme. This nursery also features a children's playground and outdoor cafe serving light meals. Call 206-842-5888 for more details.

North of Bainbridge Island on the shores of Agate Pass is the Port Madison Indian Reservation, home of the Suquamish tribe. A totem pole on Highway 305 directs visitors to the tribal museum. In August, the Suquamish celebrate Chief Seattle Days with traditional drum dances, canoe races, and a salmon bake.

Another popular ethnic stop — especially for families with Scandinavian roots — is seven miles north in Poulsbo. Norwegians settled here more than a century ago because they found the bays and inlets similar to the fjords in their native land. The annual May 17th Norwegian Independence Day celebration attracts hundreds of people, many wearing traditional costumes.

Bremerton

Bremerton Naval Museum

Location: *130 Washington Ave.*
Phone: *360-479-7447*
Days/Hours: *10 a.m. to 5 p.m., Tuesday through Saturday; 1 p.m. to 5 p.m. Sunday.*
Wheelchair/Stroller Access: *Yes*

Older children with an interest in nautical things will be fascinated by the ship models, naval weapons and military history artifacts here. Both young and old will be amazed at how much has changed in naval operations over the past century. Admission is free; tours are self-guided.

Kitsap Harbor Tours

Location: *Leaves from Bremerton's waterfront on the boardwalk*
Phone: *360-377-8924*
Days/Hours: *Various cruises leave several times daily, May through October.*
Wheelchair/Stroller Access: *Yes*
Tour boats take visitors on several different trips in the Bremerton area to see a Native American village, naval ships, and destinations north of the city. Cruise to Tillicum Village for a Native American dinner pageant on Blake Island, Fridays and Saturdays from May through September. On a clear evening, the trip offers breathtaking views of Mount Rainier, the Olympic Mountains, and the twinkling lights of Seattle's downtown skyline.

Youngsters' eyes open wide when they're greeted at the dock by costumed tribal members offering bowls of steamed clams. After eating the clams, guests are encouraged to grind the broken shells with their feet to create a white ground cover. This quiet state park is inhabited primarily by birds and deer. Activity heats up in the village, where guests dine on salmon barbequed over alder fires in a cedar longhouse — the traditional Northwest Indian way. After dinner, visitors are treated to the pageantry of Native American legends performed by ornately costumed musicians and dancers. The cruise leaves at 6:30 p.m. and returns at 10 p.m. Admission is $39.50 for adults, $36.50 for seniors, $26.50 for teenagers, $16.50 for children 6 to 12 years, $8.50 for 4- and 5-year-olds, and free to those 3 or younger.

Back in Bremerton, one of the best ways to get a look at some of the navy's finest vessels from World War II through today is aboard a Kitsap Harbor Tours boat. Though this tour is open to all ages, children younger than 8 typically don't understand the historic significance of these mighty ships. Trips leave hourly between 10:30 a.m. and 4:30 p.m. and last for 45 minutes. The narrated tour takes readers past the aircraft carriers *USS Nimitz* and *USS Midway*, and battleships *USS Missouri* and *USS New Jersey*.

Other inactive submarines, destroyers, and surface ships are also here, ready should the military need them. Though visitors would love to walk aboard these proud vessels, the ships are closed for high security reasons. Officials are working to open the *USS Missouri* for tours. Currently, the closest you can get is 300 feet away.

The ships look huge even at this distance, and you may want to bring along some binoculars for a close-up look. Tours are $6 for adults, $5 for seniors, $4 for students 6 to 12, and free to those 5 or younger.

Kitsap Harbor Tours also cruises roundtrip loops three times daily aboard a 24-knot high-speed boat between Bremerton, Keyport's Naval Undersea Museum, and Poulsbo. Depart Bremerton at 10 a.m., noon and 2 p.m. Adult fare is $9, seniors pay $8, children 6 to 12 pay $7, and those 5 or younger are free.

Yesterday's, Today's and Tomorrow's

Location: *On Bremerton's waterfront, 154 First St., at the corner of First and Washington streets*
Phone: *360-373-0802*
Days/Hours: *4:30 a.m. to 5 p.m. at the coffee shop; 5 a.m. to 6 p.m. at the deli; 11 a.m. to 7 p.m. at the soda fountain.*
Wheelchair/Stroller Access: *Yes*

Families visiting Bremerton's waterfront will discover this three-part eatery for a snack any time of day with its delicatessan, soda fountain, and coffee shop. The coffee shop opens its doors for early risers, and the soda fountain frequently keeps its doors open late for visitors who want a treat during a weekend evening family concert. Milkshakes are so thick you'll need a spoon.

Silverdale

Anna Smith Children's Park

Location: *Between Bremerton and Silverdale at the intersection of Tracyton Boulevard and Fairgrounds Road*
Phone: *None*
Days/Hours: *9 a.m. to 9 p.m., daily.*
Wheelchair/Stroller Access: *Yes*

There's a cute duck pond in the middle of this quiet park. Designed with colorful and fragrant flower beds meticulously cared for by master gardeners, this place is fun for families who like to feed ducks. A rather steep trail links this landscaped area to the saltwater below.

Bangor Naval Submarine Base

Location: *Near Keyport, north of Silverdale off Highway 305*
Phone: *360-396-4843*
Days/Hours: *Saturday tours by reservation only, beginning at 8:30 a.m. and 12:45 a.m.*
Wheelchair/Stroller Access: *No*
This 7,000-acre facility provides an inside look at how the navy trains people for submarine work. Shuttle buses that carry up to 35 passengers tour the base for three- or seven-hour tours. Nearly all parts of the tour are visible only from the bus seat because officials don't want tours to disrupt routine activity here. Since these tours are long and offer a lot of information about the eight Trident nuclear missile subs, participants must be at least 11 years old. Visitors must request reservations in writing. Groups taking the longer tour may arrange to eat lunch in the galley for about $2 per person. Obtain an entry pass at the main gate before entering.

Naval Undersea Museum

Location: *In Keyport, between Silverdale and Poulsbo, off Highway 308, go three miles east*
Phone: *360-396-4148*
Days/Hours: *10 a.m. to 4 p.m., Tuesday through Saturday.*
Wheelchair/Stroller Access: *Yes*
Visiting the new $10 million Naval Undersea Museum is a bit like being immersed in Jules Verne's *20,000 Leagues Under the Sea*. That's because the free tour here is entertaining and educational — a combination both children and parents love. Explore displays of underwater vessels and habitats designed to teach about diverse underwater life. Most children older than 5 will understand these exhibits. Young people are encouraged to search for answers to the museum's scavenger hunt-like quiz, too. Mini-subs and deep submergence vehicles are especially popular to peer into, officials say, but climbing inside isn't allowed. Other hands-on exhibits and simulations explain physical properties below the water's surface. Exhibits also demonstrate how important geology and weather conditions are to undersea life. The underwater weapons exhibit features mines and torpedoes, some dating to the Revolutionary War. Groups may make an appointment to tour the facility with a guide.

Red Robin

Location: *10455 Silverdale Way*
Phone: *360-698-4822*
Days/Hours: *11 a.m. to midnight, Monday through Saturday;
9 a.m. to midnight Sunday.*
Wheelchair/Stroller Access: *Yes*
A favorite among local families, this restaurant features more than a dozen hamburger selections, not to mention jumbo salads and appetizers. It may take some time to consider all the possible burger combinations. Some diners come just for the sweet non-alcohol fruit and ice cream "mocktail" drinks. Highchairs and booster seats are available for littles ones.

Bainbridge Island

The Streamliner Diner

Location: *In Winslow at 397 Winslow Way*
Phone: *206-842-8595*
Days/Hours: *7 a.m. to 3 p.m., Monday through Friday; 8 a.m. to
2:30 p.m., weekends.*
Wheelchair/Stroller Access: *Yes*
Treat your family to a relaxed breakfast and give them a taste of island life at this eatery. Weekend breakfast crowds are a mix of island dwellers and visitors eager to soak their pancakes with rich maple syrup or crunch on some wholesome granola cereal.

Suquamish Museum

Location: *Between Poulsbo and Winslow, off Highway 305, at 15838
Sandy Hook Rd.*
Phone: *360-598-3311, ext. 422 or 206-464-5456*
Days/Hours: *10 a.m. to 5 p.m., daily, Memorial Day through
September; 11 a.m. to 4 p.m. , Friday, Saturday and Sunday, the rest
of the year.*
Wheelchair/Stroller Access: *Yes*
Lifestyles and lives of the Suquamish people — past and present — are portrayed in this museum. It's an authentic look at tribal history and how hard the Suquamish people have worked to preserve their heritage. Part of the museum is a longhouse replica. Inside, a 15-minute video, "Come Forth Laughing," features tribal elders who tell of growing up on the 8,000-acre Port Madison Reservation and

describe white settlers' attempts to place them in non-tribal boarding schools. The museum also displays the intricate basketry created by tribal members. Children will want to caress the soft pelts of fur seals and beavers, and run their fingers along the handiwork of a hand-carved canoe. At the St. Peter's Church cemetery, you'll find the resting place of Chief Sealth (Seattle). Look for the headstone marker with painted canoes. Museum admission is $2.50 for adults, $2 for seniors and those older than 12, $1 for children 5 to 12, and free to those younger than 5.

Poulsbo

Marine Science Center

Location: *On Poulsbo's Front Street across from New Day Fishery*
Phone: *360-779-5549*
Days/Hours: *10 a.m. to 5 p.m., Monday through Saturday; noon to 5 pm., Sunday.*
Wheelchair/Stroller Access: *Yes*

Junior marine biologists will love examining plankton under a microscope, then watching their experiment on the video monitor nearby. Most of the building's exhibits are touch tanks so children get a real hands-on feel for the underwater creatures. The jellyfish and octopus are especially popular. Admission is free Tuesdays. On other days, those 13 or older pay $2, seniors and children 3 to 12 pay $1, tots 2 or younger are free, and entire families can visit for $5.

Thomas Kemper Brewery

Location: *Near Poulsbo at 22381 Foss Rd. N.E.*
Phone: *360-697-1446*
Days/Hours: *12:30 p.m., 1 p.m., 2:30 p.m. and 4 p.m., Monday through Friday; 1 p.m. and 2:30 p.m., Saturday, and 2:30 p.m. Sunday.*
Wheelchair/Stroller Access: *Yes*

Boys and girls may taste-test some of the finest root beer in the region while adults sample microbrewed beers after a free half-hour tour of Thomas Kemper Brewery. The surrounding grounds are well-groomed gardens with grassy spots ideal for picnics. This place often hosts folk singers on Saturday afternoons. In late September, the brewery celebrates an Oktoberfest, complete with specially brewed beers, oompah bands, folk dancing, and entertainment for the whole family.

Sluy's Bakery

Location: *In Poulsbo at 18924 Front St. N.E.*
Phone: *360-779-2798*
Days/Hours: *6:30 a.m. to 6:30 p.m., Sunday through Thursday; 6:30 p.m. to 7:30 p.m., Friday and Saturday.*
Wheelchair/Stroller Access: *Yes*

If you've never sampled Poulsbo bread, you don't know what you're missing. Wide slices of multi-grain loafs are baked here and sold over the counter and in select grocery stores in the region. A loaf of Poulsbo bread becomes the first ingredient for the sandwiches you may want to take on a picnic at Waterfront Park, a grassy spot within walking distance of the bakery. In the morning, consider a sweet pastry from this bakery.

Snohomish County

Snohomish County offers a wealth of diverse family activities — from horseback riding to tours of the behemoth Boeing plant. Less than an hour's drive north of downtown Seattle, this mostly rural area is filled with dozens of other delightful places for children to explore.

Using Seattle as a starting point on Interstate 5, many families first discover Edmonds, at the county's south border. Edmonds is a tidy town with hanging flowerboxes on street corners and a public fishing pier on Puget Sound. Among its 18 parks and recreational sites are the novel Sierra Park, designed for the physically challenged, and Underwater Park for scuba divers. Even families who don't scuba dive can watch the divers from the sandy beach at Brackett's Landing north of the ferry terminal. It's fun to visit after dark and watch the divers' lights cast an eerie glow from below the surface. Those bound for the Kitsap Peninsula can catch a ferry in Edmonds for a 30-minute trip to Kingston.

North of Edmonds is Lynnwood, sometimes jokingly called "Mallwood" after the Alderwood Mall shopping mecca. Lynnwood offers numerous specialty, discount and department stores, but tucked away from all this commerce is Scriber Lake, an 18-acre park with a half-mile pedestrian pathway that spans the lake. Adults pushing a stroller or teaching their children to read will take delight in this trail. Encourage your youngsters to read the signs describing the lake's birds and other wildlife.

For a more active hike, try the challenging climb to the top of Mukilteo Lighthouse on Possession Sound about 10 miles north of Lynnwood. The staircase hike is open noon to 4 p.m., Saturday and Sunday, and it's free. Built in 1905, the Mukilteo Lighthouse is a few hundred yards from the Washington State Ferry terminal where boats make 20-minute trips to Clinton on Whidbey Island.

Snohomish County's largest city, Everett, is north of Mukilteo along I-5. More than a century ago, East Coast tycoon John D. Rockefeller planned for Everett to become the New York City of the West. Today, it's a mid-sized city and home to a new Navy homeport and a colossal Boeing plant.

North and east of Everett are a number of rural towns where, in some cases, Douglas firs outnumber the residents. Marysville, a strawberry mecca north of Everett, attracts thousands of families in the early summer with dozens of U-Pick fields. In June, berry lovers can celebrate at the town's Strawberry Festival with a pancake feed and parade. To see which strawberry fields and other farms are currently operating, call the Marysville Chamber of Commerce in the early spring.

Edmonds

brusseau's

Location: *In downtown Edmonds on the northeast corner of Fifth and Dayton Streets*
Phone: *206-774-416*
Hours: *7 a.m. to 6 p.m., daily.*
Wheelchair/Stroller Access: *Yes*

Local families consider this one of their favorite restaurants because of the grand baked goods and yummy European entrees. The owner/chef collects many of her recipes while traveling abroad to promote cultural understanding with other chefs. Consider dining at this place with a child 8 or older to initiate a conversation about unique ways to learn about and respect international cultures. Booster seats are available and items can be ordered in small enough portions for a small child's appetite.

Funtasia

Location: *7212 220th St. S.W. Take I-5 Exit 179, turn west a half-mile*
Hours: *206-774-GAME*
Phone: *10 a.m. to midnight, Sunday through Thursday; 10 a.m. to 2 a.m., Friday and Saturday, Memorial Day through Labor Day; 11 a.m. to 11 p.m., Monday through Thursday; 11 a.m. to 2 a.m., Friday; 10 a.m. to 2 a.m., Saturday and 10 a.m. to 11 p.m., Sunday, the rest of the year.*
Wheelchair/Stroller Access: Yes

Drive bumper cars or gas-powered Indy go-karts, putt on an 18-hole miniature golf course, hit softballs or baseballs in an outdoor batting cage, or play state-of-the-art video games at this seven-acre indoor/outdoor amusement center. Sink a putt through the clown's nose on the mini-golf course's 18th hole and win a free game.

During the day, this place tends to fill up with children 5 to 12 years old, primarily because many of the rides and activities are restricted to those at least 42 inches tall. Children must be at least 6 to hit softballs and 8 to bat baseballs in the cages where various pitching speeds can be selected. In the late evenings, crowds here are usually teens and young adults. There's no entrance fee; games are charged per play. Save a few dollars and buy a Fun Pass or Super Fun Pass for $5 to $12, depending on the player's age and height. It's possible to reserve passes and a party table for birthday groups, too.

Sierra Park

Location: *At 191st Street Southwest and Southwest 80th Avenue*
Phone: *None*
Days: *Daily, dawn to dusk.*
Wheelchair/Stroller Access: *Yes*

Sight-impaired children and adults will discover a park in north Edmonds designed for the physically challenged. Interpretive markers with braille type describe the natural surroundings along the trail at Sierra Park. Even sighted children enjoy the stroll. Parents may use the park to teach children about ways they can help the physically disabled. The paved path is smooth and relatively flat, a plus for those in wheelchairs or pushing strollers.

Lynnwood

Chuck E. Cheese

Location: *3717 196th St. S.W.*
Phone: *206-771-119*
Hours: *11 a.m. to 9 p.m., Sunday through Thursday; 11 a.m. to 10 p.m., Friday and Saturday.*
Wheelchair/Stroller Access: *Yes*

Mechanical animal characters sing, dance and play musical instruments on three connecting stages while families munch on pizza, salads and soft drinks. A group of six may consider the $17 package the menu's best bargain. It includes a large pizza, six soft drinks, free drink refills and 25 tokens for air hockey, ski-ball and basketball hoop-shoot games for those pre-teen or older. Tokens also are good for three small mechanized rides for toddlers weighing less than 30 pounds. This place gets noisy with music and laughter in the evenings because it's popular among youngsters celebrating birthdays or post-game victories. Little ones like to get a table near the stage to watch entertainment.

Lake Serene Pony Farm

Location: *3915 Serene Way*
Phone: *206-743-211*
Hours: *By appointment only, Monday through Saturday.*
Wheelchair/Stroller Access: *Yes*

Children get a taste of the equine life atop Shetland, Arabian or Welsh ponies on guided trails here. For $6, boys and girls age 2 to 15 may ride for 30 minutes, then explore the woodsy setting on foot. An immense laurel bush on this farm becomes Never Never Land for games of hide-and-go-seek. This place is set up for indoor and outdoor picnics, so local families host birthday parties here. Call for party prices and reservations. Ask about summer riding and grooming classes as well.

Skating

Put on your skates or blades and try out the family sessions at these rinks. Besides family sessions, Roll-A-Way has so many different schedules for special programs and specific skill levels that it's best to call ahead to get details about parties, competitions, classes and open skate sessions. The same goes for Sno-King, which offers special times for broomball, hockey and competitive figure skating.

Roll-A-Way Skate Center

Location: *6210 200th S.W.*
Phone: *206-778-444*
Hours: *Schedules vary; call ahead.*
Wheelchair/Stroller Access: *Yes, for viewing*
Skate rental is included in the price of admission: $2.50 during the day and $5 weekend nights.

Sno-King Ice Arena
Location: *19803 68th Ave. W.*
Phone: *206-775-751*
Hours: *7 a.m. to 11 p.m., daily; call ahead for public skate hours.*
Wheelchair/Stroller Access: *Yes, for viewing*
Adult admission is $4, students pay $3 and skate rental is $2 each. During family skate sessions, the first adult pays full price and all other family members pay $2.

Mukilteo

Games Family Fun Center

Location: *3616 South Rd. (behind Children's World Learning Center on Mukilteo Speedway)*
Phone: *206-745-5033*
Days/Hours: *10 a.m. to 11 p.m., Sunday through Thursday; 10 a.m. to 1 a.m., Friday and Saturday during the summer; 10 a.m. to 10 p.m., the rest of the year.*
Wheelchair/Stroller Access: *Yes*
Local families pack into this indoor activity center on rainy days. Games are geared for those older than 8. Try your hand at the softball or baseball batting cages, any of seven pool tables, a wide selection of video games, or the 18-hole miniature golf course. To play mini

golf, adults pay $3, students pay $2 and those younger than 3 play for free. Prices vary on other games.

Ivar's

Location: *Ivar's Mukilteo Landing and Seafood Bar - 710 Front Street, Mukilteo; Ivar's Seafood Bar - 1520 41st St., Everett; Ivar's Seafood Bar - 9910 Edmonds Way, Edmonds*
Phone: *206-347-3648 (Mukilteo); 206-252-9292 (Everett); 206-672-2640 (Edmonds)*
Days/Hours: *Most open 10 a.m. to 10 p.m., daily (can vary in the summer).*
Wheelchair/Stroller Access: *Yes*

With three restaurants in Snohomish County, Ivar's is a favorite place among locals with a craving for seafood. The Mukilteo restaurant is next to the ferry terminal, so diners can watch the boats dock and depart. The seafood bars have a "kid's catch" with deep-fried fish fillets and French fries. For an extra treat, add a bowl of red or white clam chowder to any fish order. The restaurant and seafood bars are part of a chain throughout the greater Puget Sound region.

Everett

Boeing Plant

Location: *84th Street Southwest. Take I-5 Exit 189 west for 2 miles*
Phone: *206-342-4801*
Days/Hours: *9 a.m and 1 p.m., Monday through Friday; tickets available at 8:30 a.m.*
Wheelchair/Stroller Access: *Yes*

Visitors to Boeing's Everett plant feel like Lilliputians when looking around what's considered the largest manufacturing plant in the world. Learn how the company builds 747 and 767 airplanes and see the latest aircraft technology during this free 90-minute tour. Boeing requires children be at least 8 to take part. It's so popular that quite often those in line at 11:30 a.m. during the summer barely make it into the group leaving for the 1 p.m. tour! Tours are conducted by bus. No still or video cameras are allowed. Tour groups of 15 to 40 people should make reservations three to six months ahead by calling 206-342-4804.

Discovery Zone

Location: *1130 S.E. Everett Mall Way*
Phone: *206-290-8325*
Days/Hours: *11 a.m. to 8 p.m., Sunday; 9 a.m to 9 p.m., Monday through Thursday, and 9 a.m. to 10 p.m. Friday and Saturday.*
Wheelchair/Stroller Access: *Good for viewing*

Boys and girls 12 months to 12 years can climb cushioned walls, wade through a sea of soft plastic balls, explore a maze of tube tunnels and slide to their heart's delight in this indoor playground. There are separate play areas for toddlers and for older children. Paid supervisors are on watch, but parents of toddlers are encouraged to stick close to their child (or even climb alongside them!). It's a popular place for birthday parties, too. Call ahead to reserve a room for opening gifts and eating cake, and to arrange admission for party guests.

Everett AquaSox

Location: *Everett Memorial Stadium, 39th at Broadway*
Phone: *206-258-3673*
Days/Hours: *Call ahead for home schedule June through August.*
Wheelchair/Stroller Access: *Yes*

Peanuts, Cracker Jack and real grass give this Class A farm club an authentic baseball flavor. Some of the best seats are on the grass next to left and right fields. These spots can be better than a grandstand seat for squirmy boys and girls because it gives them more room to move around and snooze if the game runs late with extra innings.

Remind youngsters to bring a mitt because you never know when a foul ball may become a souvenir. There's a concessions stand designed for children, with steps so they can see their favorite candies over the tall counter. Older children may explore the field behind the grandstands.

Formerly the Everett Giants, this team is now part of the Seattle Mariners organization, so owners Bob and Margaret Bavasi changed the ball club's name and mascot. They selected the name AquaSox partly, they say, because of Everett's Puget Sound location and because kids of all ages love to splash in the water. The Pacific Tree Frog was chosen as mascot because its long tongue captures prey — almost like outfielders snag flyballs. Besides, say the Bavasis, "time's fun when you're catching flies."

Forest Park

Location: *Rucker and 41st streets*
Phone: *206-259-0300*
Days/Hours: *Animal Farm open 9 a.m. to 5 p.m., daily, May through September; wading pool open daily, Memorial Day through Labor Day; general park open dawn to dusk yearround.*
Wheelchair/Stroller Access: *Strollers enter from north parking lot, wheelchairs from south parking lot*

Children may help bottle feed small farm animals (most are under 3 months old) during the summer at 9 a.m., noon and 4 p.m. daily at this public park. In the afternoon, ponies offer free rides in a fenced corral to those weighing less than 250 pounds. Lines for pony rides can get long. Another popular attraction in the summer is the wading and sprinkler pool. Toddlers and children as old as 6 can splash up a storm.

Jetty Island Ferry

Location: *Catch the free shuttle at West Marine View Drive and 18th Street*
Phone: *206-259-0304*
Days/Hours: *10 a.m. to 5 p.m., Wednesday through Sunday, July through Labor Day.*
Wheelchair/Stroller Access: *No*

Children may feel like a member of the Swiss Family Robinson after riding the free ferry to Jetty Island in the summer. That's because there's a sense of both safety and adventure at the end of this two-mile-long ride from Everett. Warm, shallow water and a sandy beach await summer visitors. Jetty Island offers nature walks, crafts projects and survival adventure games aimed at 5- to 10-year-olds. The ferry leaves every half hour, but don't be surprised if three boats fill and sail before you get on.

Millstone Coffee Roasting Plant

Location: *729 100th St. S.E. (south of Everett Mall)*
Phone: *206-347-3995, ext. 232*
Days/Hours: *8 a.m. to 4 p.m., Monday through Thursday; advance reservations required.*
Wheelchair/Stroller Access: *Yes*

If a child asks where the caffeine in their favorite soft drink comes from, or wonders about the coffee brewed in the kitchen, take them to Millstone's free half-hour tour through the Northwest's largest coffee roasting plant. Watch how beans arrive from South American and African countries in burlap-style bags and are heated in hot ovens where they produce a powerful aroma. There's time to taste the coffee and watch how some are decaffeinated. Millstone sells the extracted caffeine to soda pop companies to put into caffeinated pop! Visits provide children a lesson in how U.S. companies trade with other nations who have valuable resources. Tour-goers must be at least 10 years old.

North Snohomish County

Big D's Batting Cage and Mini Golf
Location: *In Marysville at 1070 Columbia Ave.*
Phone: *360-659-4086*
Days/Hours: *Noon to 8 p.m., Monday through Friday; 10 a.m. to 8 p.m., Saturday and 11 a.m. to 7 p.m. Sunday.*
Wheelchair/Stroller Access: *OK for watching*
 Little Leaguers can sharpen their skills by selecting the speed of their sweetest pitch and swinging at 25 baseballs for $1. Reserve a cage in advance at $12 for 30 minutes or $20 for an hour. For putting, children 12 or younger pay $2.50 for 18 holes while older players pay $3.

Biringer Farms
Location: *In Marysville at 37th Avenue Northeast off Highway 529. Take I-5 Exit 195; follow two miles to Highway 529; cross Snohomish River Bridge and take the second right to 37th Avenue Northeast.*
Phone: *206-259-0255*
Days/Hours: *Vary depending on the season; pumpkin tours open in October; U-Pick berry fields open early summer; call ahead for hours.*
Wheelchair/Stroller Access: *Yes*
 Let Old Mother Hubbard tell children a story, explore the Halloween "boo barn" and find your way out of a maze of hay bales in a corn field at this pumpkin farm each autumn. On weekdays, Biringer Farms typically conducts private tours, by reservation only, for groups of at least 10 children age 3 to 8. Weekends are open to the public without reservations.
 The dark "boo barn" is mild on the thrills-and-chills scale, with no witches or ghosts, but exits are available for children who scare easily. After scurrying through a corn maze or sliding into a pile of

hay, boys and girls may pick their own pumpkin to take home. Admission is $3 to $4.50; the price includes the pumpkin. One of the largest farms in the area, Biringer is a U-Pick berry field in the early summer.

Centennial Trail

Location: *Snohomish to Lake Stevens*
Phone: *None*
Days/Hours: *Year-round.*
Wheelchair/Stroller Access: *Yes*
Bicycles, tricycles, walkers, strollers, roller skaters and even horses share this 6.5-mile paved trail through Snohomish County. It's a safe, flat place for children learning how to ride two-wheeler and for adults pushing strollers. The trail winds past horses and cows grazing at nearby farms, tractors tilling fields, and geese honking at each other around the various waterways. Eventually, planners hope to connect the trail all the way north to Arlington. To start the trail in Snohomish, drive Bickford Avenue into Snohomish, then turn east on Tenth Avenue. Go north on Maple Avenue which becomes Snohomish-Machias Road. Look for a parking lot just beyond Three Lakes Road. It's also possible to park near Lake Stevens at Bonneville Field Ballpark at the end of 16th Avenue Northeast.

Horse Country — Ponies Too!

Location: *In Granite Falls at 8507 Highway 92. Take I-5's Exit 194 to Highway 204 connecting with northbound Highway 9. Take Highway 9 to merger with Highway 92 and follow this road six miles to Horse Country — Ponies Too!*
Phone: *206-335-4773*
Days/Hours: *9 a.m. to 7 p.m., Monday through Saturday; noon to 7 p.m., Sundays and holidays.*
Wheelchair/Stroller access: *No*
Tots as young as 2 years can "getty-up" on a pony at this 111-acre equine center on the Pilchuck River. Riders no heavier than 200 pounds may prefer the guided family trail rides ranging from $15 per hour or $22 for 90 minutes. Lead-around ponies for the wee ones are $5. In the case of wet weather, there's a spacious indoor riding arena. Enjoy a picnic along the river before or after the ride. During the summer, check out the summer camps for children. Instructors teach students horseback riding and provide tips about grooming and caring for horses.

Pioneer Village and Museum

Location: *In Snohomish at Second and Pine streets, parking behind Pilchuck Shopping Center*
Phone: *None at the village, but call the Blackman Museum at 360-568-5235*
Days/Hours: *Noon to 4 p.m., Memorial Day to Labor Day.*
Wheelchair/Stroller Access: *Rough grass surfaces, but access possible*

Venture back through the history of Snohomish when you visit this restored pioneer village at the edge of the Snohomish River. Visit historic cabins, old houses and tiny refurbished shops to see what life was like in the 19th century. Boys and girls learn how settlers kept their food cold and their homes warm, and how pioneer children took baths. Admission is $1 for adults and 50 cents for seniors and students.

Snohomish Valley Ice Cream

Location: *In Snohomish at 902 First St.*
Phone: *360-568-1133*
Days/Hours: *10 a.m. to 9 p.m., Monday through Saturday; noon to 7 p.m. Sunday.*
Wheelchair/Stroller Access: *Yes*

All sorts of old-style dairy treats are served up here. Order a fresh ice cream milkshake so children may watch it whipped up in a tall metal cup with a long-arm blender. Make sure you're ready with a spoon, because these concoctions are thick. Some sundaes here are so large children may want to split them with an adult. Now that's large!

Whidbey Island

Whidbey Island is so long, it doesn't seem like it's an island. In fact, it's the longest island in the continental United States. Families driving north to south along Highway 20 will find jets roaring over Oak Harbor Naval Air Station, historic military sites that have been turned into state parks, and the waterfront charm of Langley.

Using Seattle as a starting point, drive north on Interstate 5 to Mukilteo, about six miles west of the freeway. At the Mukilteo ferry terminal, board a 20-minute ferry ride to Clinton on south Whidbey

Island. Arrive from the north by vehicle across the beautiful Deception Pass Bridge. Approach the bridge by way of Burlington from I-5, then take Highway 20 west; it gradually turns south. There's also a ferry connection to Port Townsend on the Olympic Peninsula from Keystone near Coupeville. Amateur sleuths of all ages flock to the village of Langley on the island's south end in February for the annual Mystery Weekend. Kids will think they're Sherlock Holmes while searching for clues in the oldest crime-solving event in the Puget Sound area. This weekend is open to detective wannabes who inspect a make-believe crime scene before collecting clues and grilling possible suspects at local businesses. Langley is north of Clinton, off Highway 525 on Langley Road.

About a half-hour drive northwest of Clinton on Highway 20 is Coupeville, part of the 17,000-acre Ebey's Landing National Historical Reserve. A national park ranger can provide a tour, pointing out ships sailing through Admiralty Inlet and describing the region's history. Call 360-678-4636 or 360-678-3195 for an appointment. Fort Casey, Fort Ebey, and Ebey's Landing state parks are nearby.

Three miles west, families used to seeing seafood on ice behind glass cases at the grocery store will be fascinated by the mussel farms at Penn Cove. These tasty mussel morsels are in heavy demand by the best restaurants. Look for the bivalves growing on ropes stretching across rafts linked by anchors and buoys. Oak Harbor, 10 miles north on Highway 20, is a vital cog in the Navy's air power; the Whidbey Island Naval Air Station at Ault Field is the site of tactical electronic warfare squadrons. Descendants of Oak Harbor's early Dutch and Irish pioneers keep history alive in this community with cultural celebrations each spring. Look for a Navy air show in August as well.

Chocolates for Breakfast
Location: *In Oak Harbor at 3174 300 Ave. W.*
Phone: *360-675-2141*
Days/Hours: *6:30 a.m. to 7:30 p.m., Monday through Friday; 8 a.m. to 5 p.m. Saturday; noon to 4 p.m. Sunday.*
Wheelchair/Stroller Access: *No*
This place is a chocoholic's fantasy and dentist's nightmare. Sweet pastries for all ages, and espresso drinks for adults are served in one room. Northwest jams, jellies, candies and other goodies are sold in another room.

City Beach Park

Location: *In Oak Harbor off Highway 20 at the end of 80th Street Northwest*
Phone: *360-679-5551, extension 234*
Days/Hours: *Daily year-round with some overnight camping.*
Wheelchair/Stroller Access: *Yes*

Children flock to the swings and the sliding board at this waterfront park. The town's Dutch influence is evident here with ornamental windmills nearby and lovely tulips in Holland Gardens.

Deception Pass State Park

Location: *10 miles north of Oak Harbor on Highway 20*
Phone: *360-675-2417*
Days/Hours: *Overnight camping year-round.*
Wheelchair/Stroller Access: *In some places*

There's a reason why this is one of the most used parks and campgrounds in the state. Families will find a wealth of outdoor activities at this beautiful park — from 30 miles of hiking trails to an underwater park for divers. State park officials say more than 3.5 million people use this park each year.

Half of this park is on Whidbey Island; the other half is across Deception Pass Bridge on Fidalgo Island. There are places to park a vehicle on both ends of the bridge so passengers can get out and walk onto the span. In the middle, some hikers climb over the bridge railing to hike from the top of Pass Island to the water. Makeshift routes are rough and dangerous for children. Instead, try the Discovery Trail, which starts at the Environmental Learning Center on Whidbey Island and has side trails to Goose Rock.

Fort Casey State Park

Location: *Three miles south of Coupeville, off Highway 20*
Phone: *360-678-4519*
Days/Hours: *Overnight camping year-round.*
Wheelchair/Stroller Access: *Yes*

Built in the 1850s, Fort Casey was meant to be one corner of the "Triangle of Fire," poised to defend against enemy ships attempting to sail through Admiralty Inlet in the late 1880s. The other two corners were Fort Warden and Fort Flagler. Much to the disappointment of some, no ships ever tried. The most action the fort saw was training troops during both world wars.

Today, children may re-create their own battles using old cannons, a maze of bunkers, and their imaginations. There are plenty of dark rooms beyond the gun emplacements, so bring a flashlight. When you emerge from the bunkers for fresh air, consider strolling the park's waterview trails. Two of the trails lead to Admiralty Head lighthouse, which first beamed in 1861. The lighthouse has since been moved farther from the water and now is the park's interpretive center. Inside, visitors can read about the fort's history.

Fort Ebey State Park

Location: *Off Libby Road, south of Partridge Point, eight miles south of Oak Harbor*
Phone: *360-678-4636*
Days/Hours: *Overnight camping year-round.*
Wheelchair/Stroller Access: *In some places*
It looks like Fort Ebey should have been another corner in the "Triangle of Fire," but this fort came decades later and was intended to be used as an anti-aircraft base. Like Fort Casey, it saw no action. Today it's a 640-acre park with 56 campsites. Old bunkers offer dark places for children to play hide-and-seek. Hikers can reach the beach from a steep, traversing path to Point Partridge, or two more flat paths from the park's day-use area. The park's north end features a short trail to more private walk-in campsites not far from freshwater Lake Pondilla; there's bass fishing here.

Mike's Place

Location: *In Langley at 219 First St.*
Phone: *360-221-6575*
Days/Hours: *9 a.m. to 2 p.m., daily.*
Wheelchair/Stroller Access: *Yes*
Scoot up a highchair or booster seat during breakfast and let children enjoy a bear-face shaped pancake. At lunch, the children's menu features peanut butter and jelly sandwiches, grilled cheese sandwiches, child-portion hamburgers with French fries and more.

Swing & Play

Location: *In downtown Oak Harbor off Highway 20 on Pioneer Way*
Phone: *360-675-5717*
Days/Hours: *11 a.m. to 10 p.m., Sunday through Thursday; 11 a.m. to midnight, Friday and Saturday.*
Wheelchair/Stroller Access: *Yes*
This fun-and-games stop is a place for children of all ages. Little ones may romp on gym toys. Older boys and girls should try miniature golf, basketball free-throws, fooseball, ski-ball and video games. Adults play, too. Admission is free; visitors pay per game.

Skagit Valley

Families visting the Skagit Valley in the spring may feel as if they've stepped into a picture postcard. Fields of vibrant tulips, daffodils, lilies and irises bathe Mount Vernon in fragrance and color each March, April and May. Local tours of nurseries attract thousands of visitors of all ages each year. But this fertile region, an hour's drive north of Seattle along Interstate 5, is more dimensional than a postcard scene. Nearby towns are waiting to be explored by families as well.

Consider starting in LaConner, a town of cozy bed-and-breakfast inns and shops with books, candies and gifts for children and adults. There are boat trips to Deception Pass leaving from here, too. Skagit County's oldest town, LaConner is home to the Skagit County Historical Museum (501 Fourth St.). Open afternoons, Wednesday through Sunday, the museum features vintage children's toys among the displays of old Northwest farm and logging equipment. LaConner is 18 miles west of the freeway via Highway 20.

Back on the freeway, five miles north of Mount Vernon, affordable name-brand goods — including children's clothes — are sold at outlet shops in Burlington. Look for Pacific Edge Outlet shops at the foothills of the North Cascade Mountains at the crossroads of I-5 and Highway 20.

Families bound for the North Cascades may follow Highway 20 east to Sedro-Woolley, where it meets Highway 9. Consider stopping at Riverfront Park off Township Street on the Skagit River. Shade trees make this 14-acre park delightfully cool for picnicking in the summer. Its sprawling playground is a children's favorite.

LaConner

Bunnies by the Bay

Location: *617 Morris St.*
Phone: *360-466-5040*
Days/Hours: *10 a.m. to 6 p.m. daily.*
Wheelchair/Stroller Access: *No*

Dozens of handsewn bunnies — ideal for spring and Easter gifts — wait in this farmhouse store. They're crafted at the Bunnies by the Bay store in Oak Harbor. Buy one for a cuddly collectible or a future Easter gift. Outside the LaConner store, stroll around the yard to watch the dancing whirligigs on the folk art fence.

Deception Pass Viking Cruise

Location: *109 N. First St., in Lime Dock Building*
Phone: *360-466-2639*
Days/Hours: *June through September for daily cruises; call ahead for bird-watching cruises the rest of the year.*
Wheelchair/Stroller Access: *No*

Children may think they're part of a National Geographic adventure when they board the rigid-hull, inflatable boat which takes up to 30 Viking Cruises passengers on hourly "hidden waterfront" trips between noon and dusk. Families see bald eagles, harbor seals, waterfowl and the grandeur of Deception Pass on this ride.

The same boat also takes as many as 20 passengers on two-hour excursions to Deception Pass. Admission for the shorter trip is $12 for adults and $10 for those 12 or younger. Because it's an

Photo courtesy of Jim Lippert and the Skagit Valley Tulip Festival.
Families flock to the Skagit Valley Tulip Festival to see thousands of colorful blossoms each spring.

open boat, no infants are permitted onboard. Charge for the longer trip is $49 for adults and $39 for children.

On its 49-passenger Viking Star, this cruise line also offers three-day, two-night accommodation and meal packages to Rosario Resort on Orcas Island (see San Juan Islands chapter). In the fall, winter and spring, catch a two- or four-hour bird-watching trip to the Skagit River and Skagit Bay. Passengers of all ages pay $15 for the shorter trip and $25 for the longer one. Both excursions include binoculars, so get a close look at eagles, snow geese and trumpeter swans which live here from about November through March.

The Gaches Mansion

Location: *703 Second St.*
Phone: *360-466-4288*
Days/Hours: *1 p.m. to 5 p.m., Friday, Saturday and Sunday during the summer; 1 p.m. to 4 p.m. the rest* of the year.
Wheelchair/Stroller Access: *No*

No matter how they're dressed, children feel elegant when visiting this classic mansion. In its 100-year history, the three-story house has been a high-society home, a hospital, and a boarding house. The LaConner Landmark Society restored the first floor with Victorian decor after a major fire. Curators have surprise displays coming soon to the upper floors. Admission is $2 per person or $5 for the entire family.

O'Leary Building

Location: *609 S. First St.*
Phone: *360-466-2971 (Cascade Candy Company); 360-466-1305 (O'Leary's Books)*
Days/Hours: *10 a.m. to 5 p.m., Monday through Thursday; 10 a.m. to 6 p.m., Friday; 10 a.m. to 6:30 Saturday; 10 a.m. to 5:30 p.m. Sunday.*
Wheelchair/Stroller Access: *Yes*

Chocolate sweets and reading treats share the O'Leary Building. Cascade Candy Company offers homemade fudge and truffles for the more mature sweet teeth, and chocolate suckers for the younger set. The chocolate Easter bunnies sold here are worth the trip. Next door, the shelves at O'Leary's Books brim with books and magazines. Selections for children are low enough for little ones to reach.

Museum of Northwest Art

Location: *121 S. First St.*
Phone: *360-466-4288*
Days/Hours: *11 a.m. to 5 p.m., Tuesday through Sunday (it's best to call ahead).*
Wheelchair/Stroller Access: *Yes*

Formerly housed in the Gaches Mansion, art in this new 12,000-square-foot museum, slated to open in the fall of 1995, is dedicated to the Pacific Northwest. Besides a permanent exhibit by regional artists, there are changing exhibits, including studio glass pieces. Children love the fish painting here — they get to use real fish! Ask about other special children's programs planned. The museum's store offers gifts for all ages, including kids' toys and games. Admission is $2 per person or $5 for an entire family.

Tillinghast Seed & Mercantile Company

Location: *623 Morris St.*
Phone: *360-466-3229*
Days/Hours: *9 a.m. to 5:30 p.m., Monday through Saturday; 11 a.m. to 6 p.m. Sunday.*
Wheelchair/Stroller Access: *By ramps on the first floor only*

Within its old walls, this 113-year-old shop is the Northwest's oldest operating retail and seed store. Children come here to purchase the best jack-o-lantern pumpkin seeds a few coins can buy. Adults will find some unusual and possibly rare garden assortments, too. And upstairs a year-round Christmas attic is jammed with lights, ornaments and other yuletide trinkets to make it feel like Christmas, even in July.

Mount Vernon

Padilla Bay National Estuarine Sanctuary and Breazeale Interpretive Center

Location: *1043 Bayview Edison Rd. Take I-5 Exit 231 west*
Phone: *360-428-1558*
Days/Hours: *10 a.m. to 5 p.m., Wednesday through Sunday, except holidays.*
Wheelchair/Stroller Access: *Yes*

Reach out and touch the bones, teeth, feathers and pelts of the inhabitants of this National Estuarine Sanctuary; it's one of just a few in the country. Exhibits and demonstrations at the Interpretive Center show children nature's delicate balance in the bay. Vital eel grass feeds both the birds and the sea life under the water's surface. Inside the center, peer into tanks of flounders, sea perch, sculpins, and coho and chinook salmon. Outside, walk or bicycle the 2.2-mile trail along the shoreline or grab a view from the observation deck. Plod through the mud in your boots at low tide and explore the bay from nearby Bay View State Park. This 79-campsite park offers a spacious meadow/playfield for flying kites or ball games.

Roozengaarde

Location: *1587 Beaver Marsh Rd. Take I-5 Exit 226 west on Kincaid and turn right at first stoplight. Cross Division Street Bridge. Turn left on Wall Street which angles right into McLean Road. Follow about 3 miles to Beaver Marsh Road; turn left toward windmill.*
Phone: *800-732-3266*
Days/Hours: *9 a.m. to 5:30 p.m., Monday through Saturday, and 10 a.m. to 5 p.m. March through May; 9 a.m. to 5 p.m., Monday through Saturday, June through February.*
Wheelchair/Stroller Access: *Limited; not in all fields*

Children who dig into the family flower beds with their parents will be thrilled to discover they can take home the same glorious-colored flowers blanketing the Skagit Valley each spring. Visitors to Roozengarde, the largest retailer for the Washington Bulb Company, may purchase daffodil, tulip or iris bulbs here. Others prefer to come to the fields when they are in bloom and take photographs. Daffodils start blossoming in March and tulips are dancing in the fields by April and early May. Summer visitors will find crews tilling the soil; in autumn, Roozengarde workers are planting bulbs for the next spring.

Burlington

Benson Farmstead

Location: *1009 Avon-Allen Rd., Bow (just west of Burlington)*
Phone: *360-757-0578*
Days/Hours: *April through September for daily overnight accommodations; weekends only for the rest of the year.*
Wheelchair/Stroller Access: *No*

This 17-room Scandinavian farmhouse is a bed-and-breakfast inn owned by a couple who cater to families. There's a large playroom in the granary where owner Sharon Benson teaches preschool during the week. Outside, stroll through the English garden and ask her husband, Jerry, to show you around his farm. To relax, soak in the hot tub, then get a good night's rest in preparation for a full farm breakfast complete with homemade breads the following morning.

Pacific Edge Factory Outlet Center

Location: *East of freeway at I-5 Exits 229 and 230*
Phone: *360-757-3549*
Days/Hours: *10 a.m. to 9 p.m., Monday through Saturday; 10 a.m. to 6 p.m. Sunday.*
Wheelchair/Stroller Access: *Yes*

Eyes will pop when bargain-conscious shoppers discover the great deals available at the Pacific Edge factory outlet stores. Teens old enough to buy their own school clothes will save money at the Bugle Boy store. Parents and grandparents will love the savings for littles ones at Genuine Kids (a division of Osh Kosh) and Carter's.

San Juan Islands

There's a striking mix of family relaxation and adventure offered in the San Juan Islands. Aboard Washington State ferries sailing to four of the chain's 450 islands, passengers may spot a pod of orca whales putting on a show. Once on the islands, families discover bicycling, camping, swimming and hiking.

Before venturing off on a San Juan Islands adventure, consider a stop in Anacortes, about 15 miles west of I-5 Exit 230 on Highway 20. Without looking on the map you might not realize that Anacortes is on its own island: Fidalgo, the first of the San Juans. The town's parks department, schools and radio station sponsor a Kids-R-Best Festival here in early July. It features a talent show, sports events, radio-controlled airplane displays and more — all geared to kids. Active boys and girls will want to climb and swing at the children's playground at Ninth Street and "M" Avenue.

Ferries departing Anacortes travel between Blake and Decatur islands to Lopez Island. From Lopez, the ferry leaves for Shaw Island, where most of the 200 residents are Franciscan nuns. There are no motels or inns here. Boats next sail to Orcas Island and finally to San Juan Island before returning to Anacortes. A warning about San

Juan Island ferries: watching two boats filled with passengers leave before you board is not uncommon — especially on summer weekends, when the 10,000-person population here more than doubles with tourists. It's smart to carry the current season's pocket-sized schedule and stake out a spot in line well ahead of your departure.

Those eager to bicycle in the San Juans often select Lopez. It offers the chain's most gradual slopes, but riders should still be prepared with helmets and the stamina to handle these hills. Children younger than 8 typically don't have the endurance to bike this terrain. Parents of these youngsters may want to copy what experienced bicycling moms and dads do here: pull a bike trailer or install a child-seat on the bike behind the adult's seat. Call the Bike Shop (360-468-3497) or Lopez Bike Works (360-468-2847) for rental reservations or help with repairs.

Odlin County Park and Spencer Spit State Park offer the only overnight camping on Lopez. The largest number of indoor overnight accommodations can be found at Islander Lopez on Fisherman Bay. Near the resort you'll find a gas station and grocery store for necessities.

For many Northwesterners, their first introduction to Orcas Island — the chain's largest — is the summer they spent at YMCA Camp Orkila. As adults, many return with their families to hike or bicycle 2,409-foot Mount Constitution or stake out a campsite. Orcas offers the most campsites among the islands. Some families come here to bask in the vintage old-world charm of Rosario Resort. Others prefer the stately, quiet Roche Harbor Resort on neighboring San Juan Island. It's on the island's north end. To stay at Roche Harbor Resort or moor there, call 360-378-2155 or 800-451-8910. Three pods of orca whales consider the western shoreline here a great place to dine on fish. They're often visible in September and October.

From Anacortes, some ferries are direct, but most loop to Lopez (45 minutes), Shaw (one hour), Orcas (80 minutes), and San Juan (two hours). There is a daily ferry to Sidney, British Columbia, (three hours and 40 minutes) during most of the year. It sails twice daily during the summer. Reservations are available for the Sidney sailings.

There are no reservations for the islands, so it's wise to arrive at least an hour ahead of a scheduled sailing. Ferry schedules change seasonally, so call the state ferry system at 206-464-6400 or 800-84-FERRY (within Washington state only) for a current schedule.

Anacortes

Bunnies by the Bay

Location: *2403 "R"Ave. Take "R" Avenue exit off Highway 20. Drive 20 blocks*
Phone: *360-293-8037*
Days/Hours: *Tours at 10 a.m. and 2 p.m., Monday through Friday.*
Wheelchair/Stroller Access: *Yes, but there is one step outside into the shop*

Many of the cute little bunnies that visitors may have seen while visiting the LaConner bunny shop are made right here. Watch them come to life on a free, 15-minute tour through the entire production process. Then try to resist buying one.

Scimitar Ridge Ranch

Location: *527 Miller Rd. Drive toward Oak Harbor on Highway 20; turn right at the crest of the hill near the cemetery*
Phone: *360-293-5310 and 800-798-5355*
Days/Hours: *Year-round overnight accommodations.*
Wheelchair/Stroller Access: *Yes*

Get the feel of the old West at this dude ranch. Cowboy and cowgirl wannabes will love rolling out a sleeping bag in a two- or four-person covered wagon (the four-person wagons can actually fit six) and grilling up vittles on a campfire (an adjustable height grill). Then it's time to mount a trusty steed for some horseback riding or explore the countryside on a hike. On weekends, there are free hot showers and a hot tub for adults only. Children may prefer splashing in the wading pool at the waterfall anway. Ask about dinner shows when you make reservations; show seating on summer weekends fills up fast.

Village Pizza

Location: *807 Commercial*
Phone: *360-293-7847*
Days/Hours: *Noon to midnight Sunday; 11 a.m. to midnight, Monday through Thursday; 11 a.m. to 1 a.m. Friday and Saturday.*
Wheelchair/Stroller Access: *Yes*

In the heart of downtown Anacortes, here's a delicious and convenient place to sit down and eat a pizza before catching a ferry or to grab a fully loaded pie to eat on the boat.

Orcas Island

Moran State Park

Location: *Take Horseshoe Highway north from ferry terminal to Eastsound; drive east another 13 miles*
Phone: *360-376-2326 or 360-753-2027*
Days/Hours: *Daily camping year-round.*
Wheelchair/Stroller Access: *In some places*

Camping at Moran State Park is so popular during the summer that reservations are required to secure any of the 165 campsites. Even so, it's worth the wait. First-timers often are surprised to learn that this island park isn't on the sound; it's inland with freshwater swimming beaches and rowboat rentals on Cascade Lake, trout fishing on Mountain Lake, children's play equipment, and 31 miles of hiking trails. Try the level 3.9- mile walk around Mountain Lake or the quarter-mile hike to 100-foot Cascade Falls with young children. Strong boys and girls may prefer bicycling with adults to the top of Mount Constitution. The road climbs 2,000 feet in six miles, so bicyclists need to be in shape. Those who make it to the summit consider themselves hearty, accomplished pedalers. With young children, it's better to drive here. At the summit, climb the winding staircase to the top of the four-story stone observation tower modeled after a 12th century mountain fortress. On a clear day, you can see for hundreds of miles.

Rosario Resort & Spa

Location: *On Orcas Island, 17 miles from ferry terminal, north and around East Sound to Rosario*
Phone: *800-562-8820*
Days/Hours: *Year-round for overnight accommodations.*
Wheelchair/Stroller Access: *Yes*

This majestic mansion on a rocky bluff attracts visitors with its old-style charm and waterfront setting. Once the home of shipbuilder Robert Moran, this 85-year-old estate now houses a restaurant, and exercise and relaxation facilities. On the adjacent hillside there are nearly 200 guest rooms with their own balconies. From these decks, visitors can watch boats dock at the Cascade Bay marina and seaplanes zoom across the water's surface. Encourage children to keep their eyes open for deer munching on grass outside guest rooms and on the mansion grounds. While adults enjoy a relaxing soak in the hot tub, a massage or facial, older children may swim in the indoor or outdoor pools. There are no lifeguards and the indoor pool has no wading area, so the pools are best suited for children who are either supervised, or confident swimmers.

San Juan Island

Lime Kiln State Park

Location: *West side of San Juan Island on Haro Strait*
Phone: *360-378-2044*
Days/Hours: *Dawn to dusk year-round.*
Wheelchair/Stroller Access: *No*
This park is named for the lime quarries which once dotted the hillside, bringing big limestone manufacturing business to the island in the 1880s. Now it's considered a premier site to watch orcas — also called killer whales. Late summer and early fall are prime times to view these ocean giants nibbling on marine life and salmon along the shoreline. Children adore hearing about the whales' loyal extended families, or pods. Walk down the rough trails to the bluff and stake out one of a few picnic tables for visitors. This rustic park has no flush toilets or running water.

San Juan Coffee Roasting Company

Location: *In Friday Harbor at Cannery Landing*
Phone: *360-378-4443*
Days/Hours: *9 a.m. to 6 p.m., daily.*
Wheelchair/Stroller Access: *Yes*
Previously known as San Juan Chocolate Company, this establishment is still decadently filled with chocolates. There are ice cream cones, sandwiches and desserts for all, plus espresso drinks for adults. It's fun to eat on the picnic tables outside this building on the wharf that is filled with two floors of other shops as well.

Whale Museum

Location: *In Friday Harbor at First Street and Court Street*
Phone: *360-378-4710*
Days/Hours: *10 a.m. to 5 p.m., daily, June through September;*
11 a.m. to 4 p.m. the rest of the year.
Wheelchair/Stroller Access: *No*
If you miss seeing an orca whale up close (or if you did see one and you want to know more), stop at this museum. Young children

are fascinated by the humming sound inside the museum's blue interior, because it seems as if whales are talking to them. Look at the gigantic whale skeletons mounted inside; these bones give visitors a sense of the size of these incredible mammals. Take time to explore the children's room and watch the video of whales breeding, feeding and caring for their young. Admission is $3 for adults, $2.50 for seniors and students 12 or older, $1.50 for children 5 to 11, and free to those younger than 5.

Whale Cruises

Audiences who cheered for the young boy and his big screen orca friend in "Free Willy" will find a whale-watching trip on the open water awesome. There are several reputable charter companies offering scheduled whale cruises from May through October. A qualified charter company will take visitors up close without interfering with the whale's pod (its circle of family and friends). Charter trips can vary in length and price, and some require that children be at least 6 years old. If traveling with young children, you'll want a boat with bathroom facilities. Be sure to ask about these when calling. The San Juan Visitors Information Center also can help refer you to whale cruises. Try Orcas Island Eclipse Charters (800-376-6566 or 360-376-4663 in Orcas); San Juan Boat Tours (800-232-6722) and Western Prince Cruises (800-757-6722) both in Friday Harbor; or Deer Harbor Charters (800-544-5758 in Deer Harbor).

Whatcom County

At first it seems difficult to believe that idyllic Whatcom County earned its name from the Indian word meaning "noisy all the time." But if you listen to the voices of families visiting the area's children's museum, fish hatchery, art and sports festivals, farms, and nearby Lummi Indian Reservation, you'll know that the name fits.

This pristine sector of northwest Washington bordering British Columbia is a two-hour drive north of Seattle along Interstate 5. Its largest city, Bellingham, features competitive sports and arts events open to children and adults.

In late spring or early summer, the annual *Ski to Sea* relay race and festival attracts adult competitors sking, running, bicycling and kayaking their way to glory — or at least the finish line. Young people form teams of their own to run two miles, cover a half-mile three-legged race, bicycle 3.8 miles, dribble a soccer ball a half mile, and complete an obstacle course. All participants receive a T-shirt; ribbons are awarded to second- through sixth-place finishers and first place takes home a trophy. Participants may compete in the high school, middle school, or third- through fifth-grade age divisions.

Families also may cheer for adult athletes along another route, which starts a week later with downhill and cross country skiing on Mount Baker and ends with sea kayaking on Bellingham Bay. There's a junior parade, grand parade and carnival surrounding the event. Call 360-734-1330 for more details.

For a taste of the city's cultural side, explore its books and arts programs for children. Who better than a kid to participate in the Bellingham Chalk Art Festival? On the last Saturday in August, artisans of all ages spend up to three hours drawing masterpieces on city sidewalks along Cornwall Avenue betweeen Railroad and Commercial streets. Special prizes are awarded to the best in categories for those 13 years or younger, and 14 or older (but all kids get some prize). Entry fees are $2 for children and $5 for adults. Call 360-676-8548 for registration information.

North of Bellingham to the Canadian border, towns and hamlets on side roads are dotted by towns of Dutch and Norwegian ancestry. Off the freeway, narrow coastal roads between Blaine and Birch Bay offer farm and water views en route to Birch Bay and Larrabee state parks. Both offer extensive beachcombing, camping, and other outdoor play opportunities.

With the largest fishing fleet in the state, the 3,100-member Lummi Indian Nation makes its home 12 miles south of the U.S.-Canadian border off I-5 Exit 260. A leader in the seafood industry, the tribe harvests Dungeness crabs, clams, and oysters. If possible, visit in June during the Lummi Stommish Water Festival. Visitors may sample barbequed salmon, watch Native American dancing, and cheer 11-member teams competing in war canoe races. Call 360-734-8180 for more details.

Bellingham

Bellingham Ice Hawks

Location: *In the Whatcom Sports Coliseum, 1801 W. Bakerview Rd.*
Phone: *360-676-8090*
Days/Hours: *Season runs September through March; game times vary.*
Wheelchair/Stroller Access: *Yes*

Just south of the border, this British Columbia Junior "A" hockey team scores with the best of them. Enthusiasm surrounding the neighboring Vancouver Canucks' Stanley Cup appearance has spilled over the border, and hockey is growing in popularity in Bellingham. Many Ice Hawks are in their late teens and early 20s, so this league shows young fans that hard work and talent really pay off.

Children's Museum Northwest

Location: *227 Prospect St.*
Phone: *360-733-8769*
Days/Hours: *Noon to 5 p.m., Tuesday and Sunday; noon to 8 p.m., Wednesday; 10 a.m. to 5 p.m., Thursday, Friday and Saturday; closed in September for new exhibit designs.*
Wheelchair/Stroller Access: *Yes*

Each autumn, a new exhibit arrives here and budding imaginations go wild. Museum curators work hard to incorporate local interests with educational ones. Some of the best remain for a few years as others rotate in. In the "Locomotion: Wonder of Movement" exhibit, students explore the motion of trains and the human body. They don railroad costumes and scramble on a loading dock to a model full-size historic train, much like the ones which connected Bellingham and British Columbia years ago. A newer Amtrak engine control panel allows youngsters to engineer the mighty locomotive, and a magnetized track lets them push miniature trains over hills and bridges. For toddlers there's a soft sculpture train set for climbing.

In another area, watch a skeleton mimic a youngster's motion on a bicycle while the child pumps the pedals. Nearby, boys and girls perform make-belive surgeries and extract soft-sculpture body organs and bones from another imitation skeleton. Once these pieces are out, there's an anatomical map so children know where to replace the parts. Exhibits are geared for toddlers and youngsters up to about 12 years old. Call each September for updated information. Admission is $2 per person.

Fairhaven Park

Location: *107 Chuckanut Dr.*
Phone: *360-676-6985*
Days/Hours: *8 a.m. to dusk, daily.*
Wheelchair/Stroller Access: *Yes*
    This sprawling green park is especially attractive to families with young children. The summers-only wading pool entices splashing toddlers and preschoolers between noon and 6:30 p.m. Older boys and girls flock to the swings and other equipment on the playground. A short stroll leads you to nearby fish ladders.

Lake Whatcom Railway

Location: *In Wickersham near Acme. Take Highway 9 north at Sedro-Woolley and drive 10 miles*
Phone: *360-595-2218*
Days/Hours: *Leaves Wickersham Juntion at 11 a.m. and 1 p.m., Saturday through Tuesday, July through August.*
Wheelchair/Stroller Access: *Limited; power-model wheelchairs are too wide*
    Return to the turn-of-the-century aboard this former Northern Pacific steam train as it winds the four-mile forested route in about 90 minutes. At the end of the line, boys and girls may try some "muscle propelled" motion while pumping the handcar. Admission is $10 for adults, and $5 for those 17 or younger.

Village Books and the Colophon Cafe

Location: *1210 11th St., in Old Fairhaven*
Phone: *360-671-2626 (bookstore) and 360-647-0092 (cafe)*
Days/Hours: *9 a.m. to 10 p.m., Monday through Saturday; 10 a.m. to 6 p.m., Sunday (bookstore); 7 a.m. to 10 p.m., daily, Memorial Day through Labor Day; 7 a.m. to 6 p.m., Sundays the rest of the year (cafe).*
Wheelchair/Stroller Access: *Yes*
    Book lovers frequently drive for miles to browse and buy at Village Books. Children will find their own cozy reading corner while

adults explore other titles in nooks and crannies throughout the store. Village Books shares the building with the Colophon Cafe, which serves up ice cream in superb waffle cones. A favorite here on a cold or rainy day is a "mug a mocha moo," steamed milk with hot fudge and honest-to-goodness whipped cream for children.

Western Washington University

Location: *Start at the WWU Visitors Center on South College Drive at the main entrance to campus*
Phone: *360-650-3440 or 360-650-3000*
Days/Hours: *11 a.m. and 2 p.m., Monday through Friday, except holidays and school breaks.*
Wheelchair/Stroller Access: *Yes*

University students lead these one-hour tours through several academic buildings and a residence hall, stopping at some of the best campus viewpoints of Bellingham Bay and the San Juan Islands. During the summer, when fewer classes are in session, tours are less rushed, creating more time for younger kids to spend "appreciating," or, in some cases, climbing, the nearly two dozen pieces of contemporary outdoor sculptures. Geared primarily for middle and older teens, this tour introduces prospective WWU Vikings to things to do in Bellingham and on campus during study breaks.

Whatcom County Museum of History and Art

Location: *121 Prospect St.*
Phone: *360-676-6981*
Days/Hours: *Noon to 5 p.m., Tuesday through Sunday.*
Wheelchair/Stroller Access: *Yes*

There's no better way to get a sense of this area's roots than in the Whatcom County Museum of History and Art. Exhibits rotate regularly in this three-story bright red brick building, which also houses City Hall offices. Boys and girls feel like royalty when they descend the building's staircase with its ornate, hand-carved bannister reminiscent of the Victorian era. Northwest Coastal Indian displays with ceremonial masks and hand-woven baskets, timber industry dioramas, and other changing exhibits, vividly depict the region's history. Now expanded into the adjacent former firehouse, the museum has more room for children's exhibits. The nearby Arco Building is part of the museum as well. It displays works by local artists, but this may be of more interest to adults. Admission is free.

Whatcom Falls Park and Hatchery

Location: *1401 Electric Ave.*
Phone: *360-676-2138*
Days/Hours: *8 a.m. to 5 p.m., daily; sometimes closed in March and April, so it's best to call ahead.*
Wheelchair/Stroller Access: *In some areas*
This hatchery raises fish for release into Whatcom, Skagit and San Juan waters. On self-guided tours, visitors may watch the fish in 10 outdoor ponds and seven raceways which are home to 1.5 million trout annually. If you want a guided tour, be sure to call at least two days ahead. During park hours, boys and girls 14 or younger may dip their poles in the derby pond for a chance who vie to snag a trout that they may take home. A spring fishing derby attracts dozens of youngsters to catch the biggest fish and win prizes donated by community businesses.

North Whatcom County

Berthusen Park

Location: *8837 Berthusen Park. Take I-5 Exit 270 west on Birch Bay-Lynden Road; drive eight miles to Berthusen Road; turn north*
Phone: *360-354-2424*
Days/Hours: *Dawn to dusk for day use visitors; overnight camping available.*
Wheelchair/Stroller Access: *Limited*
The Berthusens — Norwegian immigrant farmers and parents of 10 children — left this 236-acre park to the city. Today, they would be happy to see how much families enjoy it. There's fishing in the stream, hiking, a playground, and the old homestead barn and vintage farm equipment for visitors to explore. It's possible to call ahead for camping reservations.

Hovander Homestead Park

Location: *In Ferndale at 5299 Nielson Rd. Take I-5 Exit 262 west less than a mile; under the railroad trestle take a hard left*
Phone: *360-384-3444*
Days/Hours: *Park open dawn to dusk year-round; house open noon to 4:30 p.m., Thursday through Sunday, mid-June through Labor Day.*
Wheelchair/Stroller Access: *Yes, at the park; no, at the house*

Equipment that turn-of-the-century Swedish immigrants once used to till their soil is now used for climbing and playing on at this farmhouse and park. Animals are cared for by 4-H club members, and the grounds are tended by master gardeners. Admission is $3 per vehicle. When the farmhouse is open, visitors appreciate the detailed scroll woodwork and vintage decor. The homestead is adjacent to Tennant Lake Natural Interpretive Center.

Inn at Semiahmoo

Location: *In Blaine at 9565 Semiahmoo Parkway. Take I-5 Exit 270; follow Lynden/Birch Bay Road for four miles; turn right on Harborview Road then turn left on Lincoln Road.*
Phone: *800-822-4200 and 360-371-2000*
Days/Hours: *Overnight accommodations year-round.*
Wheelchair/Stroller Access: *Yes*

This upscale and relaxing resort is best suited to adults with teens, while nearby condominium rentals not connected to the resort provide an option for families with young children. At the resort, an outdoor swimming pool, exercise facility, and tennis courts are first rate. Bring your clubs for the top-rated golf course nearby.

Families with young children may prefer to fly a kite on the beach, ride their bikes to see the mile-long sand spit, or rent a boat to rock on the waves. Take some time to visit nearby Semiahmoo Park with its quaint museum detailing salmon cannery life here in the late 1800s.

Mount Baker Wilderness Area

Location: *56 miles east of Bellingham on Highway 542*
Phone: *360-734-6771*
Days/Hours: *Varies; expect some roads to be closed in winter due to snow.*
Wheelchair/Stroller Access: *In some areas*

On the west side of North Cascades National Park and Recreation Area, many families who ski or hike frequent the slopes and paths at Mount Baker Wilderness Area. Downhill and cross country skiing is open here daily in the winter, mid-November through December, with weekend hours during the rest of the season. When the snow melts, it's a spectacular hiking destination. Some trails offer blueberries ripe on the vine in late summer and early autumn.

Get an introduction to the wilderness area at Heather Meadows Visitors Center, open 10 a.m to 5 p.m., daily, July through September. Nearby, there are two half-mile wheelchair and stroller accessible hikes: Fire & Ice Trail and Picture Lake Path. Picture Lake provides countless scenes for (you guessed it) photographers. The path also features interpretive signs so families can read about surrounding plants and wildlife.

Obtain specific information about hiking within the Mount Baker National Forest from the Glacier Public Service Center by calling 360-599-2714, 9 a.m. to 5 p.m., daily, year-round, or from the Heather Meadows Visitors Center.

Mount Baker Vineyards

Location: *In Deming at 4298 Mount Baker Highway*
Phone: *360-592-2300*
Days/Hours: *11 a.m. to 5 p.m., Wednesday through Sunday; by appointment only Monday and Tuesday.*
Wheelchair/Stroller Access: *Yes, the parking lot is rough gravel*

Presses at this "mom and pop" winery crush some of the area's finest grapes. Tour group sizes are small and personal. Kids may sample non-alcoholic fresh juice while adults savor a sip of wine after a walk through the facility. Things get busy here in the summer and fall, so a call ahead is wise to make sure tours are operating.

Peace Arch State Park

Location: *Along I-5 at the U.S.-Canadian border*
Phone: *360-332-4544 or 800-624-3555*
Days/Hours: *Dawn to dusk, daily.*
Wheelchair/Stroller Access: *Yes, at the gardens*

While passing between the United States and Canada, this is a pleasant border stop to view the 67-foot Peace Arch. The monument marks nearly 200 years of peaceful relations between the two countries. In the middle of the gardened, 40-acre park, this span rests one column in Canada and the other in the United States. Youngsters can get a taste of international relations during the annual Peace Arch celebration each second Sunday in June. Thousands of children are invited to exchange flags and other friendship symbols with boys and girls from our neighbor to the north.

Tennant Lake Natural Interpretive Center

Location: *In Ferndale at 5236 Nielsen Rd.*
Phone: *360-384-3444*
Days/Hours: *Noon to 4:30 p.m., Thursday through Sunday, mid-June through Labor Day.*
Wheelchair/Stroller Access: *Yes*

These spectacular gardens next to the Hovander Homestead are an outdoor leisure destination during the summer. The sight-impaired are aided by braille signs that describe the floral scents and leaf textures through the Fragrance Garden at the Interpretive Center. After completing a half-mile of trails and boardwalks, visitors arrive at a 30-foot tower. It takes climbers with hearty endurance to make it up the last few steep steps, but the tower view is ideal for watching birds and overseeing the 200-acre marshy setting.

Wet 'N Wild Waterpark

Location: *In Blaine at 4874 Birch Bay-Lynden Rd. Take I-5 Exit 270; turn west and drive four miles to Birch Bay-Lynden Road*
Phone: *360-371-7500 (recording) or 360-371-7911*
Days/Hours: *10:30 a.m. to 7:30 p.m., daily, June through Labor Day.*
Wheelchair/Stroller Access: *For observing only*

You've never taken a real "hairpin" or "corkscrew" turn until you've tried one of the four 400-foot slides at this waterpark. Adventurous pre-teens and teens will want to whip through the "twister" or the "snake" before dropping into the pool below. Younger ones will likely prefer the three less daunting kiddie slides. A shallow pool is popular among toddlers. Adults tired of chasing kids may want to relax in the hot tub. There are concessions on site, but great picnic areas make it easy to bring your own lunch. All-day admission is $8.75 for those 6 years or older, and $5.75 after 4:30 p.m. Seniors pay $4.25, tots 3 to 5 years pay $5, and children 2 or younger are free if accompanied by an adult.

Helpful Phone Numbers:

Anacortes Visitor Information Center, 360-293-3832

Arlington Chamber of Commerce, 360-435-3708

Bainbridge Island Chamber of Commerce, 206-842-3700

Bellingham/Whatcom County Convention and Visitors Bureau, 800-487-2032 and 360-671-3990

Birch Bay Chamber of Commerce, 360-371-0334

Blaine Visitors Center, 800-624-3555 and 360-332-4544

Bremerton/Kitsap County Visitor and Convention Bureau, 360-479-3588

Burlington Chamber of Commerce, 360-755-9382

Central Whidbey Chamber of Commerce/Coupeville, 360-678-5434

Clinton Chamber of Commerce, 360-341-4545

Edmonds Chamber of Commerce, 206-776-6711
Everett Chamber of Commerce, 206-252-5181
Ferndale Chamber of Commerce, 360-384-3042
Greater Oak Harbor Chamber of Commerce, 360-675-3535
LaConner Chamber of Commerce, 360-466-4778
Langley Chamber of Commerce, 360-221-6765
Lummi Indian Nation, 360-734-8180
Lynden Chamber of Commerce, 360-354-5995
Marysville Chamber of Commerce, 360-659-7700
Mount Baker Foothills Chamber of Commerce, 360-599-1205
Mount Vernon Chamber of Commerce, 360-42-TULIP
North Cascades National Park Visitors Information Center, 360-856-5700
Port Orchard Chamber of Commerce, 360-876-3505
Poulsbo Chamber of Commerce, 360-779-4848
San Juan Islands Bed & Breakfast Inns, 360-378-3030
San Juan Islands Visitors Information Service, 360-468-3663
Sedro-Woolley Chamber of Commerce, 360-855-1841
Silverdale Chamber of Commerce, 360-692-6800
Snohomish Chamber of Commerce, 360-568-2526
Snohomish County Visitors Center, 206-745-4133
South Snohomish County Chamber of Commerce, 206-774-0507
Washington State Ferry Information, 206-464-6400 or 800-84-FERRY (in state only)

Photo courtesy of the Leavenworth Chamber of Commerce

Smokey Bear gets a warm hug from two young visitors to Bavarian-style Leavenworth.

North Cascades and North Central Washington

Almost a century has passed since Washington state leaders began planning a route over the North Cascades linking east and west. It started as separate wagon roads inching just 12 miles up on both sides of the mountain in 1896. Today, it's two-lane Highway 20, a route crossed each year by thousands of families looking for fun within the North Cascades National Park and Recreation Area, as well as other destinations on either side of the pass.

Weather permitting, Highway 20 is open April to November. When connected with U.S. 97 and U.S. 2, it's a scenic loop through Chelan country, the Wenatchee Valley and Stevens Pass to the Puget Sound region. Many families drive it to combine stops in the rugged wilderness, "Wild West" Winthrop, Lake Chelan's water wonderland, Wenatchee's fruit basket, Bavaria-style Leavenworth, and the alpine setting of Stevens Pass.

From the west, visitors to majestic North Cascades National Park and Recreation Area discover Washington's second largest river, the Skagit, home and sanctuary to hundreds of bald eagles. River float trips near Concrete and Marblemount in late January and early February are an especially popular way to watch these regal birds, but children need to be old enough to sit still in a raft for two hours or more. Call the Professional River Outfitters of Washington at 206-323-5485 to get a listing of recommended river guides.

During the summer, 5 to 13-year-olds find Saturday afternoon Junior Ranger programs at Colonial Creek Campground, 10 miles east of Newhalem. Park naturalists lead children on walks and describe the cougars, bears, deer and other wildlife and plants which make their homes here. Just east of the summit, new restrooms are complete at the renovated Washington Pass Overlook, elevation 5,477 feet. It's a welcome stop for visitors who want to stretch their legs after the long ascent.

There's an Old West feel in Winthrop and an outdoors spirit throughout the Methow Valley, an hour drive east of the summit along Highway 20. Warm summers attract horseback riders, hikers and campers, while winter snow lures cross-country skiers. After a 1993 fire gutted one of Winthrop's most historic landmarks, the town's frontier town look is being re-created. Now the 1890s-style mining town, with its Emporium stores and wooden sidewalks, is rising from the ashes with even more shops. In this setting, boys and girls imagine themselves as brave pioneers and fearless dude ranch hands. During the colder months, 175 kilometers of cross-country ski trails are groomed. Call 800-422-3048 or 509-996-2148 for more details.

To the south, just counting all the ways families have warm-weather fun on the water at Lake Chelan can keep visitors busy. With water-skiing, jet-skiing, swimming, windsurfing, sailing, innertubing, kayaking, canoeing, paddleboating, houseboating and bumper-boating, there's enough water for everyone's favorite sport. Lake Chelan is south of the Methow Valley via Highways 153 or U.S. 97, and north of Wenatchee off U.S. 97 and 97A. Only two lakes in the United States are deeper than this 55-mile-long meandering waterway: Oregon's Crater Lake and Lake Tahoe in California and Nevada. While at Lake Chelan, consider staying for at least a day at any of several places: Chelan City Park, Lakeside Park, Manson Bay Park, Lake Chelan State Park or 25-Mile State Park. For overnight accommodations, try the hundreds of campsites, resort rooms or condominiums for rent.

Farther south is Wenatchee, a place some call the "apple capital of the world." No wonder. Wenatchee-area farms grow seven billion apples annually. That's about half of all the apples grown in the entire country! A good time to visit with children is during Apple Blossom Festival in late April and early May. You'll find a parade, carnival and other entertaining events for families.

Apples, pears and other fruit trees grow on nearly all the hills and valleys near Cashmere along the Wenatchee River between Wenatchee and Leavenworth. Children are welcome in the city's Pioneer Village at the town's Chelan County Historical Museum. It's a restoration of an 1860s western community, featuring a "tonsorial parlor" (barber shop), log school, church mission and saloon.

Visitors touring the Bavarian-style village of Leavenworth may get the gnawing feeling that Julie Andrews should be running through the hills crooning "The Sound of Music." Town leaders want you to feel that way. Authentic German restaurants and treat shops, stores full of cute collectibles, and dozens of cozy bed-and-breakfast getaways make this a popular family destination. Near the village center along Front Street, boys and girls can be caught peering into shops selling itty-bitty doll house furnishings and cuddle-up teddy bears.

Favorite times of year to visit Leavenworth with families are during September's Autumn Leaf Festival, when streets resonate with oompah music, and during early October's Wenatchee River Salmon Festival. The salmon fest attracts encampments of Native Americans who perform elaborate dances to celebrate the return of healthy salmon to the Wenatchee River. It's a colorful lesson in Indian culture for children and their families of all races.

Others make an annual pilgrimage to Leavenworth's Christmas Lights Festival. Each December weekend before Christmas, adults may join children sledding in the park, competing in the snow-person building contest and enjoying sleigh rides nearby. At day's end, visitors join for the traditional singing of "Silent Night" at the town's Christmas tree.

North Cascades Loop

Lady of the Lake II and *Lady Express*/ Lake Chelan Boat Company

Location: *One mile south of downtown Chelan off Highway 97A*
Phone: *509-682-2224 (recording) and 509-682-4584*
Days/Hours: *Departs Chelan at 8:30 a.m. and returns at 6 p.m., with several stops, on Lady of the Lake II, May through October; one Chelan departure, mid-May through mid-June, and twice daily, mid-June through September, aboard Lady Express.*
Wheelchair/Stroller Access: *Yes*

Whether you prefer your ride leisurely or swift, the Lake Chelan Boat Company has the ride for you. Aboard the 350-passenger *Lady of the Lake II*, during late spring and summer passengers sail to several stops before arriving in remote Stehekin at the eastern foothills of North Cascades National Park. The smaller 100-passenger *Lady Express* makes fewer stops and takes about half the time to arrive in Stehekin. Be sure to bring plenty of film. It's about three hours to Stehekin aboard the *Lady of the Lake II*, so families will want to pack along munchies or buy a muffin, soda pop or coffee. There are bathrooms on board.

If you're riding either boat to an overnight destination, remember that adults may carry up to 75 pounds of gear while children may bring up to 40 pounds. Bicycles are transported for $13. Groups of 15 or more should call 509-682-2519 for reservations. Roundtrip fares aboard the *Lady of the Lake II* are about $21 for adults; children 6 to 11 years old pay half fare and those 5 or younger ride free. Reservations aren't needed for the *Lady of the Lake II*. On the *Lady Express*, adult passengers' roundtrip fares are about $39; children age 2 to 11 years old pay half fare and those younger ride free. Reservations are recommended for the *Lady Express*. Visitors may combine their outing with one leg of the trip on the *Lady of the Lake II* and the other on the *Lady Express*.

Lake Chelan National Recreation Area

Location: *In Stehekin at Golden West Visitors Center*
Phone: *360-856-5703, extension 14*
Days/Hours: *Stehekin Lodge open year-round; recreation area open 7:30 a.m. to 4 p.m., daily, mid-June through mid-September; noon to 2 p.m, mid-May to mid-June and mid-September through October; closed the rest of the year.*
Wheelchair/Stroller Access: *In some areas; wheelchair elevator at lodge*

When you hear the word wilderness, think of Stehekin. It's the cozy resort to escape with children at the west end headwaters of Lake Chelan and the east end of North Cascades National Park. You get here only by boat or floatplane. Stehekin offers a handful of bed-and-breakfast inns, cabins and the North Cascades Stehekin Lodge for overnight quests. Call 509-682-4494 for more details.

If you're more rugged, pitch your tent in the remote reaches of the park. There are day hikes and week-long backpacking climbs into the high country best suited for strong pre-teens and teens. Younger children who enjoy short jaunts usually have no problem hiking the two-mile route from the lodge to Rainbow Falls (even though a shuttle bus takes passengers within one block so you can ride instead of walk).

North Cascades National Park Visitors Center

Location: *In Newhalem; take I-5 Exit 232 to Highway 20; drive east about 60 miles*
Phone: *360-386-4495*
Days/Hours: *8:30 a.m. to 5:30 p.m., daily, May through October; 9 a.m. to 4:30 p.m., weekends only, Veteran's Day through April.*
Wheelchair/Stroller Access: *Yes*

Just finished in 1994, this family-friendly visitors center is an educational introduction to North Cascades National Park. Children will probably want to spend about an hour in the exhibits room, exploring animal tracks painted on walls and furniture and matching them with the corresponding animal or bird. Encourage little ones to reach into dark cubby holes and guess which animal hide or fur they're feeling. Nothing bites back!

In cozy cubicles designed for as many as seven people, watch any of the half dozen wordless videos showing various park regions. One powerful video displays the ravages of forest fires and the land's eventual rebirth. The room's sound and light-systems are timed to the video, so it seems to shake with thunder and flash with lightening on the screen.

A longer 20-minute video created by six laser-disc projectors shows scenes from changing seasons on a large screen with amazing clarity. Be to ask about the Junior Ranger Program here, too. A handout with suggested environmental activities can help 5 to 13-year-olds earn junior ranger certificates. With a certificate, they can buy a patch for a few dollars.

Seattle City Light Skagit Dams Tour

Location: *In Diablo; take I-5 Exit 232 to Highway 20; drive east about 70 miles or take I-5 Exit 208 and follow Highway 530 through Arlington to Highway 20*
Phone: *206-684-3030 or 206-587-5500 for TDD*
Days/Hours: *10 a.m., 12:30 p.m. and 3 p.m. Thursday through Monday, mid-June through Labor Day weekend; at noon, weekends only, mid-September through early October.*
Wheelchair/Stroller Access: *Yes*

For nearly 70 years, visitors of all ages have been getting a real charge out of this hydroelectric project. Seattle-area children discover the power source for their video games and stereos.

A short slide show introduces the 4 1/2-hour tour, which officially starts on a platform hoisting about 100 people 560 feet up Sourdough Mountain. There's a short paved walk to a double-deck boat on Ross

Lake, above Diablo Dam and below Ross Dam. Even the youngest visitors will enjoy this mellow, half-hour cruise. At the powerhouse, guides explain the turbine and generator activity and visitors gaze at the 540-foot structure.

After the cruise returns, guests are served an all-you-can-eat chicken and apple pie meal in a dining hall. If you prefer to eat outside, the tour offers adults a boxed lunch with a sandwich, salad, cookie and fruit; those 11 years old or younger get a piece of chicken, Jell-O, chips, cookie, and a beverage. The grassy lawns are well-groomed so there are plenty of picnic spots. Combined admission and meal cost is $24.50 for adults, $22 for seniors, $12.50 for students 6 to 11 years old, and free for those 5 or younger.

Photo courtesy of Sun Mountain Lodge and Kent Kerr
Sun Mountain Lodge guests ride horses through the Methow Valley.

Slidewaters

Location: *In Chelan at 102 Waterslide Dr.*
Phone: *509-682-5751*
Days/Hours: *10 a.m. to 8 p.m., daily, Memorial Day through Labor Day.*
Wheelchair/Stroller Access: *For observation only*
As you enter the town of Chelan, look up the hill. You'll see the water craze begin as riders of all ages shoot down nine rides and slides. Soaking in this water park's hot tub is a relaxing spot for tired parents. Admission is $10.95 for adults, $7.95 for those 4 to 7 years old, and free for those 3 or younger.

Sun Mountain Lodge

Location: *Seven miles west of Highway 20 on Patterson Lake Road between Twisp and Winthrop*
Phone: *800-572-0493 or 509-996-2211*
Days/Hours: *Overnight accommodations available year-round.*
Wheelchair/Stroller Access: *Yes*
On the east side of the North Cascades, families may select from a myriad of recreational activities at this year-round resort. Choose from horseback rides (April through October; children must be at least 50 inches tall to ride), Methow River whitewater rafting trips (May through mid-July), mountain bike tours, fly fishing classes, guided hikes to Aspen Lake and Storybook Hills, and a special Sun Mountaineers program which features games, arts and crafts, hikes and a meal for children age 4 to 10 years old (summers only). Guests also will find tennis courts, two playgrounds, a swimming pool and hot tubs. In the winter, more than 50 miles of cross-country ski trails start just outside the lodge's front door.

Wenatchee and Leavenworth

Gingerbread Factory

Location: *In Leavenworth at 828 Commercial St.*
Phone: *509-548-6592*
Days/Hours: *7 a.m. to 7 p.m., daily.*
Wheelchair/Stroller Access: *No*
Run, run, run as fast as you can, 'cuz your kids *can* catch a gingerbread man — and his girlfriend. This shop is loaded with all sorts of freshly baked cookies but it specializes in humorous

gingerbread treats. There are cookie cutters for gingerbread hula girls, trains, and gecko lizards. In the summer, gingerbread people are dressed in bikinis or swim trunks.

Hansel & Gretel Deli

Location: *In Leavenworth at 819 Front St.*
Phone: *509-548-7721*
Days/Hours: *7 a.m to 8 p.m., Sunday through Friday; 7 a.m. to 9 p.m. Saturday.*
Wheelchair/Stroller Access: *Yes*

Most families already feel like they're in a fairy tale when visiting Leavenworth, so a stop at Hansel & Gretel's makes sense. Sandwiches stuffed with imported German meats and cheeses, homemade soups that warm your bones on a winter day, and more than a dozen ice cream flavors for waffle cones are among the taste-tempting reasons to stop here.

Lake Wenatchee State Park

Location: *22 miles north of Leavenworth and 20 miles east of Stevens Pass. From U.S. 2 turn north on Highway 207 North. Drive another four miles to park.*
Phone: *509-763-3101*
Days/Hours: *Overnight camping accommodations year-round.*
Wheelchair/Stroller Access: *Yes*

Local families frequent this park year-round because of its varied recreation. In the winter, cross-country skiers, snowshoers and snowmobilers flock here to play in the powdery white stuff. When the snow melts, Lake Wenatchee State Park teems with horseback riders, hikers, campers and picnickers. At the lake's southeast corner, there's great swimming, waterskiing, fishing from boats and the bank, scuba diving, and windsurfing. Rafters paddle down the Wenatchee River into the lake here, too. During the warmer months it's smart to bring along mosquito repellant because these pests breed in local waters.

Liberty Orchards - Aplets & Cotlets Candy Kitchen

Location: *117 Mission St., off U.S. 2 about 10 miles east of Leavenworth*
Phone: *509-782-2191*
Days/Hours: *8:30 a.m. to 4:30 p.m., Monday through Friday, January through April; 8 a.m. to 11 a.m. and noon to 4 p.m., Monday through Friday, and 10 a.m. to 4 p.m. most weekends, May through December. Call ahead to confirm.*

Wheelchair/Stroller Access: *Yes*

Try to keep your child's sweet tooth — or yours, for that matter — in check after this free guided tour of Cashmere's confectionary kitchens. You'll get a free sample of candies made from locally grown apples, apricots and grapes. Tours leave every 20 minutes to kitchens where gigantic copper kettles simmer the sweet fruits before they're rolled in powdered sugar. Tours are available on Saturdays and Sundays, but since the factory doesn't operate on weekends it's best to visit on a weekday.

Lincoln Rock State Park

Location: *Seven miles north of East Wenatchee*
Phone: *509-884-8702*
Days/Hours: *Overnight camping accommodations year-round.*
Wheelchair/Stroller Access: *Yes*

Outdoor activities for a range of ages make this one of the 10 most popular parks in the state. Officials recently added children's play equipment to the grounds. Older children and adults may prefer the baseball and soccer fields, and swimming and water-skiing on Lake Entiat, created from the Columbia River by Rocky Reach Dam. There's a shallow wading area at the swimming area for kids. Most of the park's 80 picnic tables are next to the swimming beach. Three loops with almost 90 campsites are within a short walking distance the water. Some children may figure out the park was named by someone who thought the nearby basalt cliffs look like Abraham Lincoln.

Mission Ridge

Location: *12 miles south of Wenatchee*
Phone: *509-663-7631 or 800-374-1693*
Days/Hours: *Daily December through mid-April.*
Wheelchair/Stroller Access: *No*

There are 30 varying ski runs here for downhill enthusiasts of all ages and skills. Most runs are about two miles long; the longest covers five miles. For night skiers, 30 acres of runs are lit. Parents with children too young to ski may be interested in the child care provided at the day lodge. At nearby Squilchuck Ski Bowl, non-skiers may want to try the sledding and innertubing.

North Central Washington Museum

Location: *In Wenatchee at 127 S. Mission St., two blocks west of the Columbia River*
Phone: *509-664-5989*
Days/Hours: *10 a.m. to 4 p.m., Monday through Friday; 1 p.m. to 4 p.m., Saturday and Sunday; closed weekends in January and most holidays.*
Wheelchair/Stroller Access: *Yes, from the loading dock between the two buildings. Go inside and tell them visitors are waiting at the loading dock*

Bring a few extra quarters to this two-building museum because boys and girls adore watching the coin-operated, miniature Great Northern Railway trains run along the tracks here. The related exhibit describes how important railroads were to North Central Washington. Officials say children 8 years old or older seem to best enjoy exhibits here because they understand the history. Displays include a walk-through pioneer home with turn-of-the-century furnishings in the kitchen, living room and bedroom. There's also a pioneer workshop and trading store. Upstairs you'll find locally excavated fossils displayed. A skybridge links the main museum to an annex featuring art exhibits. Call ahead to find out about frequently scheduled silent movies, concerts and traveling exhibits. Suggested donations for admission are $5 per family, or $2 for adults, $1 for students 6 to 12 years old, and free to those 5 years old or younger. Parking is free a block south of the museum off Kittitas Street.

Ohme Gardens

Location: *3327 Ohme; near the junction of U.S. 2 and U.S. 97, follow 97 to U.S. 97A and follow the signs*
Phone: *509-662-5785*
Days/Hours: *9 a.m. to 6 p.m., mid-April to Memorial Day; 9 a.m. to 7 p.m., Memorial Day to Labor Day.*
Wheelchair/Stroller Access: *No*

Children may feel as if they're playing in a Swiss Alps scene straight out of "Heidi" when they run along this bluff high above the Wenatchee Valley. The late Herman Ohme landscaped nine acres here for his own family retreat in the early 1930s. Now, carefully tended wildflower gardens have replaced the sagebrush once covering this hillside. Toss a coin in the wishing well or encourage children to find their reflection in any of the five pools (no wading allowed). While walking the one-mile, rock-slab trail, families are sure to spy the numerous birds, rabbits and squirrels which call this place home. Shutterbugs will want to bring enough film to photograph views of the Wenatchee Valley, Cascade Mountains and Columbia River along the route. Admission is $5 for adults, $3 for students 7 to 17 years old and free for those 6 or younger.

River rafting

From Level 1 "float" trips to a select few Level 5 "highly technical" whitewater adventures, Washington's rivers offer a wide range of rafting excitement. The Yakima, Tieton and Wenatchee rivers are within a 90-minute drive of Wenatchee. In Western Washington, many of these outfitters run trips on the White Salmon, Green, Skykomish, Elwha, and Skagit rivers.

Most professional rafting guides won't take children younger than 12 years old. On the faster and more technical whitewater trips, some guides require passengers be at least 15 years old. But outfitters vary on ages when it comes to the Level 1 float trips, many of which waft leisurely down gentle rivers allowing passengers to enjoy the sites.

Some of these trips run about two to three hours without a stop, so children must be able to sit still that long. All require passengers to be outfitted with certified floatation lifevests. Following is a list of certified river rafting companies in the state. Most cover rivers in both western and eastern Washington:

All Rivers Whitewater and Scenic River Trips, 800-74-FLOAT
Downstream River Runners, 800-234-4644 and 206-483-0335
Northern Wilderness River Riders, 206-448-RAFT
Orion, 800-553-7466 and 206-547-6715
Wild and Scenic River Tours, 206-323-1220
Zig-Zag Expeditions, 206-282-2840

Rocky Reach Dam

Location: *Seven miles north of Wenatchee along Highway 97A*
Phone: *509-663-7522*
Days/Hours: *8 a.m. to 8 p.m., daily, mid-February through December.*
Wheelchair/Stroller Access: *Yes*

Look a salmon in the eye — if you can figure out which eye they're looking at you with — at the fish ladder here. This Chelan County Public Utility District hydroelectric project is more than just a dam. It's a three-in-one museum covering geology, local Native American history and the "Gallery of Electricity." Admission is free. When the weather is right, stake out a picnic spot on the surrounding 25-acre spread.

Sleigh Rides/Hay Rides

Location: *Most within about 10 miles of Leavenworth*
Phone: *Eagle Creek Ranch at 800-221-7433; Mountain Springs Lodge at 800-858-2276; Red Tail Canyon Farm at 800-678-4512*
Days/Hours: *Winters only; hours vary but usually daylight only.*
Wheelchair/Stroller Access: *Yes*

Snuggle up with the kids and listen to the jingle-jangle of horsebells as a team pulls your sleigh across the white powder snow during the winter, roughly late November through early March. Most rides are about 45 minutes to an hour and travel through fields and groves of aspen and fir. Some stop mid-point for a bonfire and a cup of hot cider. During the warmer months, many of these same teams lead passengers on evening hayrides along similar routes.

Stevens Pass Downhill Skiing

Location: *Off U.S. 2, 36 miles west of Leavenworth and 50 miles east of Index*
Phone: *360-973-2441*
Days/Hours: *9 a.m. to 10 p.m., daily, late November to mid-April.*
Wheelchair/Stroller Access: *Yes, in the West Lodge; some ski runs for disabled athletes*

When the snow begins to fly at Stevens Pass so do the downhill skiers. Eleven chairlifts ascend the slopes, allowing skiers to take their pick from any of 26 downhill runs. Ride the Daisy Chair to where about 10 percent of the terrain is designed for beginners. Seven of the runs are lit for night skiing. At the bottom there's a lodge for warming your toes and resting weary muscles.

If you prefer cross-country skiing, snowmobiling or showshoeing, these activities are available at Mill Creek (five miles east of Stevens Pass) and Chiwawa Road (one mile east of Highway 22/207 junction). Downhill skiing is free for children 6 or younger. There's child-care available for potty-trained kids 2 years old or older, too. Call 360-973-2441 for reservations.

Washington Apple Commission Visitor Center

Location: *2900 Euclid St., in north Wentachee near Ohme Gardens and Rocky Reach Dam*
Phone: *509-663-9600 (weekdays) and 509-662-3090 (weekends)*
Days/Hours: *8 a.m. to 5 p.m., Monday through Friday, January through April; 9 a.m. to 5 p.m., Monday through Saturday, May through December; 10 a.m. to 4 p.m. Sundays.*
Wheelchair/Stroller Access: *Yes*

Anyone who has bitten into a crunchy fresh apple, or sipped sweet apple juice will find the 18-minute video here an eye-opener. It illustrates how the state's 4,500 apple growers produce their fruit. First-time visitors are often amazed at how technical apple farming has become. Museum admission and the apple and apple juice samples at the end of the tour are free.

North Central Washington and Coulee Country

From the flat, fertile farmland of Central Washington to the mountainous wilderness bordering Canada on the north, the population is sparse. But families who live here know how to have a good time. Many visitors en route to the region's engineering masterpiece, Grand Coulee Dam, discover North and Central Washington's small communities and get a flavor of their strong ethnic cultures.

One such stop is tiny Odessa, along State Highways 21 and 28 in Lincoln County. Folks celebrate Deutschesfest here. For three days in September, the town honors its German heritage from Russia's Ukraine with authentic sausages, polka music, some contemporary dance tunes and other festivities. Children are invited to the games in the "jugend garten" (youth garden) on the street next to the Old Town Hall on First Avenue between Division and First streets. Call 509-982-0049.

To change the polka tempo to belly dancing music, visit the Greek Panayiri Festival in Soap Lake on Memorial Day weekend. West of Odessa on Highway 28, Soap Lake hosts a community party where festival-goers of all ages are invited to kick up their heels with Greek folk and line dancing, and enjoy native Greek food. Be sure to try the roasted lamb and sweet baklava dessert. Call 509-246-1821. And by the way, when inquisitive children ask how Soap Lake got its name, tell them it's because of the water's soapy alkaline, which makes it saltier than the ocean.

To the northeast, the sound of drums bounces off the nearby hills of the Colville Indian Reservation during the annual Omak Stampede in August. This week-long rodeo and Native American encampment features traditional Indian dancers dressed in full costume, cowboys competing in seven events, plus a kiddies and larger grand parade commemorating the area's roots.

For some, the highlight of the event is the stampede's Suicide Race, featuring daredevil horseback riders who plunge over a 200-foot bluff into the Okanogan River and cross its current to a breathtaking finish. It's so dangerous that several horses have been killed. Some parents find this event inappropriate for children; others consider it an age-old traditional Native American competition.

Summer is a busy time at the mighty Grand Coulee Dam. The dam's summer laser-light tours attract up to 2 million visitors each year.

About 75 miles south, Moses Lake is a mecca for waterskiers, boaters, anglers, swimmers and camping enthusiasts. Swimming is possible year-round at the new Olympic-sized pool at Moses Lake Family Aquatic Center. A hydraulic lift lowers and raises disabled youngsters and adults from the pool; it's at the corner of Dogwood and Fourth streets. Call 509-766-9246 for more details. Outside the aquatic center, skateboarders can spin their stunts on the course designed for them. Teens flock here.

When driving near Moses Lake along I-90 in December, urge passengers to keep their eyes peeled for the charming lighted Christmas scenes set up along both sides of the freeway. The scenes are erected between Quincy, at the I-90/Highway 281 intersection, and Dodson Road Interchange, 10 miles west of Moses Lake.

Grant County

Grant County Pioneer Village & Museum

Location: *In Ephrata at 742 Basin St. N. Take I-90 Exit 151/Highway 283 or I-90 Exit 179/Highway 17*
Phone: *509-754-3334*
Days/Hours: *10 a.m. to 5 p.m., Monday, Tuesday, Thursday, Friday and Saturday; 1 p.m. to 4 p.m. Sunday, May through September; closed the rest of the year.*
Wheelchair/Stroller Access: *Yes*

Imagine a pioneer barber giving a full lather shave or a jailer shackling an outlaw at this turn-of-the-century pioneer village. Children and their families who explore the village's 28 buildings, including the church, jail, bank and a homestead house, will discover some are originals moved from within Grant County to this 3.9-acre site. Youngsters may see "pioneers" (volunteers) plying their trade during the second week in June and again in late September during "living museum" days. These dates change each year, so it's best to call ahead. A petting zoo is open then, too. Admission is $2 for adults, $1.50 for students 6 to 16, and free to those 5 or younger.

YoungRiders Summer Camp

Location: *At Moses Coulee Ranch, 20 miles west of Ephrata*
Phone: *800-421-5730 and 509-754-0338*
Days/Hours: *Week-long, overnight camps mid-June through late August.*
Wheelchair/Stroller Access: *No*

Its poster reads: "WANTED! Kids, alive and well," because this summer camp provides week-long horsemanship and riding classes for children 8 to 16 years old. For about $600, YoungRiders campers sleep over in the bunkhouse, ride a horse assigned just to them, help on a cattle drive, swim, play softball, take wagon rides, and sing around the nightly campfire with others their age. All meals and snacks are included. At the end of camp, families are invited to watch a "showdeo" of skills learned during the week.

Okanagon County

Omak Stampede and Suicide Race

Location: *Downtown Omak, 60 miles north of Chelan on U.S. 97 or 60 miles northwest of Grand Coulee Dam via Highway 155*
Phone: *509-826-1002 or 800-933-6625*
Days/Hours: *Second weekend in August.*
Wheelchair/Stroller Access: *In some areas*

The rootin' tootin' Omak Stampede is more than the death-defying Suicide Race it's well known for. This week-long event features four Professional Rodeo Cowboys Association performances, kiddies and grand parades, a carnival, river raft races, a Native American encampment and tribal dance competition.

Younger children are enthralled by the color, costumes and flair of the Native American dances, while older boys and girls may learn about tribal history and lore told through dance. Visitors are welcome to browse around the teepees at the surrounding Indian village.

The town is so small that nearly all events are within walking distance. That's why many families stake out one of the more than 1,000 campsites at Omak Eastside Park and stroll to the events. Call ahead to check on ticket availability before leaving home.

Lincoln County

Grand Coulee Dam

Location: *90 miles west of Spokane via U.S. 2 and Highway 174, or about 90 miles northeast of George from I-90 via highways 283, 28, 17 and 155*
Phone: *509-633-3074 and 509-633-9265*
Days/Hours: *9 a.m. to 5 p.m., daily, year-round; nightly laser light shows during summer only.*
Wheelchair/Stroller Access: *Yes*

Though the dam is the main attraction, families should stop first at the Visitor Arrival Center. A 13-minute introductory video depicts the dam's history and its surrounding geology. The video is set to "Roll On, Columbia, Roll On," written by folk-singing Washingtonian Woody Guthrie. The tune may be old, but children will be humming it for days. Families are advised to make a bathroom stop here before leaving on the 90-minute, free self-guided tour to the powerhouse.

These days, visitors may drive on the road atop the dam, something that was prohibited years ago. From here, employees board elevators which descend hundreds of feet into the dam's inner workings. Inside, long tunnels connect spaces filled with twirling turbines and knobs, switches and buttons all designed to operate the dam. The tour makes five stops in the dam and powerhouse. You'll feel your heart start to pound as you soar inside the glass-enclosed incline elevator at the Third Powerhouse.

Perhaps the most memorable part of a Grand Coulee visit is the 40-minute laser light production projected nightly onto the dam's face. It starts at sunset, Memorial Day through September. This patriotic production opens with breath-holding quiet as blue lights illuminate the spillway before water begins gushing down. When this 4,000-foot-long dam becomes a makeshift video screen, the TV at home looks mighty small in comparison. Children will be delighted by the animated cartoons projected onto the spillway during the show.

There are several choices when searching for the best viewpoints of the display. In the town of Coulee Dam, grab a bleacher seat across from the Coulee House motel. Families with sleepy children may want to stake out a spot on the grassy lawn at the Visitor Arrival Center so they can catch a short nap before the show. Others watch it from the parking lot at the Third Powerhouse. All three have stereo systems which broadcast music synchronized with the light show.

Crown Point Vista offers views of the dam, Lake Roosevelt, and the town of Coulee Dam. Some professional photographers consider it one of their favorite camera-snapping spots. You can catch the laser-light show from this vista, too. Turn to local radio stations KEYG 1490 AM or 98.5 FM and hear the music simulcast with the lights.

For extended visits, consider renting a houseboat or camp on Lake Roosevelt behind the dam.

Rock 'n Robin Drive-In

Location: *Bridgeport and Highway 174 in Grand Coulee*
Phone: *509-633-1290*
Days/Hours: *11 a.m. to 8:30 p.m., daily.*
Wheelchair/Stroller Access: *Yes*
This place is like a scene out of TV's "Happy Days." During the summer, waitresses zip up next to your vehicle to take your order for hamburgers, French fries and milkshakes — all while on roller skates!

Photo courtesy of The U. S. Department of the Interior

A nightly light show set to music illuminates the spillway at Grand Coulee Dam.

Sun Lakes State Park and Dry Falls Interpretive Center

Location: *Seven miles southwest of Coulee City on Highway 17*
Phone: *509-632-5583 and 509-732-5214*
Days/Hours: *Park open daily with overnight camping year-round; interpretive center open 10 a.m. to 6 p.m., Wednesday through Sunday, mid-May to mid-September.*
Wheelchair/Stroller Access: *Yes*

Most popular during the spring, summer and fall, Sun Lakes State Park attracts visitors with its desert-like setting for horseback riding, swimming, trout fishing, and boating. A private park operator manages much of Park Lake; the state operates the campground and swimming beach south and east of here. With a golf course, laundromat, general store and concessions nearby, this is a park for campers who prefer not to rough it.

Youngsters old enough to understand some of Washington's geologic history will want to stop at the new Dry Falls Interpretive

Center on Highway 17, about two miles north of Sun Lakes. Center naturalists give daily talks about mammoth ice sheets which covered this land a million years ago, forcing the Columbia River to carve a new channel. Geologists say when the glaciers began retreating, an ice dam in Montana burst, sending water up to 300 feet deep over Eastern Washington. The center also features a fossilized baby rhinoceros trapped in a pre-Ice Age mudflow.

Northeast Washington

Lakes and rivers in the remote reaches of Washington north and west of Spokane make the counties of Ferry, Stevens and Pend Oreille (pronounced pond-o-ray) a magnet for the outdoors crowd. Towns are small and recreation is big.

For starters, families eager to try winter activities should call the Colville National Forest for details about snowshoeing, snowmobiling and cross-country skiing. Forest Service officials can answer questions about warmer weather camping, horseback riding, fishing, boating and hiking, too.

If you're in the south part of the Pend Oreille County on Highway 20 near Usk, make time to drive through the Kalispel Indian Reservation; it's the smallest in the country. Stop at the reservation office so officials may give you permission to tour the buffalo farm here. It gives youngsters a chance to see one of the last free-roaming herds in North America.

Gardner Cave at Crawford State Park

Location: *North of Metaline, take Highway 31 and turn west on Boundary Road; drive 12 miles*
Phone: *509-456-4169 (Mount Spokane State Park)*
Days/Hours: *10 a.m., noon, 2 p.m. and 4 p.m. tours, Thursday through Monday, May through mid-September.*
Wheelchair/Stroller Access: *No*
Oldtimers say this 1,055-foot-long limestone cave hid moonshine stills at the turn of the century. The bootlegger lost the tunnel to a Metaline storekeeper in a card game, so the story goes, and the merchant turned the land over to the state parks department. Only the cave's upper 494 feet are explorable. Visitors follow steel walkways and stairs designed to keep them from touching the

precious 9,000-year-old stalactites which grow only a half-inch every century. Natural oils in the hand kill further growth on these fascinating hanging formations, so no touching is allowed. While inside, listen carefully for the drip, drip, drip of water falling from the stalactites. The temperature can drop into the low 40s, so wear warm clothing.

Manresa Grotto

Location: *On Kalispel Indian Reservation, off LeClerc Road. Take Newport Highway to Highway 211; follow 17 miles over the railroad tracks, across the bridge and then another six miles north into Kalispel.*
Phone: *509-445-1147*
Days/Hours: *Always open but best viewing is during the day.*
Wheelchair/Stroller Access: *Yes, but it's rough*
Give children a first-hand look at a hillside cave used for religious ceremonies by both the Kalispel Indians and settlers. Visitors can see the stone altar and pews inside, then turn around and look out over the Pend Oreille Valley. Perhaps the best time to visit is the third weekend in September when a priest celebrates mass with the public. For more information about the Kalispel Indians, call the Tribal Center between 7 a.m. and 5 p.m., Monday through Thursday.

Pend Oreille Valley Train Rides

Location: *Leave from Metaline Falls Park off Highway 31*
Phone: *509-442-3397*
Days/Hours: *11 a.m., 1 p.m. and 3 p.m., weekends only, mid-June through mid-October.*
Wheelchair/Stroller Access: *Yes, for wheelchairs; strollers must be left behind and babies must be carried aboard*
Families inhale fresh air and feel the wind in their hair when they ride in any of the three open cars on this rail trip. Others prefer to stay under cover in the caboose or three coach cars. The train winds along the Pend Oreille River and makes a breathtaking stop on the trestle at Box Canyon Dam some 180 feet above the water. Autum trips are especially popular because of the brilliant fall foliage. Reservations almost always are needed about two weeks in advance for these 90-minute trips. Fares are $4 per person; infants younger than 12 months old can be carried aboard for free.

Stonerose Interpretive Center

Location: *In center of Republic, one block west of Main Street on Kean Street*
Phone: *509-775-2295*
Days/Hours: *10 a.m. to 5 p.m., Tuesday through Saturday, May through October; open 10 a.m. to 4 p.m., Sunday, May through mid-September.*
Wheelchair/Stroller Access: *Yes, but it's bumpy*
   Pack along the hammer and chisel because the kids are going fossil hunting. Nearly 50 million years ago during the Eocene Epoch — about 10 million years after the dinosaurs last roamed the earth and the Cascade Mountains were barely hills — impressions of plants, insects and fish were left in the ground at these fossil beds. Today, families come here to hunt for their own fossils after they register at the Stonerose Interpretive Center. A $1 individual or $2 family donation is suggested. Visitors may leave with up to three fossils each if they supply their own hammer and "cold" (non-wooden) chisel for digging.

Helpful Phone Numbers:

   Cashmere, 509-782-3513
   Colville National Forest, 509-684-3711.
   Douglas County, 800-245-3922, ext. 2
   East Wenatchee Chamber of Commerce, 509-884-2514
   Ephrata Chamber of Commerce, 509-754-4656 and 800-345-4656
   Grand Coulee Dam Area Chamber of Commerce, 509-633-3074
   Lake Chelan, 800-4-CHELAN, ext. 201
   Leavenworth, 509-548-5807, ext. 21
   Marblemount Chamber of Commerce, 360-873-2250
   Metaline Falls, 509-446-4415
   Moses Lake Chamber of Commerce, 509-765-7888 and 800-992-6234 (in Washington)
   Newport, 509-447-5812
   Odessa Visitor Information Center, 509-982-0188
   Okanogan National Forest, 509-826-3275
   Okanogan Tourism Council, 800-225-6625 and 509-826-1880
   Omak Visitor Information Center, 800-225-OMAK (6625)
   Republic, 509-775-3216
   Wenatchee Area Visitor and Convention Bureau, 800-554-5512 or 800-57-APPLE

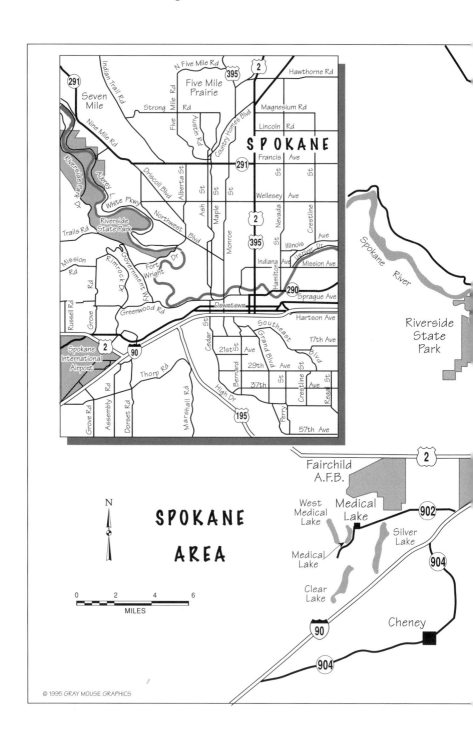

SPOKANE AREA

0   2   4   6
MILES

© 1995 GRAY MOUSE GRAPHICS

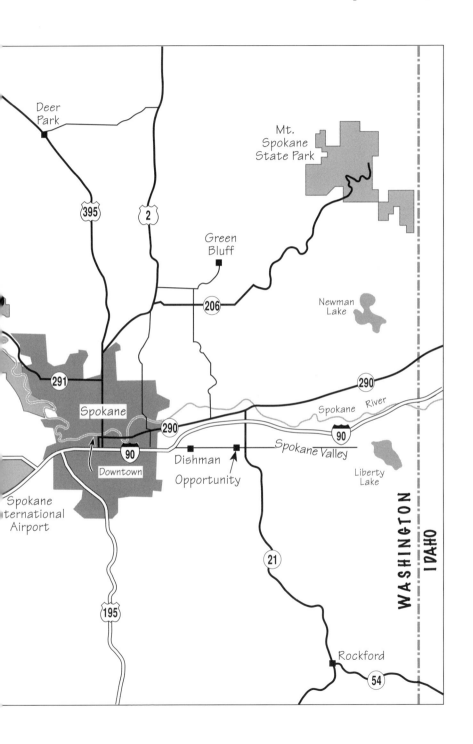

Deer
Park

Mt.
Spokane
State Park

395 2

Green
Bluff

206

Newman
Lake

291

Spokane

290

Spokane River

290

290

90

Dishman

90

Spokane Valley

Downtown

Opportunity

Liberty
Lake

Spokane
ternational
Airport

21

WASHINGTON   IDAHO

195

Rockford

54

The annual "Bloomsday Run" in Spokane's Riverfront Park is commemo-
rated by this sculpture.

Greater Spokane

The appeal of Spokane's warm spring, summer and autumn seasons is one of many reasons this city has become the largest metropolitan area between Seattle and Minneapolis. Even the city's original Native American name — "Spokan" — comes from an Indian tribe who considered themselves "Children of the Sun."

Museums here teach young visitors about the region's tribes and the early fur trappers and traders who arrived around 1807. The earliest white settlers called their town Spokane Falls and watched it become a boomtown when the Northern Pacific Railway brought people west to nearby Northern Idaho for mining.

Spokane has the distinction of being the smallest city ever to host a World's Fair. Riverfront Park, the site of the 1974 international exhibition, offers an island-like feel along the Spokane River. A favorite among children here is riding one of 54 hand-carved horses on the Carrousel designed by Charles Looff. Rides cost $1. The park is especially busy each May when the city hosts its annual Lilac Festival and Bloomsday Run. Hundreds of families line the 12-kilometer race route to cheer on the more than 50,000 runners, walkers and wheelchair racers the first Sunday in May. Later in the month, the Lilac festival's Torchlight Parade shows off Spokane's community spirit and fragrant flowers. Call 509-326-3339 for festival information.

In June, thousands of dribblers ages 7 and older try to "put the brown thing in the round thing" during Hoopfest, the largest 3-on-3 basketball tournament on the West Coast. More than 2,500 teams compete each year on nearly 160 courts throughout the city. Call 509-624-2414 for entry details.

During the city's often frigid and snowy winters, activity indoors heats up. Both ice and roller skating are popular childrens' pastimes here. Consider ice skating at Eagle's Ice-A-Rena, 6321 N. Addison (509-489-9295) or roller skating at Pattison's North Skating Rink, 11505 N. Division (509-466-8133) and Roller Valley Skate Center, E. 9415 Fourth Ave. (509-924-7655).

When it's time to relax, try the new main branch of the Spokane Library at W. 906 Main (509-626-5300). It features volumes of titles for children and young adults. The classic old Garland Theater, W. 924 Garland, is another inexpensive place to kick back with the children for a few hours. This single-screen hall shows newer movies that already have been shown at the multiplex theaters, but entices audiences with 25-cent admission on summer mornings and free refills on buckets of popcorn. Call 509-327-1050.

Great Destinations

Broadview Dairy Museum

Location: *W. 411 Cataldo. Take I-90 Exit 281 to Division Street. Drive north about six blocks, cross the Spokane River, then turn left/ west on North River Drive. The dairy is a few blocks ahead.*
Phone: *509-459-6104*
Days/Hours: *11 a.m. to 4 p.m., Monday, Tuesday, Thursday, Friday and Saturday.*
Wheelchair/Stroller Access: *Yes*

From the cow to the glass, milk travels a long way before a child drinks it. This free 45-minute self-guided tour describes how that cup of calcium gets to the grocery store. The tour details the Broadview Dairy's history, its cows, and a day in the life of a dairy farmer. There's also a seven-minute video showing the route milk follows from cow to bottling, and a viewing room where visitors can watch milk separated, processed and bottled.

Fairchild Air Force Base Heritage Museum

Location: *20 miles west of Spokane off U.S. 2*
Phone: *509-247-2100*
Days/Hours: *10 a.m. to 2 p.m., Monday, Wednesday, Friday and Saturday.*
Wheelchair/Stroller Access: *On ground level only*

Young "Top Gun" wannabes can pull the throttles and flip the switches on a B-52 flight simulator as they imagine pulling aerial stunts high above the clouds. It's just one part of the free, self-guided tour Fairchild Air Force Base offers. Outside, visitors can view nearly 700 planes and exhibits from more than 100 years of military history. There are artifacts from the Civil, Spanish-American and Vietnam wars, World Wars I and II, and Desert Storm. The tour takes about an hour. Enter through Fairchild's Main Gate and show a driver's license and proof of vehicle insurance for admission.

Cheney Cowles Memorial Museum

Location: *W. 2316 First Ave.*
Phone: *509-456-3931*
Days/Hours: *10 a.m. to 5 p.m., Tuesday and Thursday through Saturday; 10 a.m. to 9 p.m., Wednesday; 1 p.m. to 5 p.m., Sunday.*
Wheelchair/Stroller Access: *Yes*
Explore Spokane's history in detail at Cheney Cowles Museum. Permanent exhibits depict the area's original Native American residents, as well as the missionaries and fur traders who arrived nearly a century ago. New displays are introduced each six months in the art gallery. Older children studying state and local history in school are more likely than younger boys and girls to understand the significance here. Admission is $3 for adults, $2 for students and seniors, and free for children 5 years old or younger. Wednesday admission is half price between 10 a.m. and 5 p.m., and free between 5 p.m. and 9 p.m.

Eastern Washington University

Location: *Start at Shoalwater Hall near campus entrance in Cheney, 17 miles west of Spokane*
Phone: *509-359-4878*
Days/Hours: *Afternoons, October through July, by appointment only.*
Wheelchair/Stroller Access: *Yes*
Teens considering an academic future at Eastern Washington University are invited to stroll the campus on a guided tour with an "Eagle ambassador." These EWU students know the university grounds and gear the 90-minute tours for prospective students and their families. There are stops at the university's business school, a lab, a residence hall and "The Fase" — the student athletic facility built by the Seattle Seahawks when they used it as a summer training camp. Prospective students may call ahead to meet with academic advisers. They also may arrange to stay overnight as a guest in a dorm for $11 per night.

Spokane Chiefs Hockey

Location: *N. 1102 Howard at the Coliseum; will be moving to the new Spokane Arena on Mallon Avenue*
Phone: *509-328-0450*
Days/Hours: *Game times vary during September through March season.*
Wheelchair/Stroller Access: *Yes*

Ice hockey is a big sport in this city. The Chiefs play against their cross-state rival, the Seattle Thunderbirds and several other Northwest and Canadian teams in this league. Girls and boys get a kick out of seeing young men, not much older than themselves, skating to a possible spot on an NHL squad.

Spokane Indians

Location: *North 602 Havana at Interstate Fairgrounds. Take I-90 Exit 283-B north*
Phone: *509-535-2922*
Days/Hours: *Game times vary during June through September season.*
Wheelchair/Stroller Access: *Yes*

Families who enjoying watching baseball will find these Class A "Boys of Summer" offer competitive cross-state baseball rivalries with the Everett AquaSox. The closest big league team is hundreds of miles away in Seattle, so hometown fans enthusiastically support their minor league squad. Encourage children to bring a mitt because fans often take home foul balls as souvenirs.

Spokane River Centennial Trail

Location: *East from Opera House at Riverfront Park to the Idaho border; west from Riverfront to Carlson Road near Nine Mile Bridge*
Phone: *509-456-3964*
Days/Hours: *always open.*
Wheelchair/Stroller Access: *Yes*

Stretching for more than 39 miles, the Spokane River Centennial Trail's paved route is a fairly flat place for children to learn in-line skating and bicycling. Hundreds of local parents push strollers here next to walkers, joggers and bicylists who frequent the path. Dedicated in 1989 to celebrate the 100th anniversary of Washington's statehood, the trail leaves Riverfront Park at the Opera House, winding east along the Kardong Burlington Northern Bridge over the Spokane River. It passes Gonzaga University and continues north along the river through Mission Park. The jogging path follows the river bank while the bike route sticks near road shoulders. Benches along the way make it an ideal route for children who need to rest occasionally while skating or bicycling. The trail eventually stretches across the Washington-Idaho border. From Riverfront Park, the trail heads west to Riverside Park.

Places to Eat

Azteca

Location: *200 W. Spokane Falls Blvd.*
Phone: *509-456-0350*
Days/Hours: *11 a.m. to 10:30 p.m., Sunday through Thursday; 11 a.m. to 11:30 p.m., Friday and Saturday.*
Wheelchair/Stroller Access: *Yes*
Sunday is family day at this Mexican chain restaurant because the $2.95 kids' menu items are just 99 cents. These meals come with rice, beans and choice of enchilada, taco or burrito. Crayons and a placemat to color are at the table when you arrive. Many parents appreciate this place because tortilla chips and salsa are promptly delivered to the table, so hungry youngsters are satisfied while waiting for their meal. Highchairs and booster seats are available.

Chuck E. Cheese Pizza Time Theatre

Location: *100 Shadle Center, near Alberta and Wellesley*
Phone: *509-327-6623*
Days/Hours: *11 a.m. to 10 p.m., daily.*
Wheelchair/Stroller Access: *Yes*
If kids age 2 to 7 years old could design a restaurant, it would look a lot like this place. Mechanical musicians perform every few minutes for families waiting for their meal. A salad bar loaded with healthy vegetables provides an alternative to pizza. Long tables with dozens of seats make this a ready-made place for birthday and end-of-the-season sports team parties.

Ichi Shogun

Location: *821 E. Third*
Phone: *509-534-7777*
Days/Hours: *5 p.m. to 10 p.m., daily.*
Wheelchair/Stroller Access: *Yes*
Local families like to introduce their children to international food at this restaurant. Parents may find this a tasty first lesson for children as young as 5 when teaching about Washington state's growing relationship with Pacific Rim countries. Kimono-clad waitresses escort guests to their table where a chef prepares a

chicken, steak or seafood dinner at your table. The entire meal is a performance.

Old Spaghetti Factory

Location: *152 S. Monroe*
Phone: *509-624-8916*
Days/Hours: *5 p.m. to 9:30 p.m., Sunday through Thursday; 5 p.m. to 11 p.m., Friday and Saturday.*
Wheelchair/Stroller Access: *Yes, into the building, but not into the restrooms*

Hard-wood floors and vintage collectibles hanging on the walls make this pasta place feel like a museum — until you get a whiff of the fantastic spaghetti. All adult selections can be ordered in a child's portion for a few dollars less. Be sure to save room for the spumoni ice cream at the meal's end. Tables can't be reserved, but when you arrive ask the host or hostess if you can dine at a table in the train.

The Onion (two locations)

Location: *W. 302 Riverside and N. 7522 Division*
Phone: *509-747-3852 (Riverside) and 509-482-6100 (Division)*
Days/Hours: *11:15 a.m. to 11:30 p.m., daily (Riverside); 11 a.m. to 10 p.m., Sunday through Thursday, 11 a.m. to midnight, Friday and Saturday (Division).*
Wheelchair/Stroller Access: *Yes*

Local families rave about this place because it satisfies a range of appetites. At both locations of The Onion, deep-fried onion rings come in sizes large enough to wear as bracelets. An order of chocolate cake is a slab, not a mere slice. Be sure to squeeze in one of the specialty hamburgers before dessert. Items on the children's menu range from $2 to $4 and include fish sticks, chicken, hot dogs, hamburgers and peanut butter and jelly sandwiches. Highchairs and booster seats are available.

Places to Shop

White Elephant (two locations)

Location: *N. 1730 Division and E. 12614 Sprague*
Phone: *509-328-3100 (Division) and 509-924-3006 (Sprague)*
Days/Hours: *9 a.m. to 6 p.m., Monday through Thursday and Saturday; 9 a.m. to 9 p.m., Friday.*
Wheelchair/Stroller Access: *Yes*

Youngsters spot these stores from a distance by the huge white elephant on their signs. By the discount prices, you can tell these toys are used, but many children who shop here will tell you things look new to them. A super-discount room features inexpensive playthings and a separate sporting goods area sells fishing poles and other athletic equipment. Sales are cash only. It's hard to say "no" to children who beg to hop on the "baby elephant" mechanical ride; it only costs a dime.

Places to Play

Audubon Park

Location: *In Northwest Spokane at W. 3000 Audubon*
Phone: *509-625-6200*
Days/Hours: *Dawn to dusk, daily, year-round.*
Wheelchair/Stroller Access: *Yes*

When Spokane park-goers think shade, they come here. Mature trees in this spacious park are a respite from the summer sun. Most children prefer to cool off in the wading pool. Play equipment, baseball fields and tennis courts provide a wide range for outdoor activities for all ages.

Bumpers Fun Centers (three locations)

Location: *4750 N. Division at NorthTown Mall; Corner of Sprague and University streets at U-City Mall; Riverfront Park*
Phone: *509-489-4000 (NorthTown); 509-928-8445 (U-City Mall); 509-624-6678 (Riverfront)*
Days/Hours: *9 a.m. to 9 p.m., Monday through Saturday; 9 a.m. to 6 p.m., Sunday (NorthTown); 10 a.m. to 9 p.m., Monday through Friday; 10 a.m. to 7 p.m., Saturday and 11 a.m. to 5 p.m. Sunday (U-City Mall); 11 a.m. to 9 p.m., Monday through Thursday; 11 a.m. to 10 p.m., Friday; 10 a.m. to 10 p.m. Saturday; 10 a.m. to 9 p.m. Sunday, Memorial Day through Labor Day; shorter park hours the rest of the year (Riverfront).*
Wheelchair/Stroller Access: *Yes*

Amusement park officials say pre-teens especially seem to like the modern spin on this medieval-style indoor forest. Fountains and greenery give the room an outdoorsy feel, plus it's filled with 18 holes of miniature golf. The Castle room is a party center with arcade and virtual reality video games, pizza, soft drinks, and a cake for birthday guests. Arrange party details in advance. There's no admission charge, but it costs $4.25 to play golf; children 6 years old or younger play for free.

Comstock Park

Location: *In Southwest Spokane at W. 800 29th*
Phone: *509-625-6200*
Days/Hours: *Dawn to dusk, daily, year-round.*
Wheelchair/Stroller Access: *Yes*

Local families consider Comstock one of their favorite warm weather parks. It offers swimming and wading pools in the summer, a year-round playground, groomed baseball diamonds, tennis courts, and dozens of picnic tables.

Discovery Zone

Location: *1445 N. Argonne*
Phone: *509-924-0023*
Days/Hours: *11 a.m. to 9 p.m., Monday; 9 a.m. to 9 p.m., Tuesday through Saturday; 11 a.m. to 7 p.m., Sunday.*
Wheelchair/Stroller Access: *Yes*

When wet weather sets in and outdoor playgrounds look unappealing, children flock here. Boys and girls 18 months to 12 years old wade through a sea of bright red, yellow and blue balls as part of the obstacle course at this exercise center. Separate areas for toddlers keep them from being trampled by older kids who have their own sets of crawling tubes, climbing ropes, padded walls to mount, and slides to descend. Parents may join in or watch through windows in a separate, slightly quieter room. Admission is $5.50. Birthday party packages are available.

Manito Park

Location: *In Southeast Spokane at S. 1900 Grand*
Phone: *509-625-6200*
Days/Hours: *Dawn to dusk, daily, year-round.*
Wheelchair/Stroller Access: *In most places*

With the half-dozen different gardens here, spacious Manito feels like several parks in one. The rose garden and Japanese garden are among the most fragrant and children love running here. In the winter, the park's big hill is a popular sledding destination. Make new feathered friends at the Duck Pond by bringing crackers or bread to share.

Mount Spokane State Park

Location: *30 miles northeast of Spokane. Drive north on U.S. 2. At Highway 206 turn east and drive another 16 miles*
Phone: *509-456-4169*
Days/Hours: *Overnight camping accommodations June through September; dawn to dusk for day-use the rest of the year.*
Wheelchair/Stroller Access: *In some places*

Families who ski appreciate Mount Spokane's five chairlifts, which carry downhill skiers to the tops of 32 runs ranging from beginner to expert-level. South and east of the downhill area are 25 kilometers of groomed cross-country ski trails and several miles of groomed snowmobile routes. Equipment for any of these sports can be rented nearby. During the summer, 50 miles of park trails are shared by horseback riders and hikers.

Riverfront Park

Location: *507 N. Howard St. Take I-90 Exit 280A or 280B north to Spokane Falls Boulevard*
Phone: *509-625-6600 and 509-456-4FUN (recording)*
Days/Hours: *Open year-round but hours vary with five seasons and different venues.*
Wheelchair/Stroller Access: *Yes*

Some places in Riverfront Park seem bigger than life to a child. The gigantic IMAX Theatre features movies, typically with a nature theme, on a screen five stories tall with a six-channel sound system. The soaring Gondola Skyride carries riders high over the mist of the Spokane River's bubbling white waterfalls. Even the slide next to the Louff Carrousel is designed like a child's oversized wagon — and kids ride down the handle!

Besides the carnival rides and attractions remaining from the 1974 World's Fair, Riverfront Park has pockets of quiet space, too. Ducks are waiting to be fed on steps next to the Spokane River. A concrete terrace with benches near the gondola ride offers respite next to the waterfalls.

Creative boys and girls design their own adventures here. Near the sculpture of 20 Bloomsday racers, children imagine themselves as leaders of the pack. In the winter, skaters fly across the ice at Riverfront Park Ice Palace as if they were Olympic medalists. Even rolling down the grassy hills of this park becomes an adventure for a toddler. Call ahead to find out when the Spokane Symphony performs one of its free outdoor summer concerts. The final overture features a fireworks display. At some concerts, musicians perform on an anchored stage floating in the river. These are favorites for families on a tight budget. Park admission is free, but charges can range from about $1 to nearly $11 for single-ride or single-day passes on the carnival rides and other attractions.

Riverside State Park

Location: *Six miles northwest of Spokane. One access is possible from I-90 Exit 281 to Highway 2/Division Street. Follow to Highway 291/Francis Avenue and turn west. Drive to Nine Mile Road, then go another a mile and turn southwest on Rifle Club Road; drive another half mile and turn south on A. L. White Parkway. The park is about two miles away.*
Phone: *509-456-3964*
Days/Hours: *Year-round overnight camping accommodations at Bowl and Pitcher area; dawn to dusk in the rest of the park.*
Wheelchair/Stroller Access: *No*

Native American and white fur traders met near this spot almost two centuries ago to conduct their business. Today, Riverside Park attracts families coming to hike on the trails, ride horseback, or stake out one of the 101 campsites. Don't let the river's Bowl and Pitcher area fool you. Its name sounds like a fun place to play in the water, but the undercurrent is deceptively strong. Views of the basalt gorge are fantastic here, but posted signs prohibit swimming. Even the most skilled kayakers find the nearby rapids treacherous.

Play it safe and drive the family to the park's Spokane House Interpretive Center instead. A diorama tells the story of the 1810 fur trading post where business peaked in 1819 when competition drove the traders to Kettle Falls. Displays from local archaeological digs detail life before the white settlers arrived. To the east of the center, off Rutter Parkway, look for Indian Painted Rocks. Encourage children to figure out the meaning of these colored traces of petroglyphs. They can't get it wrong because the meaning is uncertain. Some think the drawings tallied successful hunting expeditions. Others are convinced they describe an important tribal meeting or a series of religious experiences.

Wonderland Golf & Games

Location: *N. 10515 Division. From I-90 take exit to Division Street/ Highway 2; drive seven miles.*
Phone: *509-468-4386*
Days/Hours: *9:30 a.m. to midnight, daily, Memorial Day through Labor Day; 10 a.m. to 11 p.m., the rest of the year.*
Wheelchair/Stroller Access: *Yes, at the outdoor miniature golf; not inside*

With indoor and outdoor activities for children 2 to 18 years old, this place is popular in any kind of weather. Castles, shipwrecks and mysterious old mansions line the lighted miniature golf courses outside. Inside, there's another mini-golf course, plus softball and baseball batting cages and nearly 80 video games best suited for pre-teens and youths. There's also the Rock-a-Fire Explosion Pizza Theatre especially appealing for boys and girls 2 to 7 years old. It features animated, mechanical animals performing toe-tapping tunes while diners munch pizza.

Helpful Phone Numbers:

City of Spokane Parks and Recreation Department, 509-625-6200

Spokane Visitor Information Center, 800-248-3230 and 509-747-3230

The Ellensburg Rodeo is considered one of the top competitions in the world.

Southeast and South Central Washington

Southeast Washington

Before it surges into the deep gorge that separates Washington and Oregon, the Columbia River rolls through a triangle on the map known as the Tri-Cities — Kennewick, Pasco, and Richland. Since the sun shines nearly 300 days each year here, families spend a lot of time outdoors.

Richland, a leader in nuclear energy production and waste disposal, celebrates its warm climate with Sunfest each June at Howard Amon Park along the Columbia River. Part of this event includes the Tri-Cities Children's Festival featuring children's music, clowns, puppets and art activities. Call 509-946-3131 for a schedule.

At the convergence of the Columbia and Snake rivers is Pasco, where explorers Meriwether Lewis and William Clark pitched camp in 1805 during their famed trek. Students may pore over exhibits here in the Franklin County Historical Museum. Displays depict the region's Native American, pioneer, and railroad history. The musuem is open from 1 p.m. to 5 p.m., Wednesday through Sunday. For more information call 509-547-3714.

In neighboring Kennewick — which means "winter haven" in the Chemanpum Indian language — the East Benton County Historical Museum details the area's pioneer history after the Lewis and Clark Expedition. The museum is open noon to 4 p.m., Tuesday through Saturday. Call 509-582-7704 for more details.

About 50 miles east of the Tri-Cities on U.S. 12 is a city that is, as they say, so nice they named it twice. Walla Walla actually earned its name from the Native American words meaning "many waters." Visitors will see fields of Walla Walla sweet onions, but don't cry if you miss the Sweet Onion Harvest Fest here in July. Just catch it next year, since it's an annual event with parades, entertainment and lots of food — with and without onions. Local farms don't offer tours because harvest season is busy and workers rush to get the onions to grocery stores across the country.

About 60 miles northeast of Walla Walla via U.S. 12 are the Blue Mountains, where skiers enjoy 23 major runs on some of the driest snow in the state. There are gradual slopes for children learning to ski and challenging terrain for more experienced downhillers. Another 35 miles of trails are groomed during the winter for cross-country skiers. Call 509-382-4725.

The Blue Mountains and Umatilla National Forest are jam-packed with hiking, camping and fishing choices in or along the Snake, Touchet and Tucannon rivers. As it weaves along the Washington-Idaho border, the Snake is considered river rafting heaven by some. Others know it as Hell's Canyon.

Jet boats cut through the Snake for day trips and overnight adventures in the 5,500-foot-deep canyon's waters, the North American continent's deepest river gorge. Most day trips are 10 hours long and involve sitting for several hours, so it's not recommended for children under 5 years old. Call the Clarkston or Asotin County chambers of commerce for recommended boating outfitters and tours.

On shore, along the 16-mile Clearwater and Snake River National Recreation Trail, take children on a geologic field trip. The trail connects the route's parks, historic sites and natural attractions along a wheelchair and stroller accessible path. It's lined by sculpted volcanic peaks and terraced basalt cliffs which are home to elk, deer, big horn sheep, hawks, eagles and Native American petroglyphs.

The largest city in this fertile wheat land known as the Palouse, is Pullman, north of Clarkston via U.S. 195 to Highway 270. Pullman is home to Washington State University, the state's second largest college. Away from campus, catch a magnificent view of the surrounding countryside at Kamiak Butte, 10 miles north on Highway 27 or Steptoe Butte, 25 miles north via U.S. 195. Or try a day jet-boating or whitewater rafting on "the River of No Return," the Salmon River. Call the Pullman Chamber of Commerce for an outfitters list.

Tri-Cities

Hanford Museum of Science and History

Location: *825 Jadwin Ave. Take Highway 240 exit north off Interstate 182 to George Washington Way; follow George Washington Way to Lee Boulevard and turn west.*
Phone: *509-376-5252*
Days/Hours: *8 a.m. to 5 p.m., Monday through Friday; 9 a.m. to 5 p.m., Saturday.*
Wheelchair/Stroller Access: *Yes*

Protons, neutrons and atoms may be over the heads of young children, but exhibits at this recently remodeled museum — formerly the Hanford Science Center — are educational for teens. New displays depicting nuclear waste tank innovations and cleanup technology show the next phase of nuclear development. Young people with an interest in engineering are particularly fascinated by this museum.

The historical section exhibits describe and illustrate Native American roots and white settlers' roles at Hanford. Most of these displays are pictorials so children don't need to be readers to understand. Boys and girls old enough to read may test their wits on computerized general science quizzes. Use your finger to select correct answers on touch-screen monitors. Operation of the museum may soon change hands, but currently admission is free.

Ice Harbor Dam and Locks

Location: *On Snake River and Lake Sacajawea. From Pasco, take U.S. 12 across the Snake River Bridge about 10 miles; turn onto Highway 124.*
Phone: *509-547-7781*
Days/Hours: *Dam open year-round; visitors center open 9 a.m. to 5 p.m., daily, April through September.*
Wheelchair/Stroller Access: *In some places*

Ice Harbor Dam, which retains the Snake River to form Lake Sacajawea, houses one of the largest navigational locks in the world. A brief video about the dam's history gives school-age children a brief lesson in hydroelectric power during one-hour self-guided tours. Browse inside the powerhouse and watch fish jump up the ladder. During the day visitors may drive their vehicle on the road atop the dam. Near the dam there's a small Native American petroglyph with a marker signifying the tribal grounds buried by Lake Sacajawea when the dam was built in the late 1950s.

The Longest Drive/Shortest Putt

Location: *In Kennewick at 6311 W. Clearwater Ave. Take Badger Road exit off I-82. Follow to 10th Avenue. Turn north on Columbia Center Boulevard then drive east on West Clearwater Avenue.*
Phone: *509-735-6072*
Days/Hours: *10 a.m. to 10 p.m., daily.*
Wheelchair/Stroller Access: *Yes, on the miniature golf course*
For the power golfer practicing a swing, there's a driving range with covered, lighted, and heated practice tees here. Nearby, little putters may practice their own swing on a miniature golf course. The Tri-Cities has more than a dozen golf courses, so this place teems with those eager to sharpen their skills. By offering a variety of golf activities, this facility tries to appeal to all golfers in the family.

Northwoods Restaurant & Storyland Golf

Location: *In Prosser, at Exit 80 off I-82, 20 miles west of Richland*
Phone: *509-786-6900*
Days/Hours: *5 a.m. to 11 p.m, daily, year-round at the restaurant; 10 a.m. to 11 p.m., daily, April through Labor Day; hours and days vary the rest of the year at the mini golf course, so call ahead.*
Wheelchair/Stroller Access: *It's tough on the gravel paths*
It's not Jurassic Park. It just looks that way at first. The 30-foot tall dinosaur statue at Storyland Golf greets visitors to this 18-hole miniature golf course in Prosser. All the features adorning this course are handmade, including the green giant and castle. Course owners operate a new family restauraunt here, too. Children's menus are available for breakfast, lunch and dinner. All kids' meals are less than $5. Highchairs and booster seats are available.

Oasis Waterworks

Location: *In Kennewick at 6321 West Canal*
Phone: *509-735-8442*
Days/Hours: *10 a.m. to 6:30 p.m., Sunday through Thursday, and 10 a.m. to 9:30, Friday and Saturday, Memorial Day through Labor Day.*
Wheelchair/Stroller Access: *Yes, for observation only*
Eleven outdoor water slides with loops galore keep children and adults cool on hot summer days at this water park extravaganza. Splash in the 5,000-square-foot swimming pool or play basketball

or volleyball on the outdoor courts. Officials plan to add two kiddie slides for the younger set. Meanwhile, this facility is best suited for swimmers, typically children 4 years or older. Adults are welcome, but are not required to get in the water. Admission is free to those younger than 4 and older than 55. Everyone else pays $12.40 for an all-day session or $9.25 for a half day after 2:30 p.m.

Red Robin Burger & Spirits Emporium

Location: *In Richland at 924 George Washington Way. In Kennewick at 1021 Columbia Center Blvd.*
Phone: *509-943-8484 (Richland), 509-736-6008 (Kennewick)*
Days/Hours: *11 a.m. to 10 p.m., Sunday through Thursday; 11 a.m. to midnight, Friday and Saturday (both restaurants).*
Wheelchair/Stroller Accessible: *Yes*

These eateries are two links in one of the region's favorite hamburger restaurant chain. Local families come here because there are more than a dozen hamburger selections. Some burgers are so large it's hard to get your mouth around the bun for a bite! Some diners come just for the sweet non-alcoholic fruit and ice cream "mocktail" drinks. Consider the heaping order of onion rings or potato skins from the appetizer menu if you're only coming for a snack. Highchairs and booster seats are available for little ones.

Sacajawea State Park

Location: *Four miles southeast of Pasco on U.S. 12, turn southwest on Tank Farm Road. In one mile, at the y-intersection, follow road east for another mile to park.*
Phone: *509-545-2361*
Days/Hours: *Dawn to dusk, daily, year-round.*
Wheelchair/Stroller Access: *Yes*

One of the state's leading recreation and education parks, this day-use facility features swimming, waterskiing, fishing, boating, and the Sacajawea Interpretive Center. The park is named after the adventurous Shoshoni woman who helped guide explorers Lewis and Clark through this region. This is an encouraging place for young people to see how women helped shape the West.

One room in the interpretive center features videos about the expedition; another room displays tools, bowls, and other items used by local Native Americans. Outside, a swimming beach on the Columbia River and nearby children's play equipment draw families during warmer months.

Three Rivers Children's Museum

Location: *In Kennewick at 873 Columbia Center Blvd. Take Columbia Drive exit off I-182. Turn south on Columbia Center Boulevard.*
Phone: *509-783-6311*
Days/Hours: *10 a.m. to 5 p.m., Tuesday through Saturday; noon to 5 p.m., Sunday.*
Wheelchair/Stroller Access: *Yes*
Children have been pouring into this museum ever since a group of parents opened it for their own kids in 1991. Junior scientists can hatch chicks from eggs, and butterflies from cocoons, but exhibits change every eight months. Climbing ramps and blocks for little hands are set aside for toddlers. Art activities are typically scheduled on Saturday mornings. Admission is $2 per person; those younger than 1 year-old are admitted free. Ask about reserving the museum for private parties on Mondays.

Tri-City Americans Hockey

Location: *In Kennewick at the Tri-Cities Coliseum, 7100 W. Quinault*
Phone: *509-736-0606*
Days/Hours: *September through March; 36 home game times vary.*
Wheelchair/Stroller Access: *Yes*
Older teens with their eyes and hopes on making the National Hockey League compete on this exciting Western Hockey League team. Locals support this squad because it's the closest thing to a professional sports team in the area. Young fans enjoy watching youths close to their age in a fast-action sport.

Walla Walla

Fort Walla Walla Museum

Location: *In Fort Walla Walla Park at 755 Myra Rd., on the west side of Walla Walla near College Place*
Phone: *509-525-7703*
Days/Hours: *10 a.m. to 5 p.m., daily, April through September; 10 a.m. to 5 p.m., weekends only the rest of the year.*
Wheelchair/Stroller Access: *Yes, for strollers; wheelchair riders may call ahead for accessible golf-cart transportation, otherwise access is difficult*
Children learn how tough it was for early Northwest settlers to pack all their belongings into a covered wagon when they try to

pack a doll house-sized wagon with miniature versions of pioneer necessities. It's part of an Oregon Trail exhibit at this museum tucked into the city park. Decades of regional history are featured here. Boys and girls pretend they're pioneers while inside the log cabins and the 1867 schoolhouse at this small re-created village. During special events, pioneer crafters and tradespeople are busy blacksmithing and baking. Call ahead for event dates. In larger buildings nearby, historical displays tell stories about the Marcus and Narcissa Whitman missionary party (see Whitman Mission listing), local Native Americans, and early farming in the region. Admission is $2.50 for adults, $1 for students age 6 to 12, and free for children 5 or younger. In pre-arranged groups of 15 or more, adults pay $1.50.

Ice-burg Drive-In

Location: *616 W. Birch St., at corner of West Birch and Ninth*
Phone: *509-529-1793*
Days/Hours: *11 a.m. to 10:30 p.m., Monday through Thursday; 11 a.m. to 11 p.m., Friday and Saturday; 11:30 a.m. to 10:30 p.m. Sunday.*
Wheelchair/Stroller Access: *Not needed; it's a drive-up*

Some of Washington's best seasonal fruits are mixed into the dandy milkshakes served here. Fresh strawberries, cherries and blackberries flavor these concoctions during the summer and fall. During other times of the year, ask for fresh bananas or pineapple. Order a milkshake by itself or with a grilled hamburger. Locals consider these burgers the best in the Northwest.

Whitman Mission

Location: *Seven miles west of Walla Walla off U.S. 12*
Phone: *509-522-6360*
Days/Hours: *Daylight hours.*
Wheelchair/Stroller Access: *No*

One of the earliest settlements on the Oregon Trail, this spot is now a memorial to the Native Americans and missionary settlers who lost their lives here. Religious teachers Marcus and Narcissa Whitman came West in 1836 to teach Christianity to tribal members, but half the Cayuse tribe later died from a measles epidemic carried by the settlers. The tribe blamed the missionaries and launched an attack in 1847, killing 13. It's a powerful lesson for children about understanding and respecting others' cultures and beliefs. If you have time, hike up to the monument on the hill and watch the sunset.

246 ♦ Discover Washington and Seattle with Kids

Clarkston and Pullman

Chief Timothy State Park

Location: *Eight miles west of Clarkston, turn north from Highway 12 onto Silcott Road; cross the brdge onto the island in Lower Granite Lake*
Phone: *509-758-9580*
Days/Hours: *Overnight camping year-round; Alpowai Interpretive Center open 1 p.m. to 5 p.m., Wednesday through Sunday, June through August.*
Wheelchair/Stroller Access: *Yes*

A graduated sandy beach on Lower Granite Lake/Snake River behind Lower Granite Dam provides a safe place for wading and swimming. Trees shade picnic tables near the children's play area. During the summer, visit the Alpowai Interpretive Center near the park entrance. Inside the center's stone building, you'll learn about the Nez Perce Indians who lived here. Artifacts recovered from archaeological digs before the dam's waters flooded this area are displayed, as well.

Ferdinand's

Location: *In Food Quality Building on WSU Campus on South Fairway*
Phone: *509-335-4014*
Days/Hours: *9:30 a.m. to 4:30 p.m., Monday through Friday.*
Wheelchair/Stroller Access: *Yes*

Melt-in-your mouth ice cream, milk shakes, and made-on-the-spot Cougar Gold cheese is sold here, direct from WSU's own dairy. Step up into the observation room so you can watch workers making the cheese; a video describes the process. Cheese made here is so popular, a separate mail order business ships blocks of it througout the country.

Palouse Falls/Lyons Ferry State Park

Location: *West of Pullman and north of Walla Walla, just off Highway 261, eight miles northwest of Starbuck, is Lyons Ferry State Park. Palouse Falls is six miles north of Lyons Ferry on Palouse Falls Road.*
Phone: *509-549-3551 and 509-646-3252*
Days/Hours: *Overnight camping April through September; day-use*

only the rest of the year at Palouse Falls; closed at Lyons Ferry.
Wheelchair/Stroller Access: *No*
"Somewhere over the rainbow" just may be Palouse Falls. The 198-foot Palouse River waterfall rushes to the Snake River through hardened lava flows. The mist rising from the drop creates a colorful aura. Columns of basalt layer the hillside. Only older children who can handle the steep hike and are accompanied by an adult should make the trail's descent. Ask a ranger about the preferred route.
Nearby is Lyons Ferry State Park where families mix outdoor recreation with an anthropology lesson. Camp overnight at any of the 52 sites on the west side of Highway 261. The park's waterfront activities are on the highway's east side. This is where you'll find the old open-deck Lyons Ferry, used for river crossings more than 30 years ago. The ferry is now tied to shore and used as a fishing dock. Nearby, a roped-off swimming beach is protected by a stone breakwater. Waterskiers venture beyond the breakwater farther into the Palouse River.
A dirt road north of the breakwater takes hikers to a gently-sloping one-mile gravel trail leading to an overlook. Signs at the overlook describe the nearby Native American burial site and the discovery of prehistoric human bones known as "Marmes Man." The remains are thought to be 10,000 years old.

Washington State University

Location: *In Pullman, tours start at French Administration Building, Room 442*
Phone: *509-335-3581*
Days/Hours: *1 p.m., Monday through Friday, when school is open.*
Wheelchair/Stroller Access: *Yes*
Cougar alumni are proud to show their offspring their old college stomping grounds, provided everyone is prepared to climb the campus hills. Children love to see where Mom and Dad studied, and hear stories about where their parents played in college. Free one-hour guided campus tours are available with stops inside the Conner Museum's collection of birds and mammals (it's the largest in the Pacific Northwest), the WSU Museum of Art, and the Jacklin Collection at the Webster Physical Sciences Building. The Webster building holds one of the world's largest petrified wood collections. Weekdays, swing by Ferdinand's creamery for a treat.

South Central Washington

Children visiting the Columbia River Gorge may need to pinch themselves to make sure they're not dreaming. In Skamania and Klickitat counties, boys and girls may think that they've returned to the 1800s — when Indians created petroglyphs near Horsethief Lake. Perhaps their imaginations will take them across a continent to England's Salisbury Plain when they stroll by a replica of Stonehenge near Maryhill. Or they may even fantasize that they're charting comets with famed English astronomer Edmund Halley at the Goldendale Observatory.

East of Vancouver along the Columbia River, travelers on Highway 14's winding two-lane road will find a variety of stops. From Stevenson to Goldendale, this is a narrow but spectacular route through the 70-mile long gorge. Encourage children to point out the more than 70 waterfalls which pour into the river along this stretch from the Washington and Oregon sides of the Columbia.

Seventy miles north of Goldendale along U.S. 97, colorful places with exotic names just roll off the tongue. Toppenish, Zillah, Wapato, Naches, Selah — these exotic-sounding places are part of the Yakima Valley, south of Ellensburg on Interstate 82.

Yakima Valley visitors will be impressed by the rich ethnic blend of Hispanic, Native American, and white residents in the region. Each group marks its heritage in the area with annual events and historic destinations.

An emerging Hispanic population in Yakima, the valley's largest city, prompted local merchants to create the Hispanic Chamber of Commerce of Greater Yakima. This chamber sponsors the Cinco de Mayo Annual Heritage Dinner each May 5, and the mid-September "Fiestas Patrias" Celebration.

In downtown Yakima, families may board the Yakima Interurban Trolley Lines for a historic roundtrip ride along city streets, past valley orchards, and across the Naches River to the Selah Civic Center. Older children receive an entertaining history lesson, and little ones get a kick out of riding in a trolley.

These rides are different from the downtown trolleys which run along Yakima Avenue and North First Street. Three commuter trolleys leave the Convention Center every 20 minutes, between 7:20 a.m. and 6:40 p.m., Monday through Saturday. When you return by either type of trolley to downtown Yakima, stop at Heritage Square. Show children how the boardwalk shops are built out of restored trains.

For Native American history, visit the Yakama Indian Nation Cultural Center in Toppenish off U.S. 97 or nearby Fort Simcoe State Park and its interpretive center. In downtown Toppenish, children like to play against the backdrop of more than 30 colorful murals painted on buildings as part of the state's 1989 centennial celebration. Maps are available at the Mural Society Office, 11A S. Toppenish Ave., between 10 a.m. and 5 p.m. daily.

In the middle of Washington state is Kittitas County. Mountainous Snoqualmie Pass borders its west side; dry hills along the Columbia River border the east. That means Kittitas County's mixed terrain offers diverse outdoor activities for families. Waterskiing and horseback riding are among the most popular. Call the Ellensburg Chamber of Commerce for a list of horseback riding companies and dude ranches.

Ellensburg is the largest city in Kittitas County. It's 36 miles north of Yakima via I-82. From Seattle, it's a two-hour drive east via Interstate 90; from Spokane, Ellensburg is a 175-mile drive west on the same freeway.

Skamania and Klickitat Counties

Baker's Dozen-n-More

Location: *In Stevenson, Skamania County, at 310 S.W. Second St.*
Phone: *509-427-7808*
Days/Hours: *6 a.m. to 6 p.m., Tuesday through Sunday.*
Wheelchair/Stroller Access: *Yes*

Some around these parts doubt the existence of the creature known as "Bigfoot," but most boys and girls love to hear tales about the reclusive furry monster who lurks in the mountains. Families who have eaten at this "home of the Bigfoot cookie" like to believe that the bakery uses a real Sasquatch's huge pawprint as the mold for mouth-watering sugar cookies. There's a variety of other baked goods available, as well.

Columbia Gorge Interpretive Center

Location: *990 S.E. Rock Creek Road, off Highway 14 in Stevenson*
Phone: *509-427-8210*
Days/Hours: *10 a.m. to 7 p.m., daily during the summer;*
10 a.m. to 5 p.m., daily during the winter (season dates vary).
Wheelchair/Stroller Access: *Yes*

At one of the newest historic museums in the state, boys and girls discover geology and wildlife through centuries-old artifacts and high-tech wizardry. They're all part of this $10.5 million center that features displays about Native Americans, white pioneers, fishing, forestry, and the river which shaped the Columbia Gorge. One favorite among children is the nine-projector slide show with powerful sounds dramatizing the floods, lava flows, and other geologic forces which carved the gorge. Other children flock to the Indian fishing platform replica next to a working indoor waterfall. Curators say youngsters 10 or older learn the most from this center. Admission is $5 for adults, $4 for students 13 or older, $3 for children 6 to 12, and free to those younger than 5.

Columbia Gorge Outfitters

Location: *Next to Skamania Lodge, off Highway 14, near Bridge of the Gods*
Phone: *509-427-2549*
Days/Hours: *Five rides daily, 10 a.m. to 5 p.m., mid-March through October.*
Wheelchair/Stroller Access: *No*

Saddle up family members 6 or older for a one- or two-hour guided horseback ride into the hills over the Columbia River. An outfitter leads groups along safe old logging roads where riders can spy wildlife along the route. Mount the horses in the corral next to Skamania Lodge. Reservations are recommended. Rates are about $20 per hour.

Goldendale Observatory State Park and Interpretive Center

Location: *1602 Observatory Dr. In Goldendale, on Highway 142, turn north on North Columbus Avenue at the light. Drive one mile to the y-intersection, then follow the road up the hill for another mile.*
Phone: *509-773-3141*
Days/Hours: *Park open 2 p.m. to 5 p.m. and 8 p.m. to midnight, Wednesday through Sunday, April through September; 1 p.m. to 5 p.m. and 7 p.m. to 9 p.m., Saturday, and 1 p.m. to 5 p.m , Sunday, October through March.*
Wheelchair/Stroller Access: *No*

Even those who missed astronomy class in school will be drawn to this powerful 24-inch reflecting Cassegrain telescope, the largest of its type accessible to the public in the United States Stargazers of all ages will enjoy the entertaining and educational presentations here, which are geared so most children older than four understand them. Tour groups of as many as 49 people watch slide shows and videos and see exhibits about telescopes and astronomy before viewing the heavens through this telescope. The telescope rests in Goldendale because it's far from the lights, air pollution, and cloudy skies of the bigger cities. Overnight use of the telescope is allowed by reservation only. Experts say stargazing is best when there's a new moon. If you come at night, dress warmly because the dome ceiling is open.

Horsethief Lake State Park

Location: *Two miles east of Highway 97 on Highway 14, about 33 miles west of Goldendale*
Phone: *509-767-1159*
Days/Hours: *Overnight camping accommodations April through September; closed the rest of the year.*
Wheelchair/Stroller Access: *No*

Encourage children to study the petroglyphs left by the coastal and interior Native American tribes who gathered here centuries ago to trade and socialize. They're on the rock walls next to the trail west of the south parking lot at this 12-campsite park. In the early 1800s, when explorers Meriweather Lewis and William Clark passed through here, it was almost like a shopping center for Indians. Today, anglers come to drop their lines for trout.

Ice Caves at Gifford Pinchot National Forest

Location: *Almost six miles west of Trout Lake on Forest Road 24*
Phone: *509-395-2501*
Days/Hours: *Always open.*
Wheelchair/Stroller Access: *No*

This maze of icy stalactites dripping from the ceiling and stalagmites growing from the Mount Adams Ice Cave floor is an eerie but exciting sight for most children eight or older who are strong climbers. The ice cave is in the Mount Adams Ranger District at the south end of the forest. It's cold and dark, so come armed with a flashlight, sturdy climbing shoes and a warm jacket.

Ladder steps in the cave's upper area descend to an underground level which is slick and sometimes narrow. The cave was formed by basalt flows from an ancient volcano. Tours are not guided, so it's best to stop first at the Trout Lake ranger station for information sheets and a map.

Maryhill Museum

Location: *35 Maryhill Museum Dr., off Highway 14, just west of Goldendale*
Phone: *509-773-3733*
Days/Hours: *9 a.m. to 5 p.m., daily, mid-March through mid-November.*
Wheelchair/Stroller Access: *Yes*

Rare and, in some cases, priceless art work collected throughout the world is displayed at this museum, which is best suited for families with young teens or those who understand fine art. Maryhill Museum is many miles from any metropolitan art center because founder Sam Hill originally intended this turn-of-the-century home to become the centerpiece of a new 7,000-acre Quaker agricultural community. But not even Hill's wife followed him here, so the wealthy businessman turned it into an art museum. After his death, Hill's friends continued collecting art for display. Today, you'll find French sculptures by Auguste Rodin and the gown Queen Marie of Roumania (now Romania) wore to the coronation of Tsar Nicholas II. Some children say the chess set collection is their favorite exhibit here. It features more than 100 antique sets from around the world.

Younger children may prefer to visit three miles east where there's a replica of Stonehenge. This columned structure is in much better condition than the original. Hill had it created to honor Klickitat County soldiers who lost their lives in World War I. Hill died in in 1931 and is buried in a crypt close by.

Maryhill State Park

Location: *12 miles south of Goldendale on Highway 97*
Phone: *509-773-5007*
Days/Hours: *Overnight camping accommodations year-round.*
Wheelchair/Stroller Access: *Yes*

Three miles east of the Maryhill Museum, families may watch skilled and wily windsurfers catch a breeze and sail across the Columbia River on their sailboards. This can be a treacherous sport, and not an activity suited for children younger than 10. Even older children are encouraged to try windsurfing on calmer waters the first few times. Two stone breakwaters creature a sheltered swimming area with a gravel beach. Nearby, there are 50 campsites.

Yakima Valley

Deli de Pasta

Location: *In Yakima at 7 North Front St.*
Phone: *509-453-0571*
Days/Hours: *11:30 a.m. to 8:30 p.m., Monday through Thursday; 11:30 a.m. to 9:30 p.m., Friday and Saturday.*
Wheelchair/Stroller Access: *Yes*
Locals voted this Italian eatery their favorite restaurant in 1993. Diners can create their own dish by scanning the list of homemade pastas then deciding which homemade sauce should top it. Some of the region's finest local wines are poured here. There is no children's menu, but half portions can be prepared for about $1 less than full serving price.

El Ranchito

Location: *In Zillah at 1319 E. First Ave., about 15 miles southeast of Yakima on I-82*
Phone: *509-829-5440*
Days/Hours: *9 a.m. to 11 a.m., Tuesday through Thursday (for tours); open until 6 p.m. daily for dinner.*
Wheelchair/Stroller Access: *Yes*
Families are invited to watch fresh corn and flour restaurant-ready tortillas being prepared on special machines three mornings a week. For lunch, many visitors crave the tacos, burritos or enchiladas made at the adjacent restaurant. After the 20-minute tortilla tour, stroll through the gift shop. Older children will admire the ornate Mexican pottery and are less likely to break anything. Satisfy your hunger at the restaurant. There is no special menu for children, but half orders are prepared at about half price. Combination plates are easy to order if you want to introduce younger children to a variety of items.

Fort Simcoe State Park

Location: *30 miles west of Toppenish on Highway 220*
Phone: *509-874-2372*
Days/Hours: *Park open 6:30 a.m. to dusk, April through September; 8 a.m. to 5 p.m., weekends only, October through March; historic buildings and interpretive center open 9 a.m. to 4 p.m., Wednesday through Sunday when park is open.*

Wheelchair/Stroller Access: *Yes, at interpretive center and most grassy picnic areas; not at historic houses*

For children, whose only understanding of soldiers and Indians comes from old movies, Fort Simcoe State Park offers a real history lesson. Once a campsite for the Yakima Indian tribe, this land was developed into a military post in 1855 after tribes and white settlers began fighting. When the conflict cooled several years later, Fort Simcoe was given to the Bureau of Indian Affairs. In the 1920s, the bureau began farm and carpentry training for tribal members and taught them to read.

Today, Fort Simcoe reflects both eras with 10 restored soldiers' barracks and an interpretive center which tells of the Indians' role here. Throughout the grassy park there are nearly 50 picnic tables, a covered picnic shelter, and playground equipment best suited for children 2 to 10 years. Fort Simcoe is at the end of a 30-mile dead-end street.

White Pass

Location: *14 miles southeast of Mount Rainier National Park and 50 miles west of Yakima*
Phone: *509-672-3100 and 509-453-8731*
Days/Hours: *8 a.m. to 4 p.m., late November through mid-February; 9 a.m. to 5 p.m. mid-February through mid-May; 4 p.m. to 10 p.m. extended hours for night skiing in late December.*
Wheelchair/Stroller Access: *Limited*

Four chairlifts carry skiers to the peaks of several challenging downhill runs. Lower slopes are ideal for kids and adults learning to ski. If grownups want some time on the slopes without younger children, consider the child-care services available daily for 2- to 6-year-olds between 8:30 a.m. and 4:30 p.m. Reservations are recommended.

At the base, there's a restaurant, general store, and a service station. Cross-country skiers will find more than 12 kilometers of groomed double-track trails.

Yakima Bears

Location: *Yakima County Stadium on Pacific Street near South 10th*
Phone: *509-457-5151*
Days/Hours: *Game times vary during the June through September season.*
Wheelchair/Stroller Access: *Yes*

Yakima baseball fans root for this Class A home team each summer. Affiliated with the Los Angeles Dodgers, these minor leaguers play against several in-state rivals, including Everett and Spokane. Many children, typically those 6 or older, will want to come to the ballpark early and watch these minor leaguers take batting and fielding practices. This is often is a good time to snag a foul ball to take home as a souvenir.

Yakima Interurban Trolley Lines

Location: *Leaves from corner of Third and West Pine streets in Yakima, roundtrip to Selah Civic Center*
Phone: *509-575-1700*
Days/Hours: *10 a.m., noon, 2 p.m. and 4 p.m., weekends only, mid-May through mid-October.*
Wheelchair/Stroller Access: *Yes*

Families can take an imaginary ride back in time aboard Yakima Valley Transit System's original electric streetcars. This two-hour roundtrip excursion between Yakima and Selah Civic Center is especially popular among children who play with model railroads of their own. The streetcars follow city streets before winding past fruit orchards, across the Naches River and past Convicts' Cave. Tell older children how criminals sentenced to heavy labor in the 1920s were forced to break rocks here.

Back in Yakima, free self-guided tours of the Yakima Electric Railway Museum are open during the trolley's operating hours. Fares are $4 for adults, $3.50 for seniors, $2.50 for kids 6 to 12, and free to those 5 or younger.

Yakama Nation Tribal Cultural Heritage Center

Location: *One mile north of Toppenish and 20 miles south of Yakima, on Highway 97*
Phone: *509-865-2800*
Days/Hours: *9 a.m. to 6 p.m., Monday through Saturday; 9 a.m. to 5 p.m., Sunday.*
Wheelchair/Stroller Access: *Yes*

Children studying Native American history in school can learn first-hand about the colorful culture of the Yakama Nation here. To remain true to their roots, in 1994 tribal leaders approved a change in their "Yakama" name out of respect to its original spelling. Everything at this Indian museum and surrounding tribal cultural center is operated by the Yakama people; tribal history is told from their perspective.

Many stories told by tribal members through photographs and dioramas about whites interferring with tribal lifestyle are sad, but

Overnight camping in teepees at the Yakama Nation Culture Center.

important, lessons for youngsters. Despite their troubled history, the Yakama are a proud people. This cultural center is home to pow-wows, which attract Native Americans from throughout the region. Call ahead for schedules and details. Museum admission is $4 for adults, $2 for seniors and students 11 and older, $1 for children 7 to 10 years old, and free to those 9 years or younger. A special $10 family admission also is available.

At the Yakama Nation Recreational Vehicle Park next to the cultural center, many families enjoy renting a campsite for their own RV or tent. Others rent a tepee for about $30. The nearby Heritage Inn is a great place to try tribal foods, too. (See following entry.)

Heritage Inn

Location: *One mile north of Toppenish on U.S. 97*
Phone: *509-865-2551*
Days/Hours: *7:30 a.m. to 4 p.m, Monday and Tuesday; 7:30 a.m. to 9 p.m., Wednesday through Saturday; 8 a.m. to 2 p.m. Sunday.*
Wheelchair/Stroller Access: *Yes*

If your family is hungry enough to eat a buffalo, bring their appetites here. The Heritage Inn restaurant serves buffalo, genuine Indian fry bread, barbequed salmon, and some of the juiciest huckleberry pie around. Children adore the authenticity, and this place gives them a chance to try new foods. The Heritage Inn serves breakfast Monday through Saturday and brunch on Sunday. It's at the back of the cultural center grounds, so don't be surprised if you're entering the facility after 6 p.m. and the rest of the center looks quiet. Just drive around behind the Winter Lodge to find the restaurant.

Yakima Valley Museum and Historical Association

Location: *In Yakima at 2105 Tieton Drive*
Phone: *509-248-0747*
Days/Hours: *10 a.m. to 5 p.m. Wednesday through Friday; noon to 5 p.m., Saturday and Sunday.*
Wheelchair/Stroller Access: *Yes*

From a covered wagon to a Supreme Court office, this museum depicts Yakima's history and diversity. Younger children may play in a vintage general store and claims shop, or try to match animals with hands-on fur samples. Older kids may prefer examining the horse-drawn vehicles collection, considered by some to be the most extensive on the West Coast. The collection includes a Conestoga covered wagon, concord stagecoaches, mailcoaches, and the Overland Express wagon; no riding is allowed. The community pays tribute here to the late Justice William O. Douglas, a Yakima native, with a replica of his Washington, D.C., Supreme Court office. Admission is $2.50 for adults, $1.25 for seniors and children 11 or older, and free to those 10 or younger.

Kittitas County

Central Washington University

Location: *In Ellensburg. Starts at Mitchell Hall. Enter campus at the corner of Eighth and D streets. Drive to second row of buildings. Mitchell Hall is the first building in the second row.*
Phone: *509-963-1215*
Days/Hours: *Call ahead for reservations, 7:30 a.m. to 4:30 p.m., Monday through Friday, during the summer; 8 a.m. to 5 p.m., Monday through Friday, fall through spring.*
Wheelchair/Stroller Access: *Yes*

Geared for mid- and older teens, the 45-minute tour of the Central Washington University campus is an outdoor walk past the institution's most important academic buildings and largest dormitories. Those with an eye for architecture will notice that part of the campus features a modern library, fine arts building, and dormitories, while turn-of-the-century homes rest just off campus along Ninth Street. If you want to look inside any of the classrooms, tell the tour office when you make reservations so they can make arrangements.

Families with younger children may prefer to stop and visit Washoe, Dar, and Tatu—who are part of the university's Chimpanzee and Human Communication Institute. Primates live in a 32,000-square-foot habitat on campus where humans communicate with them using American Sign Language. Call 800-752-4380 for details.

Ellensburg Children's Activity Museum

Location: *In Ellensburg at 400 N. Water, at the corner of Fourth Avenue and Main Street*
Phone: *509-925-6789*
Days/Hours: *10 a.m. to 5 p.m., Thursday through Saturday; 1 p.m. to 5 p.m., Sunday, September through May; 10 a.m. to 5 p.m., Wednesday through Saturday, and 1 p.m. to 5 p.m., Sunday, the rest of the year.*
Wheelchair/Stroller Access: *Yes*

One child appears to become triplets or grows 6 feet tall at the reflection exhibit at this children's museum. Many youngsters spend all their time trying on costumes and performing improvisational scenes on a stage. It's one of the permanent exhibits. Curators introduce at least one new segment of a mini-city each month so kids may play at a radio station, airport or fire station, depending on when they visit. Contents of special drawers are changed each month, also, so little ones can explore with their fingers. Toddlers play to their hearts' delight on Pleasure Island, the climbing area reserved for those 3 or younger. In the summer, this air-conditioned museum is a respite from the outdoor heat. Admission is $2 for visitors 2 or older, and free to those younger than 2.

Ellensburg Rodeo

Location: *Off I-90 Exits 102 and 109 in Ellensburg*
Phone: *800-637-2444*
Days/Hours: *1 p.m., Friday through Sunday, and noon Monday of Labor Day weekend; gates to surrounding Kittitas County Fair open 10 a.m. to 10 p.m.*
Wheelchair/Stroller Access: *Special seating for wheelchair users; special parking for strollers outside arena*

Cream-of-the-crop cowboys and cowgirls rope, ride, race and wrestle their way to the annual Ellensburg Rodeo, one of the top 25 rodeos in the world. This often sold-out event attracts visitors to watch participants from as far away as Australia, Mexico and Canada compete against U.S. riders in seven events.

Daily competitions last about four hours, so younger children may not have the attention span for the entire show. Officials say girls who love horseback riding are especially thrilled to see the professional women's barrel racing event. Another favorite among audiences is American-style bull-fighting, which doesn't hurt the bull. In this event, professional rodeo clowns go head-to-horns with the bulls for 90 seconds before they're judged on their nimble moves.

Daily show tickets range from $8 to $26, depending on seat location. Discounts are available on Friday, and any day for seniors and groups of 25 or more. Ask about covered seating if you want to be protected from the sun during part of the show. Otherwise, bring sunscreen, because it can get hot. Some of the best seating is available on Friday before many weekend visitors arrive.

Concessions are served in the stands, but no alcohol is allowed. Free parking with shuttle service is available from Central Washington University and Ellensburg High School. Arena parking lots charge a small admission and offer transportation to the front gate. Gates open at 10 a.m. Rodeo admission covers entry to the adjacent Kittitas County Fair, featuring prize-winning animal exhibits, carnival rides, and down-home cooking.

Ginkgo Petrified Forest State Park

Location: *East of Ellensburg near Vantage. At I-90 Exit 136 drive a quarter-mile north of Vantage. Turn west on Ginkgo Avenue and follow for about half a mile. The interpretive trail is about two miles northeast of Vantage.*
Phone: *509-856-2700*
Days/Hours: *Park open dawn to dusk year-round; interpretive center open 10 a.m. to 6 p.m., mid-May through mid-September.*
Wheelchair/Stroller Access: *In some areas, but it's tough*
Teens know that Ginkgo is not a new rock band. It's a prehistoric tree — now a living fossil — dating back about 200 million years to the Triassic period. Back then, ginkgo trees grew abundantly near Vantage until a lava flow wiped them out. Now visitors can find pieces of petrified wood from the ginkgo. Boys and girls visiting here feel like the big-screen's "Indiana Jones" looking for ancient clues. The interpretive center describes gingko, other minerals, and the basic geology of Washington. An interpretive trail two miles west of the center leads through a desert marked with fossil recoveries.

Sweet Memories Bakery

Location: *In Ellensburg at 319 Pearl St.*
Phone: *509-925-4783*
Days/Hours: *7 a.m. to 7:30 p.m., Monday through Friday; 8 a.m. to 6:30 p.m., Saturday.*
Wheelchair/Stroller Access: *Yes*
Soft and fluffy sourdough and cheese breadsticks are the specialty at this bakery just around the corner from the children's museum. Sandwiches are made to order and peanut butter and jelly lovers will find creations to keep them happy. Highchairs are available for little ones.

Helpful Phone Numbers:

Asotin Chamber of Commerce, 800-933-2128

Clarkston Chamber of Commerce, 509-758-7712

Dayton Chamber of Commerce, 800-882-6299 and 509-382-4825

Ellensburg Chamber of Commerce, 509-925-3137

Goldendale Chamber of Commerce, 509-773-3400

Greater Yakima Chamber of Commerce, 509-248-2021

Hispanic Chamber of Commerce of Greater Yakima, 509-952-7137 or 509-248-6751

Klickitat County Visitor Information Center, 509-493-3630

Prosser Chamber of Commerce, 509-786-3177

Pullman Chamber of Commerce, 509-334-3565

Selah Chamber of Commerce, 509-697-6877

Skamania County Chamber of Commerce, 509-427-8911

Toppenish Chamber of Commerce, 509-865-3262

Tri-Cities Visitors and Convention Bureau, 509-735-8486

Umatilla National Forest's Walla Walla Ranger District, 509-522-6290

Walla Walla Chamber of Commerce, 509-525-0850

Wapato Chamber of Commerce, 509-877-3080

Yakima Valley Visitors & Convention Bureau, 509-575-1300

Appendix
Trip Planning Resourses in Washington State

Bicycle Program/Washington Department of Transportation. A map and guide to bicycling in the Northwest is sent from Olympia. *Call 360-705-7277.*

Professional Rivers Outfitters of Washington. Seattle's Cascade Adventures mails a list of river outfitting members for whitewater and float trips. *Call 206-323-5485.*

Washington Forest Protection Association. This agency will send a 48-page, paperback guide called *A Walk in the Woods — A Public Guide to Private Forests.* Chapters describe the diversity of Washington's forests, jobs forests create, and wildlife and plant preservation. Kids fascinated by the outdoors will like the nifty charts showing how to match animal, bird, and reptile life with their tracks and habitats. *Call 800-45-WOODS, extension 405.*

Washington State Department of Fisheries. Saltwater sport fishing regulations and information is mailed in a packet from Olympia. *Call 360-902-2200.*

Washington State Department of Natural Resources. This Olympia-based agency will sell you maps and brochures describing 135 primitive recreation sites within the 5 million acres of DNR-managed land in Washington. *Call 360-902-1234.*

Washington State Department of Wildlife. Freshwater fishing and viewing information is mailed from Olympia. *Call 360-753-5700.*

Washington State Fair Association. There are dozens of fun stops throughout the summer at county fairs. Get a list with a calendar from this Moses Lake group. *Call 509-765-6080.*

Washington State Field Guide. Published by the Washington State Tourism Development Divison, this 48-page paperback guide is published three times yearly — spring/summer, fall, and winter. The guide contains complete listings of new events and activities in all regions of the state. Plus, there's a calendar of current events at the end. *Call 360-586-2088, 360-586-2102 or 800-544-1800, extension 337.* Office counselors here are from RSVP - the Retired Senior Volunteer Project. They're especially patient with children.

Washington State Lodging & Travel Guide. State tourism development division officials can also mail a thorough, 128-page bound directory with a listing of seasonal outdoor sports, camping information, helpful phone numbers, and a pull-out map and mileage chart. *Call 360-586-2088, 360-586-2102 or 800-544-1800, extension 337.*

Washington State Park Winter Recreation Office. Buy the state's 60-page "Groomed Cross-Country Ski Trails Guide" for listings of every commercially groomed trail in the state. Each listing includes the trail's description and safety information. It runs $2 to $4. *Call 360-586-0185.*

Local chambers of commerce and visitor information centers in individual cities, towns or counties. They'll mail books, brochures and maps. Phone numbers for these offices are included in this book at the end of each chapter. Some tourist officials here love talking to kids and can't wait to tell them about their child's or their grandchild's favorite park, hike or activity. In some places, fascinating tours are available at hospitals, newspapers, TV or radio stations, fire stations and police departments. Visits to libraries and public pools or recreation centers are fun nearly everywhere.

National and state parks, national forests and ranger stations. Due to state and federal spending revenue cuts, visitors are more frequently charged for travel information guides here. For national park information, call 206-220-7450. Visit or write the Outdoor Recreation Information Center at 915 Second Ave., Suite 442, Seattle, Washington 98174. *Call Washington State Parks, 360-753-2027.*

Index

Rosanne Cohn has lived in Seattle for so long that she must qualify as a native! A graduate of Garfield High School and the University of Washington, she is a leading consultant in the public relations field —currently working in the area of community relations. Rosanne and her husband, Lawrence Kahn, live in Bellevue. Their three children are grown and live in the Puget sound area.

Suzanne Hapala Monson is a Seattle area newspaper reporter and freelance travel writer. A Vancouver, Washington native, she graduated from the University of Washington before reporting for the Associated Press and The Seattle Times. She and her husband have three daughters.